Words Matter

INTERSECTIONS

Asian and Pacific American
Transcultural Studies

Russell C. Leong
General Editor

Words

Matter

CONVERSATIONS

WITH

ASIAN AMERICAN

WRITERS

Edited by King-Kok Cheung

*University
of Hawai'i
Press
Honolulu*

*in association
with UCLA
Asian American
Studies Center
Los Angeles*

© 2000 University of Hawai'i Press
All rights reserved
Printed in the United States of America
05 04 03 02 01 00   5 4 3 2 1

**Library of Congress
Cataloging-in-Publication Data**
Words matter : conversations with Asian American
writers / edited by King-Kok Cheung
     p.   cm. – (Intersections)
     Includes bibliographical references and index.
     ISBN 0–8248–2134–3 (acid-free paper). —
ISBN 0–8248–2216–1 (pbk. : acid-free paper).
     1. American literature—Asian American authors—
History and criticism—Theory, etc. 2. Authors,
American—20th century—Interviews. 3. Asian
Americans—Intellectual life. 4. Asian Americans
in literature. 5. Asian Americans—Interviews.
6. Authorship. I. Cheung, King-Kok, 1954–
II. Series: Intersections (Honolulu, Hawaii)
PS153.A84W67   2000
810.9'895'0904—dc21   99–36654
                                 CIP

Designed by Barbara Pope Book Design

Printed by The Maple-Vail Book Manufacturing Group

Contents

Introduction

KING-KOK CHEUNG

My work as an activist . . . is inextricable from what I write.
—Janice Mirikitani

The whole enterprise of writing for me is spiritual.
—Li-Young Lee

You write because you have no choice.
—Wendy Law-Yone

What does it mean to be an Asian American writer? Is it the same as being a writer of Asian descent? Or just a writer? As the epigraphs to this introduction demonstrate, the authors interviewed in this collection have remarkably different literary compulsions. Even more varied are their styles, their sensibilities, and the settings of their stories, which include Burma, Brazil, England, India, Japan, Korea, the Philippines, Sudan, Thailand, and Vietnam as well as California, Hawai'i, Kansas, and New York. Yet in this country these authors are all designated as *Asian American writers* by academics, publishers, the media—and in this volume.

Like most artists of color, authors of Asian ancestry in the

United States often face a host of assumptions and expectations. Because their number is still relatively small, those who draw inspiration from their experiences as members of a minority are often seen as speaking for their ethnic groups. Because their work is frequently treated as ethnography by mainstream reviewers, many in the Asian American communities hold them accountable for an authentic "representation." They also confront persistent stereotypes suggesting that Asian Americans may make top-notch engineers or kung fu fighters but surely not poets, playwrights, or novelists. Even writers whose works are widely read may feel ghettoized as second-class citizens in the publishing marketplace, which may accept them as good Asian American writers but still not regard them as good writers, period.

At a time when literature is largely defined by the marketplace, the popular media, academe, and various ethnic communities, *Words Matter* invites twenty authors to comment on how they would like their works to be read. They are asked to speak openly about their aesthetics, their politics, and the difficulties they have encountered in pursuing a writing career: disapproval of parents who press them to engage in more practical pursuits; cultural prohibition against exposing oneself or one's family; the absence of literary predecessors; self-contempt associated with race, poverty, gender, or sexuality; or the toll exacted by the ravages of war, exclusion, and internment. They address, among other issues, the expectations attached to the label *Asian American writer,* the burden of representation shouldered by the ethnic artist, and the different demands of "mainstream" and ethnic audiences.

This project started as an experiment on my part to bridge research and teaching, to narrow the gap between theory and lived experience, and to connect literary scholarship—a discourse that can sometimes wax abstruse and impersonal—with what my students find compelling about the literature. With the exception of Zainab Ali's dialogue with Meena

Alexander, my exchange with Paul Stephen Lim, and my conversation with Hisaye Yamamoto and Wakako Yamauchi, the interviews were conducted by graduate students from the English Department and the Asian American Studies Center of the University of California, Los Angeles. Space limitations have meant that only a small proportion of the growing number of Asian American writers have been interviewed. For the most part the selection was made by the graduate students themselves and was governed by their own lines of inquiry. I merely ensured that the volume contain a mix of poets, playwrights, and fiction writers and include immigrant and American-born authors of different ethnic origins. Time and cost of travel account for the preponderance of subjects who reside in California. We hope that future volumes can make up for the imbalance.

The special relationship between interviewer and interviewee is a distinctive feature of this collection. The graduate students are thoroughly familiar with the works of the writers interviewed and are therefore capable of asking informed questions and eliciting precious comments on specific texts. Because most of these students are considerably younger than the writers whom they are interviewing, the interviews at times come across as a probing dialogue between generations. Thus, the collection not only offers the writers an opportunity to intervene in academic debates but also gives voice to the students, whose insights inform their introduction of the individual authors and most of the questions. Many of the student interviewers are aspiring writers or literary scholars in part seeking guidance from their chosen interviewees. I sense that their passion and persistence have helped draw out some otherwise taciturn subjects and deepen the conversation. In the time that has elapsed since the interviews took place, some of the interviewers have themselves become instructors of Asian American literature or published authors of poetry and fiction.

In addition to encouraging the writers to discuss their work, the interviewers were urged to modify and expand on the following list of sample questions:

1. How did you become a writer? Was your family encouraging or discouraging along the way?

2. How comfortable are you with the label *Asian American writer*? Do you feel limited by such a term, or do you draw strength from it? Are there, in your view, particular obstacles or opportunities for writers so designated?

3. What kind of audience do you have in mind? How would you characterize the reception of your work? Do you feel a split between "mainstream" and "ethnic" readers?

4. Do you feel a sense of social purpose in your work? Do you believe in art for art's sake?

5. Does gender, class, or sexuality shape your writing? If so, in what way?

6. Which writers do you admire? Who have had the strongest influence on your work?

7. (For immigrant writers only:) Where do you consider to be your "home"? Do you feel an internal tug-of-war between your Asian homeland and the United States? Do you consider yourself to be an (Asian) American writer or a writer in exile?

The writers' divergent viewpoints—appreciating or recoiling from the label *Asian American*, claiming or disclaiming an "American" identity, accepting or rejecting social obligations—can certainly contribute to current rethinking within the field of Asian American studies. Historically, the appellation *Oriental* was used in North America both for peoples across the Pacific and for Asian inhabitants of the "New World." *Asian American*, on the other hand, is a self-designation that came into currency in the late 1960s in the wake of the civil rights and black power movements and that accentuates the American status of immigrants from Asia and their descendants. The term grew out of the frustration felt by many American-born citizens of Asian extraction at being treated as perpetual foreigners in the United States, even if their roots in this country go back several generations. Such discriminatory treatment—along with Orientalist tendencies that exoticize Asian objects, customs, and persons—has also engendered in many Asian Americans an ambivalence about their Asian heritage. Because the dominant perception of what constitutes *American* is white, mainstream, and Western, Asian Americans' desire to reclaim a distinctive ethnic tradition can seem at odds with their desire to be recognized as fully American. 5

The term *Asian American literature* first came into being when the establishment of an Asian American cultural tradition was part of the larger political struggle to gain visibility and advance social justice. According to Glenn Omatsu, in the late 1960s, "writers, artists, and musicians were 'cultural workers,' usually closely associated with communities, and saw their work as 'serving the people'" (1994, 28). Writing by Asian Americans coalesced around the theme of claiming an American (as opposed to an Asian) identity. In *Aiiieeeee! An Anthology of Asian American Writers* (1974), Frank Chin, Jeffery Paul Chan, Lawson Fusao Inada, and Shawn Wong set forth one of the earliest and most influential definitions of Asian American literature, stressing American nativity and a sensibility that is "neither Asian nor white American" (1974/1983, xxi) as the foremost criteria for such writing. But their criteria have subsequently been questioned by scholars who take issue with their masculinist bias, their marginalization of immigrant writers, and their allegedly prescriptive definition of what constitutes Asian American literature.

The editors of *Aiiieeeee!* considered "emasculation" to be one of the most damaging stereotypes about Asian Americans: "Good or bad, the stereotypical Asian is nothing as a man. At worst, the Asian-American is contemptible because he is womanly, effeminate, devoid of all the traditionally masculine qualities of originality, daring, physical courage, and creativity" (Chin et al. 1974/1983, xxx). Because they saw this affront as bound up with the suppression of a distinctive vernacular, they resolved to reclaim a specifically masculine ethnopoetics. Their androcentric solution to racist representation has been challenged by feminist critics who take the editors to task for their preoccupation with rehabilitating Asian American manhood, their homophobia, and their classification of desirable attributes as masculine (see Cheung 1990; Kim 1990; Ling 1990).

Such efforts, however, had little effect. Chin et al. made good on their commitment to re-creating a "recognized style of Asian American manhood" (1974/1983, xxxviii) in *The Big Aiiieeeee!* (Chan et al. 1991), which presents selected Chinese and Japanese heroic epics as the sources of the "Asian heroic tradition" and maintains that "authentic" Asian American writing must hark back to the ethos of these heroic tales. Three famous Chinese American writers—David Henry Hwang, Maxine Hong Kingston, and Amy Tan—are hotly denounced as "fake" by Frank Chin (Chin 1991, 2), who attributes their "popularity among whites" to their distortion and fabrication of Chinese lore. Owing to Chin's stature and influence in Asian American literary circles, his judgment is sometimes taken as definitive of the dichotomy between ethnic and mainstream audiences where evaluation of Asian American writers is concerned (although Hwang, Kingston, and Tan have their Asian American admirers, too).

Demographic flux has meanwhile extended Asian American literary boundaries beyond the compass of works by American-born writers of mostly Chinese and Japanese ancestry. Largely as a result of the 1965 Immigration and Nationality Act, which abolished quotas favoring European nations, the number of Asian immigrants has risen so sharply that it is no longer practical to insist on the primacy of American nativity. Furthermore, because of the diverse national origins of the new immigrants, the scope of the term *Asian American literature* has now been broadened to include writings by people of Bangladeshi, Burmese, Cambodian, Chinese, Filipino, Indian, Indonesian, Japanese, Korean, Laotian, Nepali, Pakistani, Sri Lankan, Thai, and Vietnamese descent. Along with this expansion came shifts in critical paradigms. One of the earlier tenets of Asian American studies was "claiming America"—highlighting the presence and contributions of people of Asian ancestry in this country. But today many immigrant writers and scholars prefer to maintain affiliation with their Asian homeland as well. The implications of claiming an American as opposed to a "diasporic" or "exilic" identity have been the subject of considerable scholarly attention. While some worry that asserting a diasporic identity may reinforce the dominant perceptions of Asian Americans as perpetual foreigners, others argue that "claiming America" only bolsters U.S. hegemony and squelches the heterogeneous concerns and sensibilities of different Asian American groups (see Gonzalez and Campomanes 1997; Cheung 1997; Koshy 1998; Lim 1997; Lowe 1991; San Juan 1995; Sumida 1997; Wong 1995).

The most radical challenge to the earlier conceptions of Asian American literature has to do with whether this literature should be "defined" at all. Given the ideological genesis of the term *Asian American*—a self-designation that implies a certain political awareness—and its subsequent use as a neutral descriptive label, as in the U.S. census, the perspectives of those who expect Asian American literature to be socially dedicated and those who believe literature to be essentially personal and experimental inevitably clash. While many scholars and students continue to expect Asian American writers to furnish material that reflects ethnic experiences, some writers have begun to balk at these assumptions. Most vocal in deploring any prescriptive formulations of Asian American literature is Garrett Hongo, who complains that writers of Asian descent are often subject to double censorship: from the mainstream society, which discourages minority protest, and from ethnic communities, which demand that these writers adopt "a predominantly political or sociological construction of Asian American identity" (1993, xxxiv). Furthermore, given the publishing establishment's tendency to value Asian American literature primarily as ethnography and the cultural nationalist emphasis in Asian American studies, works by writers who venture beyond issues of ethnicity tend to fall by the wayside—neglected by both the center and the margins. As Amy Uyematsu asks, "Why do only certain themes qualify as 'Asian American literature'?" (p. 265).

The continuing debate over the social responsibility as opposed to the artistic autonomy of the Asian American writer is evident in the recent controversy over the work of Lois-Ann Yamanaka. For two successive years, 1997 and 1998, the literary awards committees of the Association for Asian American Studies selected one of her books as the recipient of the fiction prize, but, largely because of protest from the Filipino Caucus, which found that her work denigrates Filipino Americans, her award was twice revoked. Defenders of Yamanaka criticize her detractors for failing to discern the difference between author and fictional narrator, calling for an end to tribal policing, while her critics consider such artistic defense patronizing and condescending and believe that her work reinforces the existing ethnic hierarchy and further divides the local community. The incident acutely reminds us that "words matter," not just to writers, but also to their readers, that words carry both artistic nuances and material consequences.

Never have the words of Asian American writers reached as many people as they do today. The popularity of works by Americans of Asian descent has skyrocketed in the last few decades, attracting non-Asian as well as Asian readers and making inroads into the American curriculum. High school and college instructors increasingly feel the need to include these works in their course offerings. Nor is the interest confined to the United States. Conferences on Asian American literature have been held in Berlin, Kyoto, Paris, and Taipei, and the number of overseas specialists in the field is mounting.

Despite widespread national and international interest, source material about these writers is still scarce. Most readers and instructors are familiar with only a few "big" names, such as the ones denounced by Chin; the tremendous difference among authors of various national origins and generations lumped together under the label *Asian American writers* is often overlooked. Critics, too, have a difficult time keeping pace with the expanding field. Although scholarship on Asian American literature has grown considerably, the range of authors covered is still quite limited. Furthermore, historical and biographical contextualization as well as close literary analysis have currently taken a backseat to theoretical discourse; when literary texts are tackled at all, they are often filtered through or submerged in postmodernist, postcolonialist, or Marxist critical jargon incomprehensible to lay readers. In the light of the dearth of readily accessible secondary material, this collection provides a valuable firsthand introduction to twenty writers. It enables general readers and instructors unfamiliar with this literature to become acquainted with a variety of authors and to develop an interest in their works. Specialists in the field, who have for some time tackled vexing questions of definition, identity, national allegiance, and audience, will find this volume indispensable.

The interviews presented in *Words Matter* were conducted against the backdrop of the rapid reconfiguration of Asian American studies, and American studies in general, to reflect global migrations and the diverse populations of the United

States. Besides introducing twenty writers of Asian descent and providing a forum for them to articulate their perspectives on knotty issues confronting Asian Americanists, this collection serves several other purposes. The writers' comments on their own texts should enrich the literary appreciation of students and instructors and also open up new avenues of interpretation for critics and scholars. For example, despite her problematic equation of assimilation and Americanization, Gish Jen's discussion of "good" and "bad" assimilation offers a useful angle for analyzing *Typical American,* which to date has been seen largely as a satire of the American dream; and Myung Mi Kim's observations regarding the confluence of English and Korean in her poetry take us beyond thematic concerns about crossing cultures to linger on linguistic inflections. Some of these interviews also double as oral history about the internment of Japanese Americans (Yamamoto and Yamauchi), Burma or Myanmar under totalitarianism (Law-Yone), the Philippines under American colonialism (Hagedorn, Lim), the Vietnam War (Hayslip), and the rise of the Asian American movement in the sixties and seventies (Leong, Mirikitani, Robles, Uyematsu).

This assemblage of the voices of twenty authors—individuals with unique histories and perspectives, thematic concerns and aesthetic priorities—should effectively dispel any stereotypes about people of Asian descent and testify to the difficulty, if not the impossibility, of representing the diverse groups presently collected under one heading. Can the label *Asian American* continue to bring together the many constituent groups it is meant to encompass, and is solidarity possible among them? This question is the flip side of the one raised by those critics of multiculturalism who worry about the "balkanization" of America. The multiethnic dimensions of Asian American literature and its crisis of identity also speak to the broader concerns of multicultural American studies. In the contention about American and diasporic identities can be found a microcosm of larger academic and political debates over diversity and over the inclusion and exclusion of immigrant and refugee groups. These issues underlie the very basis on which literature, culture, and art are produced, taught, and critiqued. Although Asian American literature is still seen as a subcurrent of American literature, it is fast entering the mainstream, reshaping the canon.

Some of these concerns are specifically highlighted in the titles given to the four parts of the book. "Where do we live now—here or there?"—a question posed by Jessica Hagedorn and used as the title of part 1—captures the physical or psychological shuttling between an Asian homeland and the United States that some immigrant writers have experienced. The displacement that Hagedorn found confusing when she first came to the United States she now finds exhilarating: "I'm almost happiest . . . in an airport, in between flights. The sense of a million worlds meeting in an airport." Paul Stephen Lim—another writer from the Philippines, albeit of Chinese descent—confesses that he never really feels "at home" anywhere: "When I am lecturing in the classroom at the University of Kansas, I sometimes find myself addressing the students as 'you Americans.' . . . I frequently talk about 'Us Chinese,' but never about 'Us Filipinos.'" Where Hagedorn believes that "home is in [her] head and includes forever that house in Santa Mesa," Lim (consciously echoing Carlos Bulosan) thinks that "home is where the heart is" and that his "is in America." S. P. Somtow, who is Thai by birth but who has lived in England, Holland, Japan, and divers cities in the United States, compares himself to a "chameleon" that "existed on the perimeters of each culture." He believes that his travels have a direct bearing on his choice of genre: "One of the most disorienting things of my early life was my discovery that there was no particular culture that was the way it had to

11

be. . . . Because of that, when I started writing, it tended to be in the science fiction field, where you could simply create new cultures by 'stealing' a little of this and that, mixing them up." Meena Alexander believes that it is precisely the act of crossing national boundaries that gives rise to a sense of ethnicity: "If I were living in Kerala, I wouldn't need to be Indian, I wouldn't need to be Asian. You exist as that ethnic category only . . . in a public sphere, where it's under challenge, where you're marked." For Myung Mi Kim, the sense of being between cultures permeates the language of her poetry: "I am constantly aware of this particular English I participate in—perhaps an English that behaves like Korean, an English shaped by a Korean. The space between the two languages is a site of mutation between an English and a Korean." Le Ly Hayslip faces perhaps the most acute reminder of her diasporic identity: "I am between East and West because I do not belong here and do not belong there." She recalls the traumatic experience of watching on television the destruction of her homeland during the Vietnam War and thinking to herself, "God, that could be my people, my village"; but "the Americans around me think I'm stupid because 'the Vietnamese are our enemy.'"

Janice Mirikitani's words "We came into the circle of recovery"—used as the title of part 2—express the need felt by those who have suffered personal or collective injuries to come together as a group or a community and to inspire social change through the spoken or written word. Mirikitani discloses how she comes to terms with the sexual molestation she experienced as a child when she tries to help other victims of sexual abuse. She believes that "a good poem is a good poem if it works," if it touches others. Chitra Divakaruni, president of Maitri (a domestic violence help line for South Asians in the Bay Area), also helps women who have undergone "a cycle of violence," women whose life stories sometimes enter her own fiction and poetry.

King-Kok Cheung

Al Robles deplores the dislocation and the dispersal of the Manongs, the Issei, the African Americans, the poor, the prostitutes, and all those who used to inhabit the San Francisco I-Hotel—where "the birth of our people and the community," "the poetry, the celebration," all were "woven together"—before it was torn down by land developers. He believes that poetry and other art must bear witness to "the wound" of the I-Hotel and keep alive the communal spirit. Playwright Philip Kan Gotanda laments the internalized racism of Asian American actors who accept demeaning roles; he is also troubled by those in the Japanese American community who buy into "the idea of being a second-class citizen" and by mainstream media that continue to shut out or distort Asian images. For him, the only road to recovery "is to speak out, to say what you have to say . . . to create new works—put your own works out there."

"It's like putting us in the Chinese laundries"—a simile used by David Wong Louie—conveys the frustration felt by the writers interviewed in part 3 (as well as by many others) at being invidiously categorized as *ethnic* or *Asian American* writers. "I think that translates in some people's minds as African American does still for some people—as something less than, something not as good, something inferior," Louie observes. Gish Jen explains that when she opens *Typical American* with the words "This is an American story," she is redefining the American tradition as well as making claims for her book: "As an Asian American I understood that I was going to be ghettoized, and I wanted to get out." On being referred to as an *apprentice* by the editors of the *New England Review*, Russell Leong comments that they were probably using the term to imply that "we are traveling beyond our ethnicity and learning English, or learning how to write. . . . Very patronizing." Leong himself believes that "writers of color in America help validate American writing"; hence, "the editors are the apprentices because they're learning from us."

The tendency to ghettoize is not confined to white publishers, according to Amy Uyematsu: "There are a few places where I've submitted—Asian American journals or ethnic journals—where, if I didn't do something that was specifically on a racial theme, my work wouldn't get considered." She also suspects that, when her editors asked her to remove poems about Native Americans from the manuscript of *30 Miles from J-Town*, "it was because ... I was venturing into territory where I shouldn't be." However, "as a poet I'm going to write about everything." Li-Young Lee is most emphatic about his desire not to be tagged as *Asian American:* "That classification can bring attention to Asian American writers who are overlooked because they're Asian American. But, ultimately, if we're not careful, it can be a prison because in America we have poets and then we have Asian American poets. . . . It's so important for an artist of any kind *not* to identify with a group." Lee wishes to "live in a state of 'nobodyhood,' . . . to live a life without paradigms."

Wendy Law-Yone resists ethnic classification and conventional historiography. "History, after all," she notes, "is the version of the victors. . . . Literature, on other hand, documents the version of the conquered. I'm on the side of literature"—a tag line that we take as the title of part 4. The characters created by the authors interviewed in this part are a far cry from traditional historical heroes, yet we are made to see the dreams, ideals, and strengths residing in these failed or unfulfilled lives and offered a deeper understanding of a given time and place than that afforded by official chronicles. Speaking of the protagonist of *Irrawaddy Tango*, Law-Yone reveals: "I like to focus on stories about failure. . . . [Tango] is not a successful immigrant in the generally understood sense. She does not become a CEO. But holding on to the painful past allows her ... to return to her homeland and seek ... Major Restitution." Gary Pak also roots for the disenfranchised. Asked about the maligned gay protagonist in

"A Toast for Rosita," a story in *The Watcher of Waipuna*, he replies: "The demeaning part came from the other characters looking at Rosita. Rosita was strong. The story was told from the kids' point of view. . . . Yet they were able to see Rosita through a much fresher perspective, by seeing what he did, and the honesty and pureness in his heart." Pak also reveals that the title of his recent novel—*A Ricepaper Airplane*—symbolizes the aspirations of a Korean American pioneer who dreams of going back to Korea in a plane of his own making: "Some of these dreams have been huge failures . . . [but] we have to keep on with those dreams."

Big dreams likewise turn into magnificent failures in Karen Yamashita's *Brazil-Maru*, which uncovers layers of buried history. Within the bigger picture delineating the little-known Japanese emigration to Brazil, *Brazil-Maru* zooms in on the Japanese men who opted out of the middle class to establish a commune and the Japanese women who made up the invisible workforce that sustains communal living. Similarly, in *Tropic of Orange*, Yamashita unfurls the seamy side of U.S. history, such as the dispossession of the urban poor and the exploitation of Mexican labor. Like Law-Yone, however, Yamashita prefers literature to history: "With straight history, you . . . couldn't express the emotion. You couldn't express those extra things that illustrate history. . . . I also wanted to bring in a feeling for the sense of place, that scene, the smell." The veteran writers Hisaye Yamamoto and Wakako Yamauchi both excel in capturing that special feeling. They often depict lives on the fringe of mainstream annals, but their stories are based on lived experiences, their own or others'. Yamauchi believes in telling "whatever story you have to tell"—"as long as it's honest, it's valid." Yamamoto desists from giving any advice on writing: "If people have this urge to write, they will, no matter what; wild horses can't stop them." The twenty writers interviewed here all share this unbridled impulse, although they charge in different directions.

While the part titles highlight some salient attributes and concerns of the writers, they are not meant to downplay the distinct personalities of the authors, who disagree as often as they agree with each other. Nor are they meant to limit the breadth and depth of what readers can take away from the interviews, each of which covers a wide range of topics. Readers will naturally discover for themselves many other choice morsels. As Hayslip puts it, "We need all kinds of tastes. We need all kinds of thinking to make the world go round. The choice is not up to me. It's up to the reader."

Acknowledgments

This project was made possible by funding from the UCLA Asian American Studies Center. I am particularly grateful to Don Nakanishi for his continuous support; to Russell Leong for his trust, guidance, detailed comments, and inspiring suggestions; to Brian Niiya for his encyclopedic answers to my miscellaneous queries regarding Japanese Americans; to Lynn Itagaki for her genius and devotion in overseeing the final stages of the manuscript; and to Dominika Ferens for her intelligent and exhaustive research and editorial assistance. I also thank Joseph H. Brown for his meticulous copyediting and the two readers for the University of Hawai'i Press for their encouragement and constructive criticism.

Works Cited

Chan, Jeffery Paul, Frank Chin, Lawson Fusao Inada, and Shawn Wong, eds. *The Big Aiiieeeee! An Anthology of Chinese American and Japanese American Literature.* New York: New American Library–Meridian, 1991.

Cheung, King-Kok. "The Woman Warrior versus the Chinaman Pacific: Must a Chinese American Critic Choose between Feminism and Heroism?" In *Conflicts in Feminism,* ed. Marianne Hirsch and Evelyn Fox Keller. New York: Routledge, 1990.

King-Kok Cheung

————. "Re-viewing Asian American Literary Studies." In *An Interethnic Companion to Asian American Literature,* ed. King-Kok Cheung. New York: Cambridge University Press, 1997.

Chin, Frank. "Come All Ye Asian American Writers of the Real and the Fake." In *The Big Aiiieeeee! An Anthology of Chinese American and Japanese American Literature,* ed. Jeffery Paul Chan, Frank Chin, Lawson Fusao Inada, and Shawn Wong. New York: New American Library–Meridian, 1991.

Chin, Frank, Jeffery Paul Chan, Lawson Fusao Inada, and Shawn Wong, eds. *Aiiieeeee! An Anthology of Asian-American Writers* (1974). Rev. ed. Washington, D.C.: Howard University Press, 1983.

Gonzalez, N. V. M., and Oscar V. Campomanes. "Filipino American Literature." In *An Interethnic Companion to Asian American Literature,* ed. King-Kok Cheung. New York: Cambridge University Press, 1997.

Hongo, Garrett, ed. *The Open Boat: Poems from Asian America.* New York: Anchor/Doubleday, 1993.

Kim, Elaine. "'Such Opposite Creatures': Men and Women in Asian American Literature." *Michigan Quarterly Review* 29, no. 1 (1990): 68–93.

Koshy, Susan. 1998. "The Fiction of Asian American Literature." *Yale Journal of Criticism* 9, no. 2 (1996): 315–346.

Lim, Shirley Geok-lin. "Immigration and Diaspora." In *An Interethnic Companion to Asian American Literature,* ed. King-Kok Cheung. New York: Cambridge University Press, 1997.

Ling, Amy. *Between Worlds: Women Writers of Chinese Ancestry.* New York: Pergamon, 1990.

Lowe, Lisa. "Heterogeneity, Hybridity, Multiplicity: Marking Asian American Differences." *Diaspora* 1, no. 1 (1991): 24–43.

Omatsu, Glenn. "The 'Four Prisons' and the Movements of Liberation: Asian American Activism from the 1960s to the 1990s." In *The State of Asian America: Activism and Resistance in the 1990s,* ed. Karin Aguilar–San Juan. Boston: South End, 1994.

San Juan, E., Jr. "In Search of Filipino Writing: Reclaiming Whose America?" In *The Ethnic Canon: Histories, Institutions, and Interventions,* ed. David Palumbo-Liu. Minneapolis: University of Minnesota Press, 1995.

Sumida, Stephen H. "Postcolonialism, Nationalism, and the Emergence of Asian/Pacific American Literatures." In *An Interethnic Companion to Asian American Literature,* ed. King-Kok Cheung. New York: Cambridge University Press, 1997.

Wong, Sau-ling Cynthia. "Denationalization Reconsidered: Asian American Cultural Criticism at a Theoretical Crossroads." *Amerasia Journal* 21, nos. 1–2 (1995): 1–27.

"Where do we live now—here or there?"

1

Jessica Hagedorn

Interview by

EMILY PORCINCULA LAWSIN

I met Jessica Hagedorn for the first time when I was in elementary school. I met her, not in the physical sense, but in a way that an impressionable young Filipina could never forget: in the Seattle Public Library. Every day after school, my parents used to force my brother and me to go to the library near our home until one of them could return from work. I hated reading back then because of this routine. One day, I browsed down an aisle of poetry collections and came across a simple black cloth-bound book with a black-and-white photograph of a burning guitar pasted to the front. The cover read "*Dangerous Music* by Jessica Tarahata Hagedorn" (Hagedorn 1975). I loved music, and, as a Catholic schoolgirl, I was naturally intrigued by this concept of danger. There were so few Filipino writers published in those days that I read the book over and over every time we went there. A few years later, I had so many overdue books that I couldn't check out any more, so I used to hide it in different sections of the library. I would come back the next day, and there was my fellow Filipina friend, secretly waiting for me.

Now, twenty years later, Jessica Hagedorn has emerged with so many more books and projects that you can no longer get away with hiding them in obscure parts of the library, hoping that no one will notice that they're missing. Her other poetry and prose collections include *Pet Food and Tropical Apparitions* (1981), *Danger and Beauty: Poetry and Prose* (1993), and *Four Young Women: Poems by Jessica Tarahata Hagedorn, Alice Karle, Barbara Szerlip, and Carol Tinker* (1973). Her first novel, *Dogeaters,* was nominated for a National Book Award in 1990 and was voted best book of the year by the Before Columbus Foundation. A well-known performance artist, poet, novelist, and playwright, Hagedorn was also a commentator on "Crossroads," a syndicated weekly magazine on National Public Radio. She studied theater arts at the American Conservatory Theater in San Francisco and has written numerous plays for the stage (*Mango Tango,* 1978; *Where the Mississippi Meets the Amazon,* with Ntozake Shange and Thulani Davis, 1978; *Tenement Lover: no palm trees/in new york city,* 1981; *Teenytown,* with Laurie Carlos and Robbie McCauley, 1988; *Airport Music,* with Han Ong, 1993), for television (*Chiquita Banana,* 1972; *A Nun's Story,* 1988), and for radio (*Holy Food,* 1989). In 1992, she completed the screenplay *Kiss Kiss Kill Kill,* which later became *Fresh Kill,* a movie produced and directed by Shu Lea Cheang. She performed with the bands West Coast Gangster Choir (1975–1978) in San Francisco and Gangster Choir (1978–1985) and Thought Music (1988–1992) in New York. In 1993, Hagedorn edited *Charlie Chan Is Dead: An Anthology of Contemporary Asian American Fiction.* Her second novel, *The Gangster of Love,* was published by Houghton Mifflin in 1996.

Since those library days, I've been fortunate to have met Jessica in person many times and in many places: in Seattle, where her two daughters' grandparents live; in New York, where she resides; and in Los Angeles, where I interviewed her during a recent literary festival. Her interview reflects the notion of movement, through her perceptions of home, choices, and changes in the physical and literary landscape. She is always as vibrant and animated as all the characters in her novels are.

EPL Can you tell me about the place where you were born?

JH I was born in Manila in 1949. The house that I remember was the one I lived in until we moved to this country. It was in Santa Mesa, a wonderful old section of Manila. Some of the buildings are still there—it's amazing how Manila changes so much every time I go back. I loved this neighborhood. At that time it included an old church and a lot of houses that had survived World War II. There were these big, old, crumbling houses—the kind we lived in. Ours had this garden, which to me as a child was huge, although, when I went back to look at it, it wasn't at all. There were lots of trees (a mango tree, a guava tree, a giant acacia tree), overgrown foliage, great for a kid's imagination. It had a dark, foreboding atmosphere.

I went to one of those schools run by nuns. Most people I grew up with went to these segregated schools. My brothers went to Ateneo, which is run by the Jesuits, and I went to the Assumption Convent, a very privileged school. Looking back, I had a really good education because those nuns were so strict about everything. On another level, it was incredibly repressive. I don't know what it's like now, but back then the academic standards were very high. We could write and read really well. It's quite amazing now that I'm an American, my kids go to public schools, and it's like, "Oh, God!"

EPL How long did you stay in the Philippines?

JH I lived there until I was fourteen, and then we moved. My family split up. My mother had two sisters in California, so she was drawn there. It was sort of the obvious place to go.

Jessica Hagedorn

We went first to San Diego, and we lived there for maybe four to six months. My mother went on to San Francisco and looked for an apartment because she liked San Francisco. I'm glad she did because she then sent for us and said, "Let's stay here, let's make this our base." My brothers stayed for two or three years, but they never liked it in America, so they went back to Manila, where they still live. It just never clicked for them.

In San Francisco I finished high school at a public school called Lowell. I was very lucky. We didn't know anyone, but we stumbled onto the fact that there was this great public high school, with very high standards, where you weren't required to live in the neighborhood. If you had a high grade-point average, or if you passed their entrance test, you would get admitted, and I did. Because of the education I had in the Philippines, I was way ahead of others my age. It was quite a trek for me because we were living in completely the other part of town, but I liked the independence. Even though that's not how I had been raised in the Philippines, my mother had no choice but to let me take public transportation to school. My life really changed once we hit this country, a whole other life.

EPL Can you tell me how any of this influenced your writing or your choice to be a writer?

JH I'd always known I wanted to be a writer since I was a child because my grandfather, whom I was very close to, had been a teacher and a writer, also a cartoonist. He had been interned in the Santo Tomas Camp by the Japanese, and, while he was there, he actually wrote this book with cartoons about the camps that was smuggled out, so he had a very big influence on me. There were a million other things I wanted to do, but I was very clear about being a writer.

Moving here definitely made the writing more of a necessity because I was so isolated. I began writing a lot more, just out of loneliness and the need to express my confusion about being here in this strange environment. My mother gave me one of those little typewriters. I would just start typing away little stories or poems. I didn't know what I was doing, but I just did it. I was reading a lot because I really didn't know anybody my age. I had always been a bookworm. So, once I had access to all these books in America that were cheaper and in paperback, I'd buy books all the time. San Francisco, I discovered, had all these great bookstores. It was a real adventure for me. Reading contemporary writers really inspired me. It was a scary time, too. Intellectually, I was like, "Oh, what is all this I'm finding?" It was unfiltered: I suddenly had access to all kinds of literature. My mother was encouraging. I was allowed to read anything. That was very instrumental in my development.

If I had stayed in Manila, opening up my mind would have been a slower process because I didn't have access to everything. You could get only certain books, especially in those days. You were not being hit on the head with as much stimulus. I don't want people to think that I'm speaking of the Manila that exists today. A lot more books are available there now than when I was a young child. Now there are excellent publishers that promote the Philippine writers. It's a different time there, filled with a lot of literary activity.

EPL Have you been published there?

JH I'm in an anthology of women writers that came out in 1992, called *Forbidden Fruit.* There's this wonderful writer and editor there named Tina Cuyugan and this press, Anvil Press, that publishes the younger writers that are coming up, more experimental writers. I was really happy to be in a book that had writers writing in both Tagalog and English.

EPL How has your family taken your fame as a writer?

JH Well, my parents passed away in the last two years. They

Jessica Hagedorn

were pretty philosophical about my writing; they didn't make a big issue out of it. They were used to me traveling a lot. I think they were discreet about it. For example, when the novel *Dogeaters* came out in the Philippines, they didn't tell me if it disturbed them that some people weren't too thrilled with the novel. They're [*pauses*] so civilized.

EPL Why didn't these folks in the Philippines like the novel?

JH There are always people who don't like your work. The name *Hagedorn* is not that common in the Philippines or anywhere else. So I knew my brother would immediately get asked, "Are you related to that writer?" I could just see him rolling his eyes because he's a very private person.

I think that, politically, the book was controversial. The title is very controversial. It's not a book that paints a pretty picture. Sometimes people think that literature is supposed to reflect an unreal world where everybody's noble and wonderful. My book doesn't do that, although I think it's full of love. Some people don't know how to read it; they misinterpret it. I think it hit some people in the Philippines a lot more passionately than it would people here because it's a book that hit home. My family's used to my "madness." I had already been doing stuff that's unconventional, so it's not like all of a sudden this book came out and, "Oh, God." It was more like, "Well, here we go again." My immediate family has been, for the most part, very supportive.

EPL You talk about censorship a lot. If *Dogeaters* had come out any earlier than it did, do you think it would have been censored in the Philippines?

JH You mean if Marcos had still been in power? It probably would have been even more fascinating. I wish it had come out a little earlier, but I think things come out when they're ready to. It might have been censored.

Words Matter

EPL Were you worried about that when you were writing it?

JH It occurred to me that there might be some kind of reaction that wouldn't be too healthy. I talked to my family a little bit about it because I didn't want them to be surprised. After all, they live there. They have to live with the consequences. I don't live there anymore. I come and go, so I'm in a position of privilege. So I figured that, by letting my family know what I was up to, I could at least give them some sort of warning. I did think that, with all the problems that people have to contend with back there, the least of it is this novel. It is fiction, after all.

EPL You once said, "It was a deliberate choice on my part to have one of my central characters [Joey] in *Dogeaters* be a male prostitute who is half-black, half-Filipino."[1] Can you elaborate on this?

JH I decided to create a hybrid character because I grew up in a kind of mestizo society in Manila and you write about what you know. The obvious thing would have been to create a character who is mestizo, torn between two worlds, half white, half brown. But that's not so interesting to me. What happens to all the other mixtures that are never talked about, that are not looked on so favorably? I thought about all the kids that I've seen on the streets who are the products of one-night stands. How do they survive? I'm interested in survival and endurance and how people get through very difficult situations. For me, Joey's the hero. He is noble. Other people might say, "Well, you sure picked a very negative kind of image," but I don't think so. In the face of a lot of setbacks, he manages to adapt and move on. It was a challenge to me as a writer to not go the easy route and to try to create a complex character who has a lot of obstacles confronting him. He's unwanted, his mother's dead, he doesn't even know who his father is. He's poor, he's a black American, so that's

27

already, "Uh-oh." He's not going to become a movie star in the Filipino movies because they're not interested in that. His beauty is not the beauty that Filipinos aspire to. What does he have to do in order to survive? He becomes a hustler.

EPL Of all your characters, with whom would you say you most identify?

JH I identify with Joey. I have the two main characters in *Dogeaters*, and they're both first-person narrators. There's the schoolgirl Rio, of course. Everybody goes, "Oh, is that you?" But Joey's interesting to me because he's less reactive. He acts out of necessity, so to me he's an unpredictable and exciting character. Rio's life is a life I knew, but, for me, she's more of a detached narrator, whereas Joey's the one that the immediate drama centers on. But of course all my characters are dear to me. You fall in love with all of them. That's why you create them. But, if I were forced to choose, I think I was the freest with Joey.

EPL At the end of the novel, Rio stays anxious and restless, "at home only in airports." How does this relate to you as an Asian American writer?

JH In *Charlie Chan Is Dead,* I wrote an introduction, and Elaine Kim wrote the preface. She talks about cultures that fly back and forth all the time. You have this new generation that is comfortable going home to Korea or coming back to Los Angeles and living more than one culture. Perceptions are altered. People are constantly in transit, moving all the time. I've been moving all the time since I was a child. My life was disrupted early. Before that, we traveled a lot for pleasure. We were a family who liked to go places. I always loved the sheer movement of it and meeting people in other countries or in other towns or villages in the Philippines.

So this thing about being at home only in airports is a question I bring up a lot. It was a question I brought up in the theater piece *Airport Music.* Where do we live now—here or there? The feeling of *home* and the definition of it do not mean necessarily my apartment in New York City. Home is in my head and includes forever that house in Santa Mesa. It also includes the different homes in which we lived in San Francisco as I was growing up. We moved a lot. That shaped my whole life. I was in all these different frames of mind in different neighborhoods in San Francisco. You change with each neighborhood. It affects you if you're living in the Mission or if you're living in the Sunset District, then suddenly you're in the Haight. That's like, "Whoa!" Those are little universes within the city.

I have a sense that I'm almost happiest, in a cosmic way, in an airport, in between flights. The sense of a million worlds meeting in an airport. Miami, for example—that airport to me is amazing because it's one of those major airports, what do you call those?

EPL Hubs?

JH Hub. It is a hub, where you're hearing all kinds of languages on the intercom and people are coming and going. There's a lot of crazy energy spoken in different tongues; it's this great babble. I love it. It fuels me. I'm neither here nor there. But I am somewhat rooted now that I have a family.

EPL Let's talk a little bit about your moves and that era of the sixties and seventies.

JH I moved to New York in the late seventies. For me the formative years as an artist were spent in San Francisco in the Bay Area. They were very important. I was delighted by the sheer—perhaps there's no such thing as an accident—but, by sort of accident, I met all these writers and artists.

Yesterday, I ran into one of the poets who is also a filmmaker, who used to live in the Bay Area. She lives here in LA now. Her name is Geraldine Kudaka. She was saying that back then there wasn't all this separation of mediums. We weren't as self-conscious; we were getting together and "collaborating" naturally.

I got exposed to Filipino American writers and artists who were cropping up in the Bay Area—and that was like coming home. Suddenly, I wasn't so isolated; suddenly, there were people who shared a similar sensibility. The Filipino American artists taught me a lot about the history of Filipinos in California—for example, what happened there with the Manongs—things that I was totally ignorant about because back in Manila my education didn't include the painful history of Filipinos in America.

A lot of the Bay Area artists and writers are my friends for life: Al Robles, Russell Leong, George Leong (who now works in films), Oscar Peñaranda, the Syquia brothers (Lou and Serafin), Shirley Ancheta. We were part of the Kearny Street Writers' Workshop, my first exposure to Asian America. Here were these Chinese, Japanese, Filipino, and Korean Americans getting together and forging this other, bigger identity. I was elated by it because at that time there were a lot of alliances being forged—black studies, Chicano studies—and that *Asian American* tag was politically important for us then. Cultures that don't necessarily get along are suddenly sitting in the same room, writing poems. Probably the concept of multiculturalism evolved out of this.

That was a very exciting time. Then, when I came to New York, I discovered Basement Workshop, which was the equivalent of the Kearny Street Writers' Workshop. We didn't have much funding in those days, so a lot of this creative work was done because you just wanted to do it.

EPL Can you tell me how life has been for you on the East Coast compared to that on the West Coast?

JH It's quite different. When I moved to New York in 1978, Filipinos weren't as visible there as they were in San Francisco.

I think that was one reason my mother was into living in the Bay Area, where she felt at home. Things have changed. Now you can go to Queens or Jersey City, and Filipinos are visible, and they're becoming a force to contend with, culturally and politically. New York, of course, has an incredibly diverse population, but Filipinos were never as present as they are now. I used to complain about such a basic thing as, "Where can I go to eat Filipino food?" Now you can go to such places.

Also, there's a tight-knit community of Filipino artists in Manhattan. We share the same ties to the motherland. We embrace a dual identity. When we say *home,* you're never sure if we mean America or the Philippines. Within that group, which includes actors, dancers, radio people, writers, directors, painters, and filmmakers, there are Filipino Americans who were born in this country and so have another perception. There's a difference. Maybe, on some level, I can communicate with their parents more because we're from "over there"; we're immigrants, and they're not.

When I moved to New York in 1978, there was nothing like that going on, except for Basement Workshop, which was largely a Chinese American and Japanese American arts organization. They invited me to work there, and I started a reading series. We never had any money to bring in writers from the West Coast, so it was difficult for me to present any Filipino artists because we didn't have the resources to fly them to New York or to put them up. I would always have to work with this tight budget and just invite artists who were from the New York area. But then Ninotchka Rosca, who's a novelist, an essayist, and an activist, moved to New York City. It was a start.

EPL Why did you choose to move to New York?

JH It was more exciting to me in terms of theater and film and the publishing industry. For me, New York City is the cultural capital of the Western Hemisphere. It's not a city you move to for an easy life because it's pretty harsh. But art thrives there, even in the face of obstacles. People are competitive. Audiences are more jaded and critical, so you are compelled to do your very, very best. You can't get by with as much bullshit. New York toughened up my writing.

EPL Can you talk about how your work has been received among different communities?

JH What's wonderful for me is that the reception for my work has always been cross-cultural. I was glad that *Dogeaters,* for example, was read by a lot of different people. That's the way I would like to function as an artist, that my work can reach out or that it is open to a lot of people's interpretations. It's one thing when Filipinos read the book. I don't have to sit there and explain. We have one kind of communication about it. There's a lot less mystery. I'm talking not just about the language but about the perceptions of our "goofiness" and our mysticism. You don't have to explain it. Why is it that we "get it" somehow when we read *War and Peace* or Shakespeare, for God's sake? See, I don't buy into the notion that we can read and appreciate only our own people's work. That's why sometimes I feel that, while labels like *Asian American literature* may serve to identify a certain kind of immigrant narrative, in a way they can hinder us. I'm not real comfortable with the term *Asian American writer.* But sometimes labels are necessary as marketing tools.

EPL If you were to choose a label for yourself and your writing, what would it be?

JH I wouldn't. I'm a writer. But I can't deny my gender and my ethnic identity, either.

EPL In the introduction to *Tenement Lover,* you said that you're concerned with the idea of revolution. Having said what you said about labels, do you feel that there's a sense of social purpose in your work?

JH Yes, I do. I don't think I sit down with a political agenda hanging over my head. I'm not particularly plot driven; I'm character driven. The characters I'm drawn to as a writer are invariably characters who are underdogs, and on some level there is a social purpose there. *Social purpose* just sounds so clinical.

EPL Let me put it another way. Do you feel you write "art for art's sake"? Or do you feel there's another aspect to why you write?

JH I write because I have to write. I do believe that everything is political, but I also believe that what makes it powerful is if it's personal and human. You have to dig deeper than journalism, see the soldier as a human being who is probably kind to his mother but can turn around and torture prisoners. This same man goes home to his family and is tender with his child. That to me is the challenge. If the writer concentrates on the specifics and complexities of human beings, the politics will resonate. It's not enough for some writer to say, "My God, the horrors in Guatemala," because I get that message from the *New York Times*. How does an artist elevate journalism to art? A mistake a lot of didactic artists make is thinking that it's enough to tell you, to report that this tragic event occurred. We know this because we live in a media-crazy world now. In the fifties when I was growing up, all you had to do was show me a violent image. The Vietnam War—the first war we watched on TV—turned the tide on how we "look" at things. People are bombarded with horror every day. What is my role as an artist?

EPL You were talking earlier about *Airport Music.* One line that's repeated a lot in this play is the "sad jazz of displacement." Is that you or someone else?

Jessica Hagedorn

JH In a way that's Han Ong talking about his parents' displacement. *Airport Music* is a collaboration, and there are two writers speaking on the same subject. I know that sad jazz of displacement. When I first came to this country, that was the music I was hearing. Now my displacement is more positive; it fuels and inspires me. That phrase "sad jazz" is specific to Han's story, but it's also something that we all feel, even if we've come to America of our own choosing and we're "upbeat immigrants looking at this new land where we can have more opportunity." There's still this sadness of "Hey, you've left home," even if you've come here under the best possible circumstances. It's a beautiful phrase that we can relate to, all of us.

EPL How did *Airport Music* come into being?

JH I had seen Han's work in New York. I'd heard that he was Chinese-Filipino and that he'd just come here recently, so I was intrigued. He was young and new in this country, and yet he was already such a presence in Los Angeles. So I went to see his one-man show at the Public Theatre, called *Symposium in Manila*. He performed as if he were giving a lecture and slideshow on multiculturalism. It was very funny. I thought, "Well, here's a kindred spirit." He definitely has his own style, but the way he tackles themes is both familiar and refreshing. His writing is crisp, pop-culture influenced, and smart. I asked Han if he also wrote fiction because I was gathering material and was interested in finding new writers to include in *Charlie Chan Is Dead*.

Han said, "As a matter of fact, I'm working on a novel."

I said, "Why don't you send me a couple of choices. Let me look at different excerpts." He did, and I chose one. Han came back to New York to do another solo piece called *Corner Store Geography*, which was about Los Angeles. It was much more physical than his other work. I put it in the back of my mind that one day we'd have to do something together. I hadn't been doing any performance work, mainly because I was editing the anthology, I had a new baby, and I was trying to finish my second novel. To me, that was enough. But Akila Oliver from the LA Festival called to invite me to come and do a reading and panel. I thought, "Oh, I don't want to do a reading. Let me do something to challenge myself." I proposed to do a work in progress. I hadn't written one; I hadn't even asked Han if he was interested in collaborating. But I said, "There's this writer who is based in LA I'd love to work with. Akila knew who Han was, and she was excited by the idea. I thought, "Oh no. Now I have to write it, and we have to rehearse, and I have to ask Han if he wants to do this."

Well, it all worked out. I forced myself to return to the stage. *Airport Music* grew from being a one-night event in LA to a full-length piece at the Public Theatre in New York and then at Berkeley Rep in California. It's great fun for me because writing is solitary and performing is not. I hadn't performed in so long that it was a nice way to kick myself into coming back to the theater. It's a public way of dealing with your writing in a grander format. You have lights, music; you can "play" with props.

EPL How much more will you add?

JH I don't know; I had this idea yesterday when we went to Russell Leong's party. These stories started happening, and I thought, "Oh, we have to add this." Who knows? Things always happen to me at the last minute that we add to the show. It's part of the fun of it; it keeps it fresh. Like those jokes you heard that happened in the elevator that day, so we added them.

EPL Which ones?

JH The one about the Yuppie. What is a Pilipino or Pinoy Yuppie? A Puppie!

Jessica Hagedorn

EPL This humor is in your second novel, *The Gangster of Love.*

JH Yes. The original title was *Yo-Yo*. It takes place largely in America, so the theme and landscape are different. It's a story of family and a friendship between two women artists who are very close to each other. It's also about making art and what that means in this particular time. Art is a very difficult subject to write about. Then it's about the yo-yo because I have this fascination with the Filipino yo-yo champions who used to do the exhibitions. Those guys were sharp. They were beautiful. To me, they were a kind of matinee idol, running around the country showing off. Yet, underneath, there was this horrible tension because they had to travel to places where segregation was imposed and they were attacked. The yo-yo's a metaphor.

I have an excerpt of it in *Charlie Chan Is Dead*. This particular chapter actually takes place in LA, in West Hollywood. I have a character who is an aging Filipino actor. The excerpt I chose was the one where his niece goes to visit him in Los Angeles and he reflects back on his career. He doesn't work a lot anymore, but I have him being one of the original dancers in *West Side Story*. Because he's Filipino, he's had the job of playing every person of color in every Hollywood movie. That's the only kind of work he can get, even though he's an accomplished dancer, a great singer, and a good actor. He's forced to play Indians. His name is Marlon Rivera. He names himself after Marlon Brando.

EPL You were talking about moving from one culture to another and Marlon "passing." Does that reflect you and your identity?

JH It's a source of frustration. I'm always appalled that people know so little about where I come from, literally and figuratively. Even if they know I come from the Philippines, most Americans have no idea what that means. Americans know so little about the culture and the landscape of one of their former colonies. It's an amazing thing to me because we always know so much about everybody else. I get disgusted and mad, but, other times, cultural confusions have been a source of liberation. For example, people from Mexico can accept me as a person who feels at home in their culture. There are a lot of connections that we have, even though Mexicans are different. I can enter the culture as a sister.

Sometimes the mislabeling of me has come, not out of malice, but out of assumptions about a certain way I look. It happens in the Philippines, too. When I start speaking Tagalog, people who don't know me go, "Where are you from? Are you Filipino?" And I go, "Yes. And I can look like this." They have an idea of what you're supposed to look like if you call yourself a Filipino. I know I can get away with calling myself this mixed person, but I feel good identifying myself with the place I was primarily born and raised. Yes, I have some Chinese blood; yes, I have some white European blood in there; but that's not what nurtured and raised me. What are we going to do, measure these things? It's been a constant source of, let's say, mixed emotions for me, this "passing" for this and that. It's also amusing. When I first came to New York, there weren't that many Filipinos. Well, what's the next thing? People would look at me and go, "She must be Puerto Rican," so I would find that very funny. Sometimes I'd say, "Sure!"

At Lowell High School in San Francisco I had a really good friend named Richard who was Filipino. He had no trouble identifying me as a Filipino. He walked right up to me and said, "Pinay ka ba?" I looked at him and said, "Yeah! How did you know?" I had already been so inundated by the other kids at Lowell, who were primarily Chinese and Jewish and always asked me if I was Chicana. There were maybe three Filipinos at Lowell back then. I was used to people ask-

Jessica Hagedorn

ing stupid questions. Richard didn't. He must've smelled it or something.

EPL If there's anything that you could change in your life, in your career, what would that be?

JH There's nothing I would change. In my life, there are things that I would change—there are people who died too soon or died tragically, and I wish they hadn't, but that's life. It's full of those tragedies. I would wish that they hadn't had to go that way. I would wish my parents were still alive, but perhaps this was a time when they had to go. My career—I have no regrets. If I had to do it over again, maybe *Dogeaters* would have been a longer book. I longed to keep writing it, but I was also impatient because I wanted the book out. If I had to do it over again, maybe I would have kept writing and said *Dogeaters* will come out when it comes out. There was more I wanted to explore, but there was also this sense that I could end it. So I did.

Note

1. Jessica Hagedorn, "The Exile within/the Question of Identity," in *Asian Americans: Collages of Identities: Proceedings of the 1990 Cornell Symposium on Asian America: Issues of Identity,* ed. Lee C. Lee (Ithaca, N.Y.: Cornell University, Asian American Studies Program, 1992), 25–29.

Selected Works by Jessica Hagedorn

Chiquita Banana. In *Third World Women.* San Francisco: Third World, 1972.

Four Young Women: Poems by Jessica Tarahata Hagedorn, Alice Karle, Barbara Szerlip, and Carol Tinker. Edited by Kenneth Rexroth. New York: McGraw-Hill, 1973.

Dangerous Music. San Francisco: Momo's, 1975.

Where the Mississippi Meets the Amazon. Written with Ntozake Shange and Thulani Davis. Produced by the New York Shakespeare Festival Public Theater, New York, 1978.

Pet Food and Tropical Apparitions. San Francisco: Momo's, 1981.

Dogeaters. New York: Pantheon, 1990.

Teenytown. In *Out from Under,* ed. Lenora Champagne. New York: **39** Theater Communications, 1990. With Laurie Carlos and Robbie McCauley.

Tenement Lover: no palm trees/in new york city. In *Between Worlds: Contemporary Asian-American Plays,* ed. Misha Berson. New York: Theatre Communications Group, 1990.

Airport Music. By Jessica Hagedorn and Han Ong. 1993.

Charlie Chan Is Dead: An Anthology of Contemporary Asian American Fiction. New York: Penguin, 1993. Editor.

Danger and Beauty: Poetry and Prose. New York: Penguin, 1993.

Fresh Kill. Directed by Shu Lea Cheang. Produced by the Airwaves Project, 1994.

2

Paul Stephen Lim

Interview by
KING-KOK CHEUNG

I saw Paul Stephen Lim's play *Mother Tongue* when it was staged by the East West Players in 1988. I was so impressed by its use of English composition lessons to introduce flashbacks and to advance the plot, its suspenseful revelation of the mother's tragic story, and its bold treatment of homoerotic material that I wrote the playwright to express my admiration. Rereading the play recently, I was also struck by how much it resonates with current debates in Asian American literary circles over claiming an "American" or a "diasporic" identity. The protagonist, David Lee, was born in Manila but was denied Filipino citizenship because his parents are Chinese. His decision to become a naturalized American citizen sparks a heated confrontation with his mother, whose other son was killed by American soldiers at the end of World War II.

The protagonist's predicament concerning nationality parallels that of the playwright, who says that he never feels "at home" anywhere. Lim was born in Manila of Chinese parents in 1944. He emigrated to the United States in 1968 but did not become an American citizen until 1982. He earned his

B.A. and M.A. in English at the University of Kansas, Lawrence, where he is currently an associate professor of English. He is the author of a collection of short stories, *Some Arrivals, but Mostly Departures* (1982), and eleven plays. *Conpersonas*, his first play, was judged best original script in the 1976 American College Theatre Festival. *Woeman* (1978) and *Flesh, Flash and Frank Harris* (1980) were both produced off Broadway in New York, *Points of Departure* (1978) and *Mother Tongue* (1988) at the East West Players in Los Angeles, and *Homerica* (1985) in Leicester, England (for publication information, see the selected bibliography). *Figures in Clay* was given a staged reading at the 1990 Modern Language Association convention in Chicago. *Report to the River* (1997), his latest play, won top prize in the playwriting competition at the Edward Albee Theatre Conference (June, 1999). Lim is also the founder, artistic director, and producing coordinator for the English Alternative Theatre (EAT), a group whose primary objective is to nurture the work of his playwriting students. In 1996, at the Kennedy Center/American College Theater Festival (KC/ACTF) festival in St. Louis, Lim was awarded a gold medallion from the Kennedy Center for his work with student playwrights.

   The following interview began in June 1997 when I taught a graduate seminar for the Multicultural Literary Institute in the English Department at the University of Kansas, Lawrence; it was later completed by email exchanges after my return to Los Angeles. Getting to know Lim better was my bonus for visiting the University of Kansas. He was full of stories about his own family members, local Lawrence residents, other writers and artists, and his (male) dog, Imelda, who actually figures in *Figures in Clay*. But I came away with the feeling that his talent has been insufficiently recognized in Asian American cultural circles, partly because he is "hidden" in Lawrence, and partly because many of his plays do not revolve around Asian (American) characters. What he said of

Paul Stephen Lim

Taiwanese American director Ang Lee is also true of himself: "The world is . . . his oyster."

KKC What was it like for someone of Chinese descent to grow up in the Philippines? Now that you are an American citizen, do you consider yourself Chinese American or Filipino American?

PSL Because they were (and continue to be) a minority group that controlled the economy of the Philippines, the Overseas Chinese were feared, hated, and reviled when I was growing up in Manila from the forties through the mid-sixties. However, as a member of this minority group, I was taught that we were superior to the Filipinos, not just economically, but also intellectually, culturally, etc. Thus, I was not encouraged to develop friendships with people other than other very boring (in my opinion) Overseas Chinese. Here, in America, I consider myself Asian American in general (to include my Philippine background) but Chinese American in particular. There are no Philippine restaurants in Lawrence, Kansas, and I do miss some of the Philippine foods I grew up with. But, if I had to choose between Philippine cuisine and Chinese cuisine, the latter would win out . . . and we are what we *eat*.

KKC What was your education like in the Philippines? What did you like and dislike the most?

PSL All through elementary school, I went to an English-language Jesuit school in the morning and then to a Chinese school in the afternoon to learn Mandarin. I hated the Chinese school because it made me feel like even more of an outsider. As for the choice of the English-language schools I went to, my parents wanted the best for me. In those days, for boys from good families, *the best* meant either the Jesuits or the Christian Brothers. So I had the Jesuits for elementary school, the Christian Brothers for high school, then back to the Jesuits for the first two years of college, before I would drop out of school altogether. My teachers told me early that I had a gift for writing, and they all encouraged me to develop the gift. In high school, I not only edited the high school paper and yearbook but also started to contribute "human interest" articles to the local newspapers and magazines.

KKC Did you decide to be a writer then? Was your family supportive?

PSL I was twelve or thirteen when I began to dream of a life as a writer. My parents had no idea what I was doing in school. I was getting very good grades in all my classes, and that was all that mattered to them. They thought they were getting their money's worth, and of course they were. My parents had no great interest in art or literature. Their spoken English was merely serviceable. And so, ironically, as I began to grow as a writer in the English language, so would my alienation from my parents and the rest of the Overseas Chinese community in the Philippines, which was largely a merchant class interested only in commerce, not art.

KKC Both Jessica Hagedorn's *Dogeaters* and your own *Mother Tongue* describe the pervasiveness of U.S. cultural imperialism in the Philippines. Were you enamored of American pop culture?

PSL Oh, yes. Absolutely. We sang all the songs, read all the books and magazines, saw all the movies and TV shows. Something many of us did up through our early teenage years was to write our favorite American movie stars care of their movie studios in Hollywood, asking for their autographed pictures. Among my childhood treasures were the pictures I received from Doris Day, Jeffrey Hunter, Audrey Hepburn, Troy Donahue, Jean Simmons, James Dean, etc.

Paul Stephen Lim

KKC When and why did you come to the United States? Do you remember your first impression of this country? Any big surprises?

PSL Pure and simple, I wanted to go to the source of the language I wrote and dreamed in, to where the art was being created. In the Philippines, we had to wait weeks, sometimes months and years, before we would get a chance to read the books and magazines, to see the movies and plays, that were "current." I wanted to have it all, and quickly.

I did not know what it actually meant, the idea of the Philippines being a colony of the United States, until I arrived in the United States. Once I was in America, I found it difficult to shake off "the colonial mentality." Yet the moon was not bigger in America. Not everything was better in America. The biggest surprise for me was that not all white people were teachers or artists or intellectuals. To this day, it makes me uncomfortable to deal with white people who are not bright or well educated, who are in fact quite ignorant and stupid.

KKC Now that you have spent almost three decades in the United States, do you feel at home in your adopted country, or do you still feel "homeless"?

PSL Quite truthfully, I never really feel "at home" anywhere. When I am lecturing in the classroom at the University of Kansas, I sometimes find myself addressing the students as "You Americans" instead of "We Americans." I frequently talk about "Us Chinese" but never about "Us Filipinos." Carlos Bulosan says, "Home is where the heart is." My heart is in America.

KKC Looking back, do you feel you were lucky to grow up in the Philippines, where there seemed to be a greater tolerance for homosexuality than in China?

PSL I have no way of comparing the two cultures because I did not grow up in China. In the Philippines, even though "the *bakla*," the homosexual, was very visible in the society, he/she was still very much the stereotypical object of fun and sometimes ridicule, as in Western society. The *bakla* was the flamboyant, effeminate homosexual, usually a couturier, a hairstylist, a florist, an antique dealer, etc. Macho teenage boys who participated in homosexual sex were not thought to be *bakla*. Because of the high premium that the Roman Catholic Church placed on the virginity of women, it became permissible for the boys to "play" with each other until it was time for them to get married. Homosexuality was merely a phase that many boys went through because "good girls" were not available for sex. As for the Overseas Chinese, I'm not sure if there was tolerance or intolerance for homosexuality. The subject was never discussed in my household, and thus I don't know what attitudes toward homosexuality there might have been. Occasionally I would hear some of my elders referring to someone as being "half ram, half ewe." That was the term used to describe the homosexual, but, to my childhood ears, the term was not used with scorn or derision.

KKC As you said, gay people are often stereotyped as effeminate, and so are Asian American men in the United States. Do you agree with David Henry Hwang that Asian men are perceived as effeminate even in the American gay quarter?

PSL In America, stoicism is often confused with weakness and passivity, so there is a great deal of truth in David Henry Hwang's identification of the Butterfly syndrome in many East-West relationships. Also, rightly or wrongly, perhaps because America is such a *big* country, most Americans prefer to have *big* things—big houses, big yards, big cars, big breasts, big penises. While I have never seen their respective appendages, it wouldn't surprise me greatly if Bruce Lee were "bigger" than Bruce Willis or Jack Nicholson "smaller" than Jackie Chan.

Paul Stephen Lim

KKC Have you encountered any racism or homophobia at Lawrence?

PSL Lawrence, Kansas, is no different from the rest of America, and I'm sure racism and homophobia exist here. But, to my knowledge, I have not been the specific target of such hatred. This may be due to the fact that I live in a fairly protected academic environment, surrounded by people who are fairly enlightened. If any of my colleagues or students are in fact racist and/or homophobic, they simply wouldn't be open about it, for fear of being considered politically incorrect or, worse, having lawsuits brought against them.

KKC When I saw *Mother Tongue* back in 1988, I was struck by its bold articulation of a gay Asian American identity, especially considering that you were writing in the Midwest. How did the audience—both in California and in Kansas—respond to the homosexual material in the play?

PSL My recollection is that the audiences in Los Angeles and Kansas seemed more interested in my depiction of the behavior of the American military in Asia during World War II and the Vietnam War. The only time there was a discussion of the homosexual material came after the staged reading of the play this past summer at the University of Hawai'i in Manoa. I was not present at the reading or the discussion, but the director, Chris Millado, emailed me that the audience was very uneasy about the professor in the play even daring to contemplate a sexual relationship with one of his students. In this case, I think the audience was merely responding to the issue of sexual harassment. Race and gender had nothing to do with it, I think. This same audience would have been equally upset with David Mamet's *Oleana,* wherein a white male professor is accused of harassing a white female student.

KKC David Lee in *Mother Tongue* finds it difficult to tell his mother about his sexual orientation. Is it because the mother is Chinese or Christian or both? Is silence really better?

PSL David Lee in that play would have difficulty talking to his mother about anything that truly mattered to him. He has been so alienated from his parents by his Western-style education that he really has nothing to say to her or to discuss with her. The subject of his sexual orientation simply would not come up, just as he would not discuss art and literature with her. This isn't a question of David being "dishonest." In this case, "honesty" would serve no purpose whatsoever, and silence is golden.

KKC The mother in the play, who is a devout Christian, nevertheless observes traditional Chinese rituals at her husband's funeral. Is such religious hybridity common in the Philippines?

PSL Yes, but I'm not sure this is unique to the Chinese in the Philippines, who want the best of three worlds, the Buddhist, the Confucian and the Christian. Don't the Japanese do the same with Buddhism, Shintoism, and Christianity? The Filipinos call such people *seguratistas,* people who want "to be sure" they are included among the winning team, whatever that team might be.

KKC What about yourself? Do you have any religion?

PSL When I was young, I fell in love with the rituals of the Roman Catholic Church, but Pope John XXIII changed all that. While I no longer belong to any particular church or religion, I continue to believe in goodness and doing good.

KKC You once said that *Mother Tongue* is all fact, but it is also all fiction. At the climax of the play, David Lee learns that his brother Nelson was burned to death when some drunken American soldier threw a grenade at him at the end of World War II. Did you make that up?

Paul Stephen Lim

PSL With some of my plays, when I'm asked if they are "autobiographical," my glib reply is, "All of it, and none of it." The story of how Nelson died is one I grew up with, sorrowfully. I have a scar on my right knee that my mother tells me is from the blast of the grenade that blew Nelson to bits. I would be dead, too, if a servant's body had not shielded me from the blast. In real life, the name of the brother who died was Arthur. Ironically, my mother had named him after the son of General MacArthur. My mother had heard on the radio that the general had a son named Arthur MacArthur.

KKC Can you give an example of how you convert the raw material of life into a scene in the play?

PSL I worked as a copywriter in Manila for seven years, first for J. Walter Thompson Co., then for Philippine Advertising Counselors. The advertising campaigns used in *Mother Tongue* and *Figures in Clay* for Pond's cold cream, Philippine Standard [the Philippine version of American Standard, the company that manufactures toilets], and Philippine Air Lines were real advertising campaigns that I had worked on and that had been used by those clients. I "borrowed" these for the plays because they helped show David's wit and expertise and also because some of the key words used in those advertising campaigns actually helped advance the plot. For example, the use of the phrase *the old guard* versus *the new guard* becomes crucial in revealing the relationships in *Figures in Clay*. I prepared the advertising campaign for Universal Travel and Tours in *Mother Tongue* as though it were for a real client. I had fun doing it.

KKC *Figures in Clay* revolves around an interracial and intergenerational triangle stalked by AIDS. Is there any particular message you wish to convey through that play?

PSL The three men in *Figures in Clay* are at a crossroads physically, psychologically, spiritually, and at least two of them don't seem to know which road to take. Thus, they are in limbo, in stasis, inert. It is a terrible situation for anyone to be in. Anyone who has ever had unsafe sex can only wait and hope that the tests will come up negative. This is the only time in life when being negative is good. Being positive leads to death.

KKC You said they are at a "crossroads." What are their options?

PSL I'll try to answer the question, albeit in a roundabout fashion. In *Figures in Clay,* one of the characters talks about the "dilemma" one faces when one is halfway through reading a book one isn't particularly enjoying. To give up on the book is to admit that the time already spent on the book has been wasted. To carry on reading could ultimately prove rewarding, or not. In this sense, analogously, the men in the play are at a "crossroads" in their relationship.

KKC What inspires you to write? Do you feel a sense of social purpose, or is it art for art's sake? Or the pursuit of "truth"?

PSL All the above. I take writing very seriously. Even when I am punning or being frivolous, I am serious. I firmly believe that everything in life is political.

KKC How do you feel about the label *Asian American writer/playwright*? What kind of audience do you have in mind when you write? Do you feel a split between mainstream and ethnic audiences?

PSL I just said that all life is political. To call oneself an Asian American writer means that the writer wants to be identified as such because of his or her politics. My ethnic heritage and background makes me an Asian American writer, but my material is not always Asian American. Being Asian American is just part of what I am. It is not the sum total of me. My politics go beyond being Asian American or being gay.

Paul Stephen Lim

KKC Can you tell us more about your politics? What concerns you most right now?

PSL Among other things, *Report to the River* concerns itself with the "river" that separates the rich and the poor, the haves and the have-nots, in our society. If I were to make a list of the things that truly make me angry, it would be filled with all the terrible divisions in life that separate us, especially in areas dealing with race, gender, and social class.

KKC There are few Asian (American) characters in your plays except in *Mother Tongue, Points of Departure, Homerica,* and *Figures in Clay.* Is that because Asian American topics are too close to home?

PSL If the material calls for the characters to be Asian, then they are. Because I am living in the heartland of white America, where I have few contacts with other Asians, especially in the arts, I don't find myself thinking about Asian or Asian American themes as frequently as I might if, for example, I were living in Hawai'i or California.

KKC How do you go about writing a play? Do you start with a plot or characters? Do you already know how the play will end when you begin writing?

PSL It varies from play to play. But most of my plays got written because there were stories in my mind that would not rest or go away. For the most part, I know how my plays are going to end, but sometimes there are surprises, even for me. The play I just finished writing this summer, *Report to the River,* took me somewhere completely unintended and unexpected. I had no idea it would end that way, but it did, and I'm pleased.

KKC Isn't *Report to the River* based on a true event?

PSL Yes. But, unlike Truman Capote's use of real events in

In Cold Blood, the true facts I was working with actually led me somewhere else, so that the true facts in the play became less important than the fiction I was creating.

KKC I want to know more about the fact and your fiction. You use *Rashomon*-esque techniques very effectively in this play. The different versions of "what happened" in *Report to the River* also remind me of Maxine Hong Kingston's depiction of what happened to her No Name Aunt. Why do you create these versions? In your own mind, which of them is "true"?

PSL I am very much a fan of Kurosawa. Even more than *Rashomon,* my favorite Kurosawa film is *High and Low,* based on the novel by Patricia Highsmith. The four versions of how the boy died in *Report to the River* are based on the actual case, wherein the man accused and convicted of killing the boy gave four different versions of how the boy died. According to the psychiatrists and clinical psychologists who testified in court, the man was suffering from a mental disorder called *fixed delusions.* He would forget all previous versions of the story he had told as soon as he fixated on a new version. After studying all the court transcripts and interviewing the man for over sixteen hours, I still didn't know which of the four versions to believe, and so I decided to change the fourth version, to make a quantum leap from a "satanic killing" by the "Antichrist" as represented by the letter *A* that had been carved on the boy's chest to other things that might also have been symbolized by that letter *A,* such as America itself. For me, the play is not just a "murder mystery." I hope I don't sound too pretentious when I say that the play is a mirror I am holding up to America. My play *Homerica* also did this.

KKC Be pretentious. What kind of mirror are you holding up to America?

Paul Stephen Lim

PSL *Homerica* was written in 1977, and I meant it to be an epic overview—like the *Odyssey*—of the American family—past, present, and probable future. Being Chinese, and having been raised to believe in the sanctity of the family and the clan, I was unhappy with what the Republicans are now calling the breakdown of family values in America. I'm a Democrat, and I identified the problem long before anyone had ever heard of Dan Quayle. As for *Report to the River*, I think it goes without saying that the play shows us our insatiable obsession with crime and violence—as a society, we cannot seem to get enough of O. J. Simpson, JonBenet Ramsey, Andrew Cunanan, etc. These are our new media heroes.

KKC The theme of violent death recurs in your work, for example, *Conpersonas, Mother Tongue, Report to the River*. Do you know why you are drawn to this particular theme?

PSL I hadn't realized it was a recurring element in my work. You are the first to point it out. I've always thought of myself as being fairly sanguine and pacific by nature. It's odd, however, that the word *sanguine* now means "cheerful" and "optimistic" when its original meaning was somehow related to "blood." I have never hit anyone physically, only verbally, which is not to say that you cannot draw blood verbally. Be that as it may, perhaps all this physical "repression" seeks violent and bloody release in my creative life.

KKC Who are your favorite writers, and which have the strongest influence on your writing?

PSL I was a voracious reader as a child. In one week, I'd have read *The Wizard of Oz* and *Crime and Punishment*. Among prose writers, I greatly admire Graham Greene, William Faulkner, William Saroyan, John Fowles, James Baldwin, John Cheever. Among dramatists, Shakespeare, Ibsen, and Chekhov. Almost everything by Tennessee Williams and

Arthur Miller. And the early work of Tom Stoppard and Harold Pinter.

KKC What about among writers of Asian descent?

PSL Carlos Bulosan, Nick Joaquin, Li-Young Lee.

KKC I also wonder whether Freud has been a strong influence because so many of your works attribute the protagonist's angst to his unresolved relationship with his parents, especially his mother?

PSL Like it or not, Freud is now part of the Judeo-Christian culture. When I was in high school, I seriously thought about going to medical school and on to psychiatry, but it wasn't meant to be.

KKC I went to your talk about father-son relationships in the films of Ang Lee. Yet there are hardly any father-son relationships in your own work except in "Flight" [in *Some Arrivals*]. Would you care to say anything about your own relationship with your father?

PSL After my mother lost her first two children, she took over my upbringing, and that upbringing did not allow very much contact with my father by way of normal father-son activities through sports and the like. My father allowed my mother to live in her paranoia and to raise me the way she did. He retreated into silence; and my greatest regret in life is that I never really knew him, never really had a genuine conversation with him. Oddly enough, when I look at myself in the mirror these days, it is his image (and maybe also his spirit) I see staring back at me.

KKC In the same talk you also mentioned how happy you were to come across Ang Lee's films, to see real Asians instead of stereotypes such as Charlie Chan or Fu Manchu. Do you think that is something you yourself have done and want to do, to create some believable Asian (American) characters?

Paul Stephen Lim

PSL Ang Lee is an artist. With *Sense and Sensibility* and *The Ice Storm*, he is going beyond the Asian and the Asian American. The world is now his oyster, as it should be, and I am so happy for him. And for "us," too.

KKC Tell us something about EAT. In what sense is it alternative theater?

PSL In addition to producing plays by my playwriting students in the English Department at the University of Kansas, the English Alternative Theatre [EAT] produces plays that are not particularly "commercial." These are mostly plays by people of color, plays by women, plays by gays and lesbians. We are also alternative in the sense that we have no permanent home or venue. We are gypsies, and we frequently use alternative, nontheatrical spaces for our performances.

KKC Tell us the difference between writing a story and writing a play. Which do you find the most exciting or challenging?

PSL In prose fiction, a writer can readily enter the mind or consciousness of a character and report truthfully what that particular character is thinking or feeling. This is not easily achieved in the theater. Hamlet's "To be or not to be" speech is a good example. Here, Shakespeare is forced to use a prosaic device, not a theatrical device. If Hamlet is merely thinking these thoughts, we would not be able to hear the words inside his head. On the other hand, we do not ordinarily go around speaking out loud to ourselves in this fashion, so the device seems awkward, artificial. I used to derive great pleasure from writing short stories, but these days I find it more challenging to tell the same stories on a stage.

KKC How do you feel about writing and performing plays in the heartland of America?

PSL Working in Lawrence, Kansas, is both a plus and a

minus. The plus is that there is no great pressure to succeed commercially. Ultimately, I work to please myself and can only hope that what pleases me will also please others. The minus is that, for the same amount of work, so few people get to see the final product here. For example, if *Report to the River* were being performed in Los Angeles or New York City instead of Lawrence, Kansas, the production would be reviewed by the *Los Angeles Times* or the *New York Times* instead of the *Lawrence Journal-World,* and more people would know about the play, and maybe more people would see the play, and maybe more people would be moved intellectually or touched emotionally by my work.

KKC The protagonist in "Flight" often watches his own life as though he were a character in a story or a movie; he allows his emotions to surface only "in the dark of movie houses or between the pages of books" [1982, 16]. As a playwright and director, do you sometimes feel a similar estrangement from or objectification of yourself?

PSL Yes. Even when I am an active participant in a scene, I am always watching myself watching.

KKC Yet you say you cry every time you think about the need to euthanize your pet, Imelda, who has cancer. . . .

PSL Truthfully, I am quite embarrassed to be feeling this way about a dog. There must be something very wrong with me that I cannot or do not allow myself to feel this way about people I know. By the way, it will interest you to know that, two days ago, I drove to a pet shop in Topeka and bought a fifteen-week-old female keeshond. Her name is MyKee. I did this in the hope that Imelda will teach the new puppy how to behave in this house, that maybe Imelda will pass on some of his own good nature to the new puppy, that maybe the puppy will give Imelda a new lease (leash?) on life, but the truth is I did it for me. When the time comes and Imelda has to be euthanized, I think it will be easier on me if there is already another puppy in the house. My friends are more confused than ever that Imelda is a "he" and that MyKee is a "she." Gender be damned, I say.

KKC What would you say to someone who wishes to become a playwright? Any words of wisdom?

PSL You will have the best of times, the worst of times. Also, seriously, there is little money to be made writing for the theater; so be prepared to find some other way to pay the bills while you are writing.

Selected Works by Paul Stephen Lim

"Pulchritude." *Solidarity* (Manila) 8, no. 9 (1974): 80. Poem.

"Relationships in the Making." *Bridge: An Asian American Perspective* 3, no. 4 (1974): 39. Poem.

"Alternatives." *Philippine Panorama* (Manila), 13 July 1975, 30. Poem.

"Ode to Discipline." *Irish Times* (Dublin), 21 April 1975, 8. Poem.

"A Portrait of the Filipino Male as Impotent." *Philippine Panorama* (Manila), 17 August 1975, 8–9. Essay.

Conpersonas: A Recreation in Two Acts. New York: Samuel French, 1977.

From *Points of Departure. Bridge: An Asian American Perspective* 5, no. 2 (1977): 27–29. The whole work has appeared as *Some Arrivals, but Mostly Departures* (1982).

Some Arrivals, but Mostly Departures. Quezon City, Philippines: New Day, 1982.

Flesh, Flash and Frank Harris: A Recreation in Two Acts. Louisville, Ky.: Aran, 1985.

Hatchet Club. In *Plays,* vol. 1, ed. Cj Stevens. Baton Rouge: Oracle, 1985.

Homerica: A Trilogy on Sexual Liberation. Louisville, Ky.: Aran, 1985.

Woeman: A Recreation in Two Acts. Louisville, Ky.: Aran, 1985.

Figures in Clay: A Threnody in Six Scenes and a Coda. Louisville, Ky.: Aran, 1989.

Mother Tongue: A Play. Louisville, Ky.: Aran, 1992.

"He Takes with Him Memories of Ourselves." In *Dreamtime: Remembering Ed Ruhe, 1923–1989,* ed. Robert Day and Fred Whitehead. Chestertown: Literary House, 1993.

Report to the River. Lawrence, Kans.: English Alternative Theater, 1997. Play.

3

S. P. Somtow

Interview by
RAHPEE THONGTHIRAJ

A Thai European American writer, S. P. Somtow was born in Thailand in 1952. He has written books ranging from science fiction to fantasy and horror novels. He grew up in various European countries and was educated at Eton and Cambridge, where he received his M.A. in English and music. Somtow first made his name as a postserialist composer; his work has been performed, broadcast, and televised on four continents.

In the late seventies, he began to write speculative fiction and won the 1981 John W. Campbell Award for best new writer as well as the Locus Award for his first novel, *Starship and Haiku* (1981). He has also won the Daedalus Award for his historical novel, *The Shattered Horse* (1986). His young adult novel, *Forgetting Places* (1987), was selected as an outstanding book of the year by senior high school students participating in the national Books for Young Adults Program. His short fiction has twice been nominated for the Hugo Award (the science fiction equivalent of the Oscar) as well as four times for the Bram Stoker Award (for horror). *Vampire*

Junction (1984) is widely believed by critics to be of importance in the modern "splatterpunk" movement.¹

Having lived in Thailand, Japan, Holland, England, and the United States, Somtow is, like one of the characters in his autobiographical *Jasmine Nights* (1994), "a creature of two worlds." Somtow describes how Justin, the novel's protagonist, struggles to reconcile his cultural differences to reconnect himself to his native roots and absorb his Thai European culture. At the beginning of the story, Justin perceives himself as solely "English"; he prefers to think of himself as an adult Englishman who is knowledgeable in the classics. Perhaps Justin rebels against his native culture because he cannot understand how his Thai heritage is a vital part of his identity. His great-grandmother warns him that he has internalized the European standards and lost the values of his Thai culture:

> Now, listen to me, my child. Contrary to what you may have led yourself to believe, you are not English. I know you are a creature of two worlds . . . but the path you must take lies between them. Think of your chameleon. Perhaps his death is a sign. Perhaps it is you who must absorb his spirit now, my child, you who must learn to change the colour of your soul. If you don't learn this, I promise you that you will spend the rest of your life adrift, clinging to planks, without ever catching sight of land. (p. 5)

Because Justin tries to suppress his cultural identity, he remains a lost soul. His wise and sensitive elder encourages him to take a long-awaited journey in which he will experience a metamorphosis. For Justin to find a balance between the European and the Thai cultures, he must take the path that "lies between" them to gain self-knowledge.

Like his young protagonist, Somtow denied his Thai heritage and identity yet could never escape from the truth. It has

S. P. Somtow

taken years for him to integrate the disparate parts of his life in order to accept who he is. While his father collected degrees and became a diplomat, Somtow lived and traveled all over Europe and Asia. With his diverse cultural background, Somtow felt he "was always . . . shifting from one culture to the next."

From his childhood to his young adulthood Somtow lived like a recluse, protected from the outside world. As he describes his childhood experiences, he reflects on the loneliness and painful alienation he experienced while growing up in Thailand. Although as a child he attended school in Europe, he returned to Thailand when he was seven but continued his "classical" or "European" education there. Like Justin in *Jasmine Nights,* for most of his childhood Somtow refused to speak Thai and to accept Buddhist values. Sheltered in his family's huge upper-class estate, and surrounded by only Thai-speaking relatives, the young Somtow, an Anglophile, felt culturally alienated.

Desperately trying to suppress his "other" culture and past, Somtow at first wrote only infrequently about his personal experiences in Thailand or his tricultural dilemma. But, after writing *Fiddling for Waterbuffaloes* (1986), which reflects the cultural alienation he often felt while living in places such as Japan or his homeland, Somtow began to explore his past, setting a number of stories in Thailand, including "Chui Chai" (1991), a Frankenstein story about AIDS in Bangkok, and *Jasmine Nights,* which satirically portrays the lifestyles of Thai high society in the sixties.

When I first spoke with Somtow on the phone about interviewing him at his house in Sun Valley, outside Los Angeles, he wryly warned me, "It's the house that everyone hates." As I approached the house, which resembled the mansion in the "Munsters" television show, I was not surprised to see a large, unkempt lawn, hovering trees, and a worn-out mailbox. Before I entered the house, Somtow greeted me with a

Words Matter

Sawadee krap (*hello* in Thai) and asked me to remove my shoes. Surrounded by dinosaur relics and cluttered bookshelves full of his published works and science fiction magazines, we began our casual interview over warm cups of coffee.

RT You began writing science fiction in 1977. Why did you pick this genre?

SPS Though my first career was as a composer, I turned to writing science fiction as a way of working myself out of a block that I had in music. I enjoyed reading science fiction as a kid. It was another part of my unconscious that had never been given a voice before, and the other one [his musical voice] had become dumb. I guess [my unconscious] was forced to speak.

RT Can you describe the character development and theme of your first critically acclaimed science fiction novel, *Starship and Haiku*?

SPS It's a very strange novel. It's a postholocaust novel, which is unfashionable now that the cold war is over. The postholocaust novel is a genre in science fiction. *Starship and Haiku* is a novel in which the only surviving civilization is Japan. The daughter of the Japanese interior minister is contacted by a whale, and the whale reveals that the Japanese race is a result of genetic experiments performed by whales of the past. The revelation leads to a big wave of suicide by the Japanese. The Japanese are not entirely human because the whales created them. It's a very surreal novel, rather apocalyptic. It's also full of these strange satirical things. The main character is a woman, and her relationship with the whale is central to the story. She is a very strong woman in a very submissive culture. The Japanese culture has reverted to a more medieval one, so it's much more repressive. It's a feminist novel in a way.

S. P. Somtow

RT What kind of science fiction did you read as a child?

SPS Theodore Sturgeon's *The Skills of Xanadu,* published in the late sixties, and Ray Bradbury's works.

RT How does your cultural background influence your science fiction?

SPS When I was writing science fiction, I used a lot of my background, but I disguised it. For example, in *Starship and Haiku,* there's this hundred-page dinner party. As a consequence of what these people are saying, entire planets are being destroyed. It's in the context of an elaborate game that the people at the dinner party are playing, replete with a long description of the foods they are eating. This really is a veiled reference to the enormous family gatherings of my childhood at which the fates of many people were being discussed at great length and decided on.

My experiences and travels have a great influence on my writing, although a lot of it is not necessarily that obvious. One of the most disorienting things of my early life was my discovery that there was no particular culture that was the way it had to be. I was always changing or shifting from one culture to the next. Because of that, when I started writing, it tended to be in the science fiction field, where you could simply create new cultures by "stealing" a little of this and that, mixing them up. So it was sort of an anthropological task as it were. It was only very slowly that I moved into the realm of more realistic fiction. I felt I needed to rely less and less on spectacle and develop new ways of looking at the human condition.

RT What do you mean by "shifting from one culture to the next"?

SPS I spent my entire life in various cultures, thus was forced to adjust very rapidly. I was like a chameleon, and I existed on the perimeters of each culture.

RT Has it been a struggle for you to write on "Asian" topics?

SPS It took about ten years for me to write about Thailand. First, I had to remember my history, which came flooding back to me. In 1978, when I returned to Thailand, I became very involved with traditional Thai music. This is what began the process of reconnecting to my Thai culture. After my involvement with Thai music, I became a professional writer. I did not write about my Thai culture for ten years. My parents did not encourage me to write about it. Yet I did write about other Asian cultures from an alien perspective. I wrote about the Japanese culture, which is just as alien to me as the Thai culture. Science fiction is cultural anthropology. As a science fiction writer, I'm always transplanting real cultures that I encounter into futuristic settings. Consequently, I have incorporated many elements of Thai culture in ways that are unrecognized.

RT Does *Jasmine Nights* represent ways of reexamining and reclaiming your sense of identity and history?

SPS Seeing oneself as a chameleon is an alien way of looking at the concept of self. When I was a kid, I used to think of myself as English, like Justin in *Jasmine Nights,* which is a story of someone set right in the middle of a complex alien culture. And the only way Justin can connect to his culture is to see how it relates to other "alien" cultures. He has to dig deeper into his past to find the connections.

RT Your works have expanded to include science fiction, horror novels, and books for young adults. You haven't written science fiction for seven years. Why did you move away from it?

SPS I've become disenchanted with science fiction. Much of my short fiction simply deals with subject matter that is too provocative to be taught in high schools, like *Forgetting*

Places, a story about teenage suicide, which ironically was voted best work of the year by high school students, according to a survey done by the University of Iowa.

RT Why are you disenchanted with science fiction?

SPS I am not actually disenchanted with it, but there is a ghettoization of science fiction. It is not taken seriously.

RT In 1984, you wrote your first horror novel, *Vampire Junction,* viewed by Robert Bloch as of great significance in the "splatterpunk" movement.[2] *Moon Dance* (1989) was nominated for the American Horror Award. Would you say something about *Moon Dance?*

SPS It's a great immigration saga about a family of werewolves who settled in the United States in the sixties. It's sort of a combination of the great American novel with extremely graphic horror and kinky sex. The werewolves are a Freudian symbol of the beast within. I made the werewolves behave exactly like wolves do in real life; when they're in human form, they mark their territory. The alpha female is the only one that can mate. I established complicated human analogues for all the different things the wolves actually do in the wild. I've tried to transfer this to a civilized Victorian society. Since most of the setting of the book is in South Dakota, I had to do extensive research. I spent a lot of time speaking to many Native Americans and learning the native languages long before *Dances with Wolves* was made.

RT How do you write your stories? Where do you derive all this creativity from? Is writing a novel or a short story a long process?

SPS No, I take hardly any time to write. That's the oddest thing. It takes me a long time to think of the characters, settings, and themes. Yet, when I write, the ideas come out. I seem to receive the words directly from somewhere. But I

Words Matter

realize that I can easily write without taking a lot of time because the words of great authors from my classical education were beaten into me when I was too young to understand them.

RT Who is your main source of inspiration? Which authors have influenced you the most?

SPS When I was very young, I spent a lot of time reading works by Shakespeare and the Greek tragedians. In my small way I try to follow or imitate the way Shakespeare was reinventing the language. I try to write as though the English language is being discovered for the first time.

RT When you write your stories, do you see yourself as a detached observer?

SPS The whole point of writing today is to place ourselves within the mind of the character. It's sort of method writing. So you try to become who the character is in that particular setting. I don't suddenly change the point of view around the character in some intense scene. I use multiple viewpoints, but I never suddenly jump from one viewpoint to another in the middle of a scene. I think it's bad style.

RT Does your audience play a role in your writing? Is your audience largely "mainstream"? Is there a particular effect you want to create in the audience?

SPS My audience is largely American and European. Most of my readers do not think of me as other than an American writer. Ever since I stopped trying to please my readers my audience has grown larger. Now I do whatever I want, and I find my work has become more popular. I don't take any reviews seriously, whether they're critical or uncritical. You have to trust yourself.

Everything I write is subversive to a certain extent. Any writer who deliberately imparts a moral to a story is not a

S. P. Somtow

writer. You don't deliberately set out to write a moral story. If you do, you're a teacher, not a writer. A writer just shows, not show and explain. When I write, I'm always trying to show people aspects of reality they have missed.

RT What do you mean by not trying to please your audience?

SPS The publishing industry is a political game. Publishers package books and place labels on them. I prefer my books to be read for what they are. That's why I wrote *Jasmine Nights* without any labels. Initially, *Jasmine Nights* was rejected by every publisher. They stated that I was not a "mainstream" writer and can't be writing this kind of book now. The rejection letters stated that the book was not "politically correct" because *Jasmine Nights* portrayed Thais as rich and sophisticated and Americans as poor and culturally backward. The novel was published by Hamish Hamilton, a prestigious publisher in England, and was later bought by American publishers, who were waiting in line to publish it.

RT Have you found it difficult to publish? Are there particular obstacles or opportunities for an Asian American writer?

SPS It hasn't been particularly hard. Thais are not an oppressed minority. There are many Asian groups that have been oppressed, but I don't think Thais are. There have been few stereotypes and misconceptions about Thais because they are more invisible than other Asian groups. For example, people see Koreans as owning mom-and-pop stores. But Thais are more invisible, like in Middle America, which has no idea of what Thais are like because they have not seen enough of them. The clichés and preconceptions are shifting. Thais seem to be subjected to the general clichés that many Asians are subjected to. I think Thais are sometimes perceived as a bizarre cross between the wild, dark, sexual creatures and the prudery of individuals. Thais own restaurants, and the "Land of Smiles."

RT How comfortable are you with the label *Asian American writer?*

SPS I do not believe it's good for any writer to be called anything other than a writer. I do not mind being called an Asian writer, but being labeled just as a writer gives me more freedom. I want to be perceived as a writer, not as an Asian writer. I feel dishonest exploiting the Asian connection. It seems like a cheap way to gain fame. Because I spent very little of my life in Thailand, I didn't feel that qualified to talk about it. Thus, I spent the first ten years of my literary career trying to avoid any ethnic labeling. It was actually rather a struggle to write about Asian things. As I grew older and spent more time in Thailand, I became more and more Asian. It's a complex relationship between me and all the members of my family. I have a very large and complicated family, just like the one in *Jasmine Nights*. Because I never felt comfortable speaking or writing about my ethnicity, I never felt particularly involved in it. Now, I'm more comfortable speaking Thai.

Notes

1. The term *splatterpunk* was coined in 1986 during a debate over what constitutes "horror" literature. According to Louis J. Kern, "splatter literally refers to brutal sexual violation, dismemberment, and slaughter. Depictions of torture, fear, and pain raise the following questions: 'What does it mean to be human? and what are the limits of human consciousness?'" Splatterpunk literature transgresses literary and theatrical conventions through uses of shock, spectacle, and fear. According to Kern, "Splatterpunk, or the 'new horror' . . . is an aggressively confrontational literature of contemporary alienation," not to be subsumed under "classic horror literature" ("American 'Grand Guignol': Splatterpunk Gore, Sadean Morality, and Socially Redemptive Violence," *Journal of American Culture* 19 [1996]: 49, 47).

2. Robert Bloch, *S. P. Somtow: A Biography* (New York: Spectrum; Hollywood: Shapiro-Lichtman, n.d.).

Selected Works by S. P. Somtow

Starship and Haiku. New York: Pocket, 1981.

Vampire Junction. London: Gollancz Horror, 1984.

The Shattered Horse. New York: TOR, 1986.

Forgetting Places. New York: TOR, 1987.

Aquila and the Iron Horse. New York: Del Rey, 1988.

Symphony of Terror. New York: TOR, 1988.

Aquila and the Sphinx. New York: Del Rey, 1989.

Fire from the Wine-Dark Sea. New York: TOR, 1989.

Moon Dance. New York: TOR, 1989.

"Chui Chai" (1991). In *The Year's Best Fantasy and Horror: Fifth Annual Collection,* ed. Ellen Datlow and Terri Windling. New York: St. Martin's, 1992.

Fiddling for Waterbuffaloes (1986). Eugene, Oreg.: Pulphouse, 1992.

I Wake from a Dream of a Drowned Star City. Axolotl, 1992.

Jasmine Nights (1991). New York: St. Martin's, 1994.

The Riverrun Trilogy. Atlanta: White Wolf, 1996.

Vanitas: Escape from Vampire Junction. New York: TOR, 1996.

The Vampire's Beautiful Daughter. New York: Simon & Schuster, 1997.

4

Meena Alexander

Interview by

ZAINAB ALI AND DHARINI RASIAH

Born in India, raised in India and North Africa, educated in England, and now living in New York, Meena Alexander has clearly lived the Indian diasporic experience. As this interview reveals, her work parallels the transitory nature of her life, moving from poetry to prose, fiction to memoirs, essays to testimonials, and consistently infused with politically charged issues, ranging from a rape in Hyderabad, to love during the Gulf War, to racism in the United States. Labels defy her experience. She draws strength from her multiple identities and writes from the borders of a number of communities. As she notes (in an unpublished interview with Dharini Rasiah), "Many of the issues I address in my writing have come quite precisely from this intense, yet edgy relationship with my communities."

This interview was a collective effort, started by Dharini Rasiah but conducted mostly by Zainab Ali. As a writer and an artist, we were interested in discussing what it means to be writing within several different contexts. Our own work explores the lives of South Asian women living in the United

States and captures the predicaments within which we are placed, voluntarily or not. Alexander sorts through similar complexities in the lives of displaced people, of new immigrants, of the politically persecuted. She has a deep sense of justice that permeates much of what she writes. But it is her poetic imagination that shapes her writing and gives it a fluidity and intensity that reveals her passion for life.

ZA I noticed that you write in different genres—poetry, fiction, memoir, literary criticism. You've also moved around: you were born in India, and then you moved to Sudan and then to England and then to Manhattan. And you speak many languages: Malyalam, English, Arabic, Hindi, and French. How does all that intersect with your art and affect your choice to write in so many different genres?

MA What an interesting question! I have never actually conceptualized it like that, but, now that you've said it, it sort of makes sense. Perhaps you are suggesting that there is some connection between speaking different languages and writing in different genres? One thing that I do remember is that, when I was a child, we would go back every year from North Africa to India and we would stop in Bombay. Malyalam I could never forget because it's my mother tongue so it is very deep inside me; but my Hindi, which I had known from childhood, sort of got overlaid with Arabic. It was as if there were not room in my head for each of them simultaneously. In other words, I could speak them separately but not at the same time. So, when I got to Bombay, I would start speaking some Hindi, and it would sound like Arabic; then I would switch to Arabic, and then somehow it was that same region of the brain, almost like a map of languages. Is that in some way like writing in different genres? Perhaps there is some connection.

I was asked to write a response ["Rights of Passage"] to

the editorial statement of a new journal called *Interventions: The International Journal of Postcolonial Studies*. It's edited by Robert Young at Oxford. When I started the prose piece, a short essay really, I felt I was writing a particular sort of language, but then I switched very quickly to include a poem I had written ["Brown Skins, What Mask?"] as well as a line or two from a poem I have just completed called "Rites of Sense." Now using the poems is not just for illustration. I need the discrete music of poetry there, on the page, to make a filter for my thoughts. I need to embed that in the run-on lines of prose reflection. The book *Shock of Arrival* is a more elaborate form of this.

That seems to be the way my mind works. It's finding different points of access to a difficult terrain, but the mental geography is one and the same. Tolstoy said that some writers are like hedgehogs; they just know one thing. And other writers are like foxes; they know a lot of things. I feel I'm like the hedgehog. I know only one thing and have only one or two interrelated problems that I keep getting at in different ways. I don't think of myself as someone with a multitude of questions; I think of myself as most like a landscape I'm making a palette out of, layering. A palimpsest of self . . . that's how I reach time and the density of experience. I remember how as children we also used to have to shift our clothing when we went from Europe to Sudan to India. I'm used to these changes in the garb. And it's a kind of freedom for me to be able to do that. I would feel terrible if somebody said write only this or only that. Yet I basically think of myself as a poet.

ZA You do? I always think of you as a novelist.

MA In a way it really doesn't matter. People who read my poetry in India and who write about my poetry really have not read any of my prose except perhaps *Fault Lines*. I started as a poet. But, because some people are doing dissertations on

Meena Alexander

my work now, they are bringing it together. But still I don't know how all these things work in one's head.

ZA You think that, even though you are writing in different genres, you are still attacking the same issue?

MA I think so. All my life as a writer I've been touching the complexities, sometimes evading them. It has to do with a postcolonial geography, a geography of displacement. You can look at it in terms of my experience as a child, as a woman growing up, or as someone who is living in a racialized world in the United States. There are many ways of looking at it, but there are certain issues that keep coming up.

ZA Before we discuss your different books, I want to ask you about your father because I was fascinated to learn that he was a meteorologist. And I imagined in your household your father always gazing at the stars and you gazing at the migrations of the world and at how you yourself are moving from one continent to another, switching languages, switching clothes as you've said. How might his presence have influenced you?

MA He's been very, very important in my life. He did mathematics, physics, meteorology. His concern with the weather and the changes has been extraordinarily formative for me. He taught me the names of the clouds, the names of the stars, and I knew that his work was always bound up with something that was global and shifting and beyond the edge of perception. In other words, you couldn't ever predict with accuracy. He made me aware of the limitations of science, even as he believed in it as a scientist. From him I also developed a fascination with shifting forms. He has this real passion for clouds and the shapes of clouds. When we went back to India from Sudan, he was very involved in something called the World Weather Watch. There were these huge satellites bringing in data about the monsoons. I've always been fascinated by monsoons, partly because of Kerala, where we lived, but partly because my father taught me a kind of reverence for what might be frightening natural occurrences like terrible thunderstorms. He always called them nature's glory. He's also quite religious, so he had this enormous sense of the ultimate goodness of everything that occurs even if it is destructive in part. That is something I value deeply even though I don't have quite that sense of cosmic awareness that he has.

ZA And your mother?

MA My mother is not a scientist; all her life she has been a housewife. I've just finished this poem called "Rites of Sense" in which I talk about how my mother taught me how to live in her father's house and sweep the threshold, fold a sari, raise a needle, and stitch my woman's breath into the mute amazement of sentences.

ZA Can you explain "the mute amazement of sentences?"

MA This idea is something I did learn from my mother. On the one hand, there's always the sense that, if you're a woman, you should not speak, you should not reveal your emotions. At the same time, she taught me the decorum of a certain kind of traditional living. I sort of combine the two, but the sentences come out mute. A sentence is not just what you write; it's also a life sentence. I got a conflicting set of messages from my parents. My father always wanted me to work. He said, If you're a woman, you should work, which is the opposite of what my mother believed in: a woman should never work outside her home.

ZA And then to move on and write a memoir. Do you feel you betrayed her in some way?

MA Well, I think she was not pleased. She did feel betrayed in some ways. The *Malayalam Manorama*, which is one of the leading Indian newspapers, did a spread on me and titled it something like "Kerala Girl Goes West." It was all in Malayalam. People who had read it would sometimes call on my parents. My mother was actually pleased about this and would serve them tea. It's as if what I did, in some small way, became part of the community. Over the years she has accepted that I'm a writer. Which doesn't mean that she reads what I write. I wouldn't assume that she would want to or even that she should.

ZA But it's good to finally get her approval?

MA I shouldn't presume that: approval. There's a part of her that's proud of me, but I don't think she's comfortable with it. It would not be truthful if I said she is comfortable and happy and proud. She's ambivalent. She realizes that my work is there and people read it. And, when I go to Kerala, people come from the newspapers to interview me, and she's pleased. An interview came out in the *Hindu* last month, and my father of course immediately sends me the cutting, but my mother—you can hear it in her voice—doesn't believe that women should display themselves.

Something of that conflict surely also enters into one's self? There's all this complexity to what it means to live as a writer, as a writing woman. There was once a time when the office next door to mine at Hunter College was occupied for two semesters by Philip Roth. I went to these wonderful lectures he gave on the European novel, was particularly impressed by one on Primo Levi; the clarity, the pain of that historic experience haunted me. The barbarity of what happened. And, once, we were talking about borders, and I said to Philip Roth (this was before I became an American citizen), "I have this fantasy: if only I could swallow my green card, no one would stop me at the borders!" He wanted to see my green card, so I pulled it out and showed it to him. Perhaps he had never seen one before. I will never forget something he later told me: "Meena, if you're a writer, all you have is your life;

you really don't have anything else." I cannot evade that truth, though I think there have been times I've wanted to. We can go only so far with our invented realities. At the end we come back to the soil of our own experience. Who can tell how far that takes us or how far that draws us back?

ZA It's a gamble.

MA But in a sense you don't have anything else. That's the scary part. That's what I meant about being a hedgehog. You just have that, and you're forever approaching it, and sometimes odd things come out because each moment of perception, each act of writing gives you a different piece.

ZA Let's speak about *Nampally Road*. Since we are talking about gender issues, I want to move on and talk about the novel in which twenty-five-year-old Mira returns to India from Britain to teach poetry. The India—the Hyderabad—she returns to seems very different from the one she left; she is entering a very political landscape now. Can you describe that climate?

MA There's an enormous turbulence but also the possibility of a positive change. This was just after the period of emergency, 1975–1977, when civil rights had been withdrawn, and there really was a sense of a restoration of democracy. We were acutely aware of what it might mean to have democratic rights taken away and what it might mean to assert one's civil rights, including the civil rights of women. For me it was both bewildering and enormously exciting. For Mira this is the world she is from, a world in which what she says could count even if only two or three people listen; the boundary between art and the political world is in some ways taken away. And that is one of the energizing things about her experience as I see it.

ZA But at some point she begins to question the necessity of teaching poetry in India.

Meena Alexander

MA It's true because she's teaching not just any poetry; she's teaching English poetry and poetry from the canon. I think that she, like myself, has a helpless love for Wordsworth. In fact, I've just written an essay on Mary Wollstonecraft and female life writing. It's the bicentenary of her death and of the birth of Mary Shelley. I ponder what this enormous love for Wordsworth is. It's almost an impossible love because it's this idea of a native place, of a particular language, of a simple life—none of which is possible for someone like me—and in a sense all of which is written over the Anglican world of which he was a part. The connection with Wordsworth is also a deep one because of the whole question of memory that he foregrounds. But, when you live in a time of enormous turmoil, you think, What's the use of any of this? That's something Mira had to confront.

ZA What prompted you to portray the rape of a woman by the police?

MA It actually happened in Hyderabad when I was there. There was this Muslim woman, Rameeza Be, who was gang raped by the police, and at the time there were a number of such incidents occurring all over India. The police had unchecked power—a real issue of police brutality—and women's groups were starting to organize all around the country, protesting. This particular case became a very famous one in India. A famous jurist called Lotika Sarkar from Delhi actually enacted what is called the Bill of Custodial Rape as a direct result of the Rameeza Be episode, arguing that, if a woman is raped in a police station, a particular kind of case can be made against the police because she is in their custody and is supposed to be protected. Somehow the rape of Rameeza Be became a catalyst for a lot of the unrest that was swirling around Mira's world, and the question arose of what kind of meaning one's history can have in such a world.

ZA When you fictionalized the rape, were you worried about what the Indian press might say about you?

MA No, I wasn't worried at all. My father was worried. He said, "Oh, Meena, if you come back, they'll *gherao* you." I don't know if you know what *gherao* means: it is when you make a circle around somebody and prevent her from moving. A form of attack. Actually, the press was very kind in the sense that the book was taken seriously, and the reviews were by and large positive. And a lot of people read that book. I was in Delhi in the fall of 1996 for a meeting that the Sahitya Akademi [the National Academy of Letters in India] had put together, a chance for writers and artists to discuss the dangers of communal violence in India. The gathering was called in the aftermath of the brutal destruction of Barbri Masjid, a mosque in Ayodhya, by Hindu right-wing groups, and the growth of ethnic violence against minority communities was very much in our minds. What would it mean to build a secular, multicultural India? It was in that context that a professor who was teaching the book and had written about it came up and spoke to me. He said, "You realize of course she's a Muslim woman." And I said, "She is, but, when I wrote it, I hadn't thought about that in particular. But of course she's a member of a minority, and she's violated. I realized that, for this Muslim gentleman, the book was important in a particular way. After Barbri Masjid, the book is read differently.

ZA That is true because the political climate has changed.

MA It has changed. It was the femaleness that I was concerned with, but the fact that she's Muslim is also relevant. Because of the polarization that has happened recently in India, these issues are read differently.

ZA When you come up against issues like those, young writers might be interested to know how you might overcome obstacles. For instance, you mentioned your mother's ambivalence about your writing, and talking about the political climate of our homeland, and being here outside it.

MA I don't really have a strategy. I write about what touches me deeply. And there's no rule. You can't say, You ought to write about this but not about that. For instance, when Safdar Hashmi, the young Marxist playwright, was killed in Delhi, I was not in Delhi, I was in New York, but I knew people who knew him, and it touched me very deeply, the idea of this radical who was killed as he was performing a play. I wrote two poems about it, and the same two poems were published here, in India, and in Britain. They were published in many places, and then last year—the fiftieth anniversary of India's independence—I was in Kerala, and I received an invitation from the Sahitya Akademi and Professor Satchidanandan, the secretary of the Akademi, who said, "Please come and read your poems." I was overwhelmed. I thought: My god, to read at the Sahitya Akademi on Independence Day is a great honor. I got very nervous, and I thought: What should I wear, how should I do my hair? And then I said to myself: Don't be a total idiot. They're not inviting you because of your hair or what you wear. They're inviting you because of your poetry. I would just read exactly what I wanted to read.

I read the poems about Safdar Hashmi's murder[1] and my poem "Paper Filled with Light," and people gave me a wonderful response. It was a powerful moment for me because, when I finished, Krishna Sobti, one of the older Hindi writers, got up and took a red flower, a gladiolus, from the table where the chairman, Bhisham Sahni, was sitting and gave it to me, and she embraced me. A number of the writers there were from the older generation, the Partition era. And I thought, I was sitting in New York writing this poem, but it's all right. I'm doing what I'm meant to do. It was a very, very moving and amazing moment for me because where we live we're so marginal. A poem can travel; the imagination does in fact move over boundaries. I'm an Indian writer; I'm also an American writer. It's all a question of multiple boundaries and affiliations.

ZA It might also help if writers writing across cultures would try to create what you had described as your "born-within" audience—the listening part of yourself—so one is not concerned about what the academics or the critics might say.

MA Obviously it does affect us. We're human beings, and, if we get bad reviews, we get distressed. But I think that, for me as a writer, I had to struggle against censorship from childhood on, so writing has always been a struggle. There has never been someone saying, "Yes, go ahead and write and publish and do well in your poetry." My father did encourage me; my mother didn't, and I internalized that nay-saying. You don't assume that telling the truth or telling the truth of art is going to be something that will necessarily gain you acceptance.

ZA Unlike *Nampally Road*, which moves chronologically in time, *Fault Lines*, your memoir, moves circularly in the sense that you arrange the events on the basis of theme rather than chronology. Did this form arise from looking back on your life and not being able to place it in a very rigid, linear pattern?

MA Yes, what you're saying does make sense. In *Nampally Road*, I made the decision just to have a moment of time, in just one place—carefully bounded. Whereas *Fault Lines* does have to do with layerings of time and place, and the only way I could move through that complexity was by using some of these techniques of association where you move through theme and image rather than chronology.

ZA Almost like poetry.

Meena Alexander

MA I suppose. Yes.

ZA You call your memoir *Fault Lines,* which seems to reflect your particular interest as a writer in describing the shifting ground of loyalties and identities. Can you describe the importance of fault lines for you?

MA There were years when I was a teenager who decided to be a writer, but then I always felt it impossible because I thought to myself: All the great writers have lived in just one place all their life, and they've always been within a certain tradition. I was very upset by this because I felt it was not possible for me to keep on being a writer in the sense of writing a whole body of work because my life was in so many different pieces. And then I came here. I left one world, and there was another I didn't quite understand. Gradually it came to my awareness that there were many people like this in the world, that it wasn't just me, that in a sense the world was always changing and shifting. I wasn't a creature beached out of time. My experience and the structures of my experience might be meaningful to other people. You have to have that hope somewhere; otherwise, you can't really write. You have to hope that someone somewhere will understand what you're saying.

ZA Do you think that writing for you then was an effective means of piecing together your fractured life of being constantly uprooted?

MA Only insofar as I was actually writing. Once a book is finished and published, it doesn't work for me anymore. I have to start from scratch all over again. It's one of the hardest things about being a writer. You can't be like a professor and say, "Yes, I've written book number one on Wordsworth; now I'll do book number two on Coleridge and number three on Keats." You can't do that. As a writer you are always beginning, and so you have to learn humility because you just

Words Matter

start again and again and again. It may be the same ground, and you may get better at your craft, but you still have to go to that scary place of starting all over. Adrienne Rich says somewhere that, if you're a poet, you have to go for where the fear is. That makes a lot of sense. You have to go precisely for those parts of your experience that are unintelligible even to you and to raise the possibility of making sense out of them. Obviously you can't just do that all the time—that is too exhausting—but you have to set that instability, that unknown, within the framework of the known, the experienced, and the sharable world. It can change the sense of the world.

ZA David Mura said that, when he writes, he knows he's writing well when he is writing things about which he feels he's going to lose his entire family if he publishes them. He says it's that fear that keeps him writing because he knows then that he's telling the truth.

MA Yes, I do admire David's work very much. There's a kind of edge to it, and this is why it's so hard. There has to be that edge because you're really out on a limb, even to yourself, or to the part of yourself that would judge you.

ZA Your daughter has inherited fault lines of her own. In your memoir, you write about how she makes a drawing of her family and the preschool teacher is confused because she doesn't seem to know the difference between Indian and Native American.

MA Isn't that amazing? So many people don't. I went to Maine, maybe two or three or four years ago, to give a reading at a college there. I wrote a little about it in *The Shock of Arrival,* but in a cryptic form. Before the reading, the students came up to me and were very apologetic and said, "Look at the newspaper." And in the student newspaper there's a picture of me in a sari, and underneath it said

"Native American poet." And I said, "What happened?" They said, "Well, we put *Indian,* and the editor thought it was politically incorrect and switched it to *Native American.*" So I began [the reading] by saying that I was honored to be considered Native American but that I wasn't; then I spoke about the white man's naming patterns. There are some parts of this country where Asians are so invisible.

ZA Yes, particularly South Asians.

MA South Asians, yes. Because people don't know if you're Arab, or Puerto Rican, or Native American, or Indian. I was very surprised when this happened to my daughter, but then I realized that it isn't as uncommon as we might think.

ZA So what do you think your daughter's challenges will be in this new geography?

MA There will be enormous challenges. I think she'll just take them and get pleasure from them as she goes along. I mean, that's what I hope for her. Just the other day—she's now eleven going on twelve—she was in tears. I asked, "What's the matter?" She says, "Oh mama, what am I going to do?" She said all her friends are being "fake Indians" now. They're all doing henna, and wearing *buttus* [a dot worn on the forehead by some Indian women], and you know these shops have a kind of quick do-it-yourself henna and sell *buttus* and Indian skirts for $50.00. She said, "They're all being fake Indians, poseurs. I'm a real Indian, and I don't even have an Indian skirt." I said, "Don't worry, sweetie. We were in India all summer, and the reason you didn't buy a skirt was that nobody wore them there!" You see how it can work when there's this whole Indian chic at the moment with the teen group? Obviously you have to negotiate these things, and it's hard when you're young because you have to struggle through them. You think, "I'm real, but nobody sees me."

ZA It seems that America's the only culture that can turn other cultures into a fad: bring them in, use them up, and then throw them out and bring in another country.

MA It's pretty hard when you're eleven. But I think at some level you have to learn how to cope with it. And then of course it passes.

ZA I agree. When I was growing up—I grew up in Minneapolis—everyone was of Scandinavian descent; everyone thought that I was mixed or that I was a light-skinned black.

MA Or did they think you were Native American?

ZA They didn't; they couldn't see outside their tiny geography.

MA Yeah, these things are very complicated, and how one makes sense of them, and how the sense marks you, and then how you become a writer, or how you live your life. We pay with our life; that's how we make art.

ZA Yes, and you write that in your memoir. You say that ethnicity is "a violence from within that resists fracturing."[2] Why do you consider it "a violence from within?"

MA Because it comes out as a result of this almost inimical questioning. If I were living in Kerala, I wouldn't need to be Indian, I wouldn't need to be Asian. It comes into existence in a public sphere, where it's under challenge, where you're marked.

ZA In *Manhattan Music,* your most recent novel, when Sandhya first arrives in Manhattan from India, she feels directionless. What kind of issues is she facing as a new immigrant?

MA Through her character I'm trying to deal with a set of voiceless experiences that have to do with feeling that nobody knows what you are, and, because nobody knows what you

Meena Alexander

are and nobody recognizes you, you cannot be yourself. She really has no context in which to put her old experience of life. She's also married, and she doesn't seem to have a real place in this marriage. It's not a partnership for her but something she has drifted into. What also haunt her are the memories of India. For Sandhya this dislocation is something that really cuts her off from a past and won't allow her the space of entry into new life. The book is about how she tries to enter a new life and in the end succeeds. It's almost a rite of passage, the kind of psychic difficulty she goes through; her trying to kill herself is like trying to kill that part of herself that couldn't live because she hadn't integrated her experiences.

For women coming here from India it is particularly hard: the old ways of living are no longer valid, and you haven't really been taught as a woman to branch out on your own. She has nowhere to go outside the house, but the house doesn't nurture her. She doesn't have a broad-based house; she lives in this isolated nuclear family. She's too scared to take a job; she's stuck.

ZA This fear of moving around and the isolation she feels within the nuclear family compared to the extended family at home are all feelings that any immigrant would feel coming to America, leaving strict and rigid rules behind and coming to a place of boundless freedom. No one's taught her the responsibilities of living in a place where there's so much freedom and she has to navigate and learn that herself.

MA Exactly. She does not have a sense at the beginning of what it might mean to live her own life. Her cousin, the one who works in New Jersey who's a social worker, is a very different character. Sakhi has a project; she's fired by certain passions to help other people. And Draupadi, Sandhya's alter ego, is a Caribbean Indian woman who is a performance artist. But Sandhya is all alone, and for me she is a poignant character because there's a longing in her, which I have seen in people, particularly women who've come here and really don't know what to do. I've felt that at some point in my life coming here.

ZA I agree. And yet what's fascinating for me is the concept of America. When I go back to Hyderabad or travel abroad, a lot of people think, Wouldn't it be great to have all that freedom!

MA But freedom for what?

ZA Exactly. And then you arrive here, and that concept is made reality, and suddenly you just become paralyzed. You seem to be saying that neither the rigid rules nor the freedom is the answer, really. What then would you say is the alternative?

MA The alternative is not the absolute freedom because the freedom is also, remember, within a racialized society, and she has to confront what it means to be an Indian here in the United States because she can't be a white person. There's a bit very early where she thinks she could wash off her skin color and become like Marilyn Monroe. She's trying different ways and finding they can't work for her. The question is, What does work? I think it's in Manhattan, through her connection with Draupadi, that she goes through a dark night of the soul and comes out the other end. There are characters in fiction where they just sort of end-stop. I didn't want her to just stop. Then I worried: Was I forcing a possibility of life on her? I did agonize over that as a writer. I could see the anguish inside her, but I didn't want it to end her life. And, in a way, Sakhi helping her, rescuing her, enables her—almost like a newborn creature—to come out of the park. The park is very important because there's a pool of water there and she looks in and sees her face. If you remember the overture to the novel, the monsoon flood ends with Draupadi saying, "Who would hold up a lamp so she could see her eyes see-

Meena Alexander

ing?" [p. 4]. So in a sense she comes to the possibility of self-awareness, which for me is very important for any freedom we conceive.

ZA In an interview with Dharini two years ago, you said about *Shock of Arrival* that you try to capture how the moment of entry into the United States enters the imagination.

MA Such a wonderful statement! I had forgotten it. It's true because isn't that what happens to Sandhya Rosenblum when that moment is spread out through months and years? It's that process of transformation, of self-transformation, of knowing not only how to live your life in a place where you can invent yourself but also how to live your life in a place where, ethnically, you're racialized. You have to understand which possibilities are and aren't available to you. Above that, there is something ontological. In the imaginary, the idea of arrival in America is a big moment, a moment that, because of the immigrant nature of this country, is always returned to. It has to do with a suspicion of the past that one sees in the American psyche. Yet, without history, we really can't live. Emerson wrote that we have no need for memory, which had to do with cutting away from Europe. But, if you cut away from your past, what happens to your present?

ZA You don't have a present.

MA Yes. So that is part of what *Manhattan Music* is. Remember Draupadi keeps quoting Emerson, saying, "We have no need of memory." She's making up her own credo. She's a strange lady.

ZA In a sense, we all do that. We have all these credos to live by, in order to exist. But, with Sandhya, I found her progress of assimilation amazing; even though she arrives here as an adult, she seems very quickly to go through what I know I went through as a child: this wish to wash my skin away.

MA She's older. Her name, *Sandhya,* is that time at dawn or before dusk. It's that in-between zone. I want to convey that sense of in-between-ness through her.

ZA She has an affair with Rasheed, an Egyptian scholar, and she subsequently attempts suicide when he leaves her. In the American context, this may be seen as a woman's weakness. What is it for her?

MA For her it's the intensity of her passion—she feels she's given herself to him—and then it's a very Indian thing also, this idea of passionate love, even if the love is doomed. She feels she has no life apart from him at that point. Part of her passionate self had never come out before, neither in India nor in the United States. I very carefully set the novel during the Gulf War. It's passion in a time of violence, in a time of war. There's an anthology called *Blood into Ink*[3] that contains the writings of Arab and Indian women, South Asian and Middle Eastern women; it includes translations from the Arabic from Lebanon and other countries. I wrote a preface for it called "Translating Violence," and I wrote that at the same time as I was working on the novel. That short essay is also in *Shock of Arrival.* There is a connection between the ruminations there and the novel, in the sense of the whole question of what happens to passion in a time of violence.

ZA Similarly, in *Nampally Road,* there's a dense political backdrop. I know that, for you, the political and the arts seem to be woven together in many ways. Could you tell us whether there's a social purpose behind your work?

MA That's a very, very hard question. Our passions exist in the world, and yet at the same time, when we write, we're alone. Both are important to me. My imagination does come to life most vividly when there is that interface between what is very intense and personal and what is public and contested. That may have to do with the way I was brought up: I was raised by Indian nationalists, and I was brought up on stories of Gandhi and Satyagraha, his political nonviolent resistance. Then as a child I moved to Khartoum, and I was always aware of being at the borders of war, within a space of political turbulence. So the idea of a space that was free of political turmoil hadn't ever been available to me. It's not as if I was born in—let's say Oregon—and lived there all my life. Maybe there is a longing somewhere for a very simple world, but it's just not there for me. What I try to do is give voice to these very simple human experiences of longing and love and loss—all the stuff that makes us what we are—but within this complicated, unstable world, shifting within diasporic and migrant spaces, where identities are contested, where they cannot be taken for granted. Because that's the world I know. It's not something that I feel I should write about; it's just what I have.

ZA Talking with Dharini, you said that often you "feel driven by a deep sense of social purpose, sometimes painfully." What specific social purpose?

MA I do believe at some level in a kind of radical humanism, that all human beings have certain inalienable rights—which is why I love living in America. It's a democracy. Whatever visionary power my work has allies itself to that ideal. Now, I don't think writing should be a political project; I don't believe that at all because I think that would diminish it. But I do hold on to some vision of social justice and equality. I have a poem called "Art of Pariahs," which is in *River and Bridge* and also in *Shock of Arrival;* I wrote it as a response to a series of racial incidents in New York City. At the end there's almost a longing that people could exist, as it were, freed of their skin. Of course you can't.

ZA What are you working on now?

MA I'm working on a series of new poems. I'm actually working on a whole new book of poetry, an autobiographical book that has some poems set in Kerala, some here in Manhattan, and also has some that deal with transit lounges and migrancy. I'm also making notes for a new book of prose. I'm at the moment not entirely sure if it's going to be fiction or memoir. I'm hovering between the borders of one and the other, and I'll just use whatever form seems best for me—but I do want to draw in some of these questions of childhood and travel. And, in a file I've opened in my computer, I didn't put *novel,* and I didn't put *memoir;* I deliberately put *prose book.* I'm always living on the borders of something. It's a struggle for form, and I try to figure out what fits, right?

ZA In *Shock of Arrival* [pp. 1–2], you say, "Coming to America, I have felt in my heart what W. E. B. DuBois invoked. Two souls, two thoughts, in one dark body." And you go on to say, "But now at the tail end of the century, perhaps there are many souls, many voices in this one dark body." What nuances have you captured in this?

MA These are the buried voices that we have to give voice to through our art, the voices that were buried and mutilated and hidden. What is unitary we have done with—we don't need that anymore in terms of looking at life. We want the multiple, the polyvocal, because in this century, certainly, the hegemony of the one has always been frightening and destructive. Whatever simplicities we might aspire to in our art and in our life have to be based on this very complex and calibrated harmony of many voices.

ZA Now that we are coming into the new millennium, what do you see as the new fault lines for all our children and the incipient and evolving ethnic communities?

Meena Alexander

MA I would hope that our children will be able to take a lot more for granted than we can, in terms of the right to community, the right to happiness, the right to choose whom to be with, where to be, when to be. I would like to wish that many of these barbed wires that we see in the world would disappear because we've understood that cycles of violence don't work. For our children, I hope there will be more psychic space to build creative lives, and not just deal with legacies of violence, so that in the millennium we talk about many voices, voices that can also deal with celebration and reparation. The twentieth century has been a difficult century considering the ethnic crises in the former Yugoslavia, Sri Lanka, parts of India. All that violence based on ethnic hatred has to be healed. So I wish that it would be a time of healing for our children, where it doesn't matter what color your skin is or whether you're Indian, or Arab, or African, or Latvian, or Irish (because, after all, the idea of *white* is also a construction), that these things should diminish and fall away.

Notes

1. The Safdar Hashmi poems appear in *River and Bridge* and are reprinted in *Shock of Arrival*.
2. Unless otherwise specified, all such quotations are from an unpublished interview with Dharini Rasiah.
3. Miriam Cooke and Roshni Rustomji-Kerns, eds., *Blood into Ink: South Asian and Middle Eastern Women Write War* (Boulder, Colo.: Westview, 1994).

Selected Works by Meena Alexander

The Bird's Bright Ring: A Long Poem. Calcutta: Writers Workshop, 1976.

I Root My Name. Calcutta: United Writers, 1977.

Without Place. Calcutta: Writers Workshop, 1978.

Stone Roots. New Delhi: Arnold-Heinemann, 1980.

Dear Preferred Cardholder:

The enclosed Bank Check is real and pre-approved in y
Preferred Cardholders, like yourself — who will benefit fro
fraudulent charges will be made by credit card thieves this y

When you cash or deposit the enclosed check, you will re
credit services information, a money-saving list of No-Fee an
Instant Cash Rebate — Yours to Keep — as our gift to you
Guarantee. Plus as an added bonus, you will receive a Free c
credit files contain some sort of error, so it's important for yo
errors, omissions or out-of-date information that could negativ

Stop and think for a second! What would you do if one o
travel and entertainment cards was lost or stolen? Or worse y
purse was missing! Could you remember the names and credit
that under law you can be held liable for up to $50.00 on each c
or more on your debit or cash cards*.

This unique program provides around the clock protection for
card protection plan is the professional solution to the epidemic p

It's 24-hour protection you can't afford to be without. If you c

...ber and we will block the use of your existing cards and

...ts of the Credit Card Protection Agency.
...ly cash or deposit the $3.25 check, your instant cash
...efore the void date printed on the face of the check and

...ided by American Express, Citicorp, Shell Oil and Bank
... services with the Agency are only 87 cents per month —
...84 months — that's seven full years for only $73.08.
...u are protected by our No-Risk Guarantee. Just call the
... to receive a full refund for any reason. Of course, the

...e spaces provided on the reverse side of your rebate
...otection kit, including warning labels, wallet-size card,
...dit information will be sent to you by return mail.

Sincerely,

Michael J. Cassells
President

...o-Risk Guarantee and reserve your Free Credit Report for your
...ate Check prior to its expiration date.
our potential liability under law.

House of a Thousand Doors: Poems and Prose Pieces. Washington, D.C.: Three Continents, 1988.

The Storm: A Poem in Five Parts. New York: Red Dust, 1989.

"Introduction." In *Truth Tales: Contemporary Stories by Women Writers of India,* ed. Kali for Women. New York: Feminist, 1990.

Nampally Road. San Francisco: Mercury, 1991.

"Paper Filled with Light." *Grand Street* 10, no. 3 (Summer 1991): 99–101.

"Transit Lounge." *Michigan Quarterly Review* 30, no. 4 (Fall 1991): 636–646.

Night-Scene, the Garden. New York: Red Dust, 1992.

Fault Lines: A Memoir. New York: Feminist, 1993.

"Brown Skins, What Mask?" In *River and Bridge* (1995). Reprinted in the coda to *Manhattan Music* (1997).

River and Bridge: Poems. New Delhi: Rupa, 1995; Toronto: TSAR, 1996.

The Shock of Arrival: Reflections on Postcolonial Experience. Boston: South End, 1996.

Manhattan Music: A Novel. San Francisco: Mercury, 1997.

"Rights of Passage." *Interventions: An International Journal of Postcolonial Studies* 1, no. 1 (1998–1999): 14–17.

5

Myung Mi Kim

Interview by
JAMES KYUNG-JIN LEE

Myung Mi Kim was an hour late to an early evening poetry reading in February 1996, one that celebrated the release of *The Bounty*. She was held up in the infamous Los Angeles rush-hour traffic. When she finally arrived, a few in the audience had gone home, but a good twenty or so remained— some avid readers of Kim from the beginning of her published career, others listening to her poetry for the first time. Kim read from both *The Bounty* and her forthcoming book, *DURA;* it was a performance that was guided by the reign of silence, punctuated by the sharpness of words. Silence acted as a filter, distilling her thematic concerns to a single utterance, so that the force of Kim's poetic voice could be evinced but never fully known.

Kim's poetry continually strives to move beyond scripted ideas of language, identity, history, and narrative. She and her poetry both want to, and do, resist attempts by others to delimit what are ultimately for her spurious labels. Whether she is being referred to as a Korean American poet, a woman poet, a Bay Area poet, or a postlanguage poet, Kim wants to reject all labels. Yet, at the same time, just as she is aware that getting somewhere necessitates being bounded by available paths—or freeways—she is also acutely aware that her poetry is girded and delineated by political scripts, narratives of history. This tension between the flights of her poetic imagination and the structure of narrative traffic makes Kim's poetry dynamic, not only for where it goes, but also for how it gets there.

Kim came to Los Angeles partly for a small California book tour promoting *The Bounty,* partly to finalize plans for the release of *DURA,* and partly to visit her mother. During the 1995–1996 academic year, Oberlin College (her alma mater) stole her away from San Francisco State University, where she is a professor of creative writing, to be an artist in residence. Her poems have benefited from what she calls the *anthologizing phenomenon,* including both Asian American *(The Forbidden Stitch, Premonitions)* and "avant-garde" American *(Primary Trouble)* collections. We met to talk a day after the poetry reading, in between her morning interview with a local Korean newspaper and a meeting with the Sun and Moon Press folks. Our conversation represented a short stopover, assessing where her work was at that point, where it was moving, but our talk was also a pause to remind ourselves that where we are is always the beginning and end point of our searches.

JKL I remember when you read from *Under Flag.* What kind of differences have you been trying to think about, post-*Under Flag*?

MMK I think what I am trying to teach myself in recent work is ways of extending and furthering the investigations I began in *Under Flag:* what is the subject's relationship to narrativity, to the demands and nuances of "telling," and, perhaps more significantly, to *rendering* experience. I'm tracking what

Myung Mi Kim

appear to be distortions in time (or linearity, or chronology) and ways to suggest that these may be closer to the way perception actually takes place. "Post-*Under Flag*," as you put it, I feel I'm exploring the interplay between prosody (sound value, rhythms, cadences) and "time"—perception. I'm attempting to listen for the "speed," "duration," and "music" of perception taking place.

JKL How did it feel to get to the kind of moments where what one might call *extraneous narratives* fall away? How did it feel to write in that way?

MMK It's a lesson in staying as close as possible to that first move or push toward language. How does it feel to write this way? I would say it's as if I am listening—at (or in) an act of attention.

JKL How does this relate to your interrogation of English?

MMK Perhaps it's in (or through) this state of attention that the possibilities for "interrogation" exist at all. I am aware of trying to address/hear/notate in an English that is inflected by a Korean. I am aware of an "English" that pulls in, relates, and simultaneously disarrays questions of authority and knowledge. If it's possible to say so, I am interrogating the questions of translation between cultures and languages and in particular the kinds of resemblances and contaminations that inform how language(s) systematize and engender notions of power. In a more visceral way, I am constantly aware of this particular English I participate in—perhaps an English that behaves like Korean, an English shaped by a Korean. The space between the two languages is a site of mutation between an English and a Korean.

JKL Like a third language?

MMK Yes, a language beyond what is systematically Korean and English—a language called into service to hold the space created out of the conversation between the two locations—a language that necessarily sets in motion questions around resemblance, contamination, boundary.

JKL You have said elsewhere that coming to the United States at the age of nine really affected you and your writing. How, and why?

MMK If I had come any earlier, I think my sense of Korean would have been a lot less formed. If I had arrived any later, my sense of Korean-identified experiences, facts, realities would have been much louder. But it strikes me that there's something about being nine or so, where you have enough access to the language that you feel a connection to the culture it's located in, but you have yet to live out the complexities of participating in that culture fully. And, yet again, that culture is embedded in you somehow. In this strange region of knowing and not knowing, I have access to Korea as a language and culture, but this access is shaped by rupture (leaving the country, the language). When I engage "Korea"—what resemblance does this have to any "real" place, culture, or the language spoken there? So, in this effort and failure of bridging, reconfiguring, shaping, and being shaped by loss and absence, one enters a difficult negotiation with an Imaginary and a manner of listening that to me *is* the state of writing.

JKL A friend of mine wanted me to ask you this: On the one hand, you're dealing with language as such. But, on the other hand, there are moments in the text where you name a place, name an event. So it really brings it back to a particular incident and calls to attention a certain audience. To say, for example, *Kwangju*[1] calls into attention certain kinds of audiences with certain kinds of knowledge. So she was wondering (and I'm wondering as well), How do you imagine your audience?

Myung Mi Kim

MMK There are multiple identities and forces that constitute an audience. An audience is not (can't be) monolithic. Perhaps there's a tendency to think of multiple audiences occurring in isolation from each other—the implication being that there is little "translation" between and among audiences. (Maybe this is what I'm picking up in your question? In other words, how are we to understand this idea that only "certain kinds of audiences with certain kinds of knowledge" would know about Kwangju?) I'd like to propose that there is no one audience toward which one writes (or toward which I write) but that the very act of writing is an approximation of the possible conversation *between* "audiences." If I imagine an audience at all, I am imagining possibility. And residing inside this possibility are various communities (or audiences, if you will)—Korean, Korean American, fellow writers, etc.—that complicate and challenge, support and enliven questions of responsibility, recognizability, and so on.

As far as a reference such as Kwangju is concerned, even though its specificity may not carry to every reader, if the text (the maker of the text) is alert, attentive at the scene of writing, I believe that the terms operating behind/underneath a reference to any single event are carried through all the elements included on the page—so there would be a way to read Kwangju even if one didn't know much about the particulars of that event. In the imagery, cadences, rhythms, formal shapes, and so on presented in the poem, a ground of associations will emerge that readers will be able to build on.

Here, I'm trying to place the task of the poem or of writing as one that revivifies and augments the circuitry between and among what are thought of as distinct groups or audiences or cultures, and this is where language—every utterance—is political. The poem is a lived demonstration of the meaning of culture, language, history. If the poem's references, methods, articulations are not immediately transparent or scrutable, and if meaning happens line by line, increment by increment—that's absolutely fine and perhaps only real because "meaning" is emergent—it is a process. Of course, talking in this way reminds me that I'm often asked, "Don't you want to be Amy Tan or Maxine Hong Kingston and have people read you and buy your books widely?"

JKL That brings me to the whole question of commodification of a certain idea of what a Korean American or an Asian American work should be.

MMK Yes, and that's a complicated issue. There has to be a way to problematize the issues of who gets published, who gets read, whose work gets distributed, whose writing comes in and out of view. What's of concern to me is the anthology phenomenon, like Korean American this or gay/lesbian that. When categories are perpetuated, when experience is "thematized" (reduced, in other words), what can result is a kind of dismissal. I would hope what I am doing in my work is raising questions about how the location of Asian American, Korean American, immigrant, female, and so on can resist commodification.

JKL Part of the political impulse of Asian American writing has to be in a certain sense insurgent. I was wondering what you think about how that Asian American scene works today, if it's losing the initial emphasis to break open boundaries.

MMK Any movement that can name itself has already begun to erase itself. Asian American writing that declares its allegiance to the insurgent needs to examine vigilantly how and in what manner it continues to enact the meaning of insurgency. As we have seen in different instances (what is Marxist, what is feminist, what is ethnic studies at this point?), atrophy, co-optation, or institutional "legitimation" is a very real force. It works quietly, efficiently to undermine even the invention

Myung Mi Kim

of insurgency, let alone its expression. It takes constant (re)engagement to keep applying in yet unexplored ways what we call *Asian American* and *insurgent* and *activist.*

JKL Who are the people who make you vital still? Who are the folks that move you on, not necessarily forward?

MMK The ones who help me stay vigilant, alert, engaged? Maybe I can best answer that question by answering some of my current reading. I'm reading and have been reading the work of Maurice Blanchot closely. The propositional quality of his investigations seems so rich and open. Reading his *Infinite Conversation* in conjunction with Edmond Jabes' writing, especially *From the Desert to the Book,* has been particularly instructive.[2] On a different kind of trajectory, I am reading about/around geopolitical space and the politics of time in some sort of tandem with my desire to track the history of scientific knowledge. Another arena of reading for me right now involves research into what we'd have to call *Korean shamanism,* but I mean more specifically the chants associated with *mudang.* Among other things, I'm fascinated by the very sound of these chants. I continue to read, of course, in and around those poems that enact a translation between world and language—that is, the task of being a historical subject. Here I find myself returning to George Oppen's work again and again. As you can see, no one kind of reading or writer or thinker marks what I look toward. But what these create or suggest collectively—that's vital.

JKL One of the things that struck me was your phrase [in *The Bounty*] "that domain's supreme prosperity" [p. 45]. Throughout your work there's this constant articulation of land, territory, domain. So I'm wondering how you think about questions of land and space because politically that's really important. Then, when you do use those words, they seem to have a really imperialist or masculinist gesture to them.

MMK Yes, I am calling attention to a property-laden, proprietary, militaristic language of discovery and of taking. The imperialistic or masculinist gesture is clearly an agent in the work but one that I would hope serves not to polarize but to problematize how we undergo an examination of a complicated sign such as *imperialism.*

JKL The question of land has to do with how you see questions of vision. In *Under Flag*, you say, "widest angle of vision before vision fails to mean" [p. 37]. How do the questions of property, land, political space relate to thinking about new kinds of vision?

MMK You are bound by time and space and where you are located. So, if I'm sitting at my window, I am bound—

JKL You are always implicated—

MMK Yes, I've been thinking about how you see—given the boundaries of where you are, of wanting to push beyond the limitations of where you are and also having to acknowledge how you are informed by this limit.

JKL Does that relate to questions of women's bodies, or woman's body as a kind of landscape, and thinking about how that coheres with questions of space, questions of history?

MMK I'm not sure this will even begin to answer your question—but I have been thinking in particular about the site of reproduction, mutation, standardization, as well as liberation. I've been thinking also about the way anatomy emerges as a science around the time of voyages to the "New World." The idea of looking at the body—more, looking inside it—

JKL Dissecting it—

MMK Yes, to inculcate a culture of dissection (discovering/owning/naming).

Myung Mi Kim

JKL You read yesterday a poem about the hummingbird and how you were looking at the idea of the hummingbird. That, once you claim it and name it, it's destroyed. Is that connected to thinking about women and the female body?

MMK Whether it's a historical moment, a question of Asian American identities, thinking through the female body, or seeing a hummingbird, there's a way in which the charge of writing, the charge of participation in language, is always approximate, so the naming does not fix and erode but may resonate and continue to charge—

JKL History is that which has been done. But what you seem to do is rearrange it, to recharge it.

MMK So that it becomes available, visible, circulating, embodied. There is no present possible without a past, and the transmutation between these points is where experience resides—where the perplexity of living happens.

JKL I am interested in a passage from your book *DURA*. It has to do with that section where you talk about the Korean man who was killed during the LA uprisings. Edward Lee has become an indelible mark in recent Korean American history. It's clear to me that he's affected you in a certain way. Considering something as traumatic as the LA uprisings, how do you deal with those emotionally laden moments of crisis?

MMK Perhaps I should begin by saying that I'm certain that I haven't begun to "deal with" the LA riots. The section you're referring to incorporates the voice of Edward Lee's mother from the documentary *Sa-I-Gu*.[3] I was tremendously moved by this devastatingly clear voice of a mother who has lost a child. I wanted to honor this voice. And this section of the poem is an initial attempt—one that I would hope is revisited throughout various sections of *DURA*. So, yes, the crisis, the emotion, the urgency, if you will, enters, but I am also wondering how this crisis—the LA riots—must prompt thinking about the forces that have produced it. There's this crisis moment expressed as the LA riots and what does that make available to us? How is it possible to interpolate between the crisis and the forces that have produced it (the entire complex of historical, economic, and political conflu-ences that shape an event). So there's the work of recogniz-ing the fact of an event, the fact of a crisis (the death of Edward Lee, the LA riots), and the accompanying work of understanding that the crisis must lead into a negotiation with an entire historical/political continuum.

JKL The last words in *The Bounty* are really haunting. "Synaptic unruly enter." Are you thinking about questions of violence there?

MMK My first instinct in answering this question is to posit that any utterance is violent as it is political, as it has every potential to liberate (or not)—the question of how one might enter human discourse under the largest possible terms. Unruly, ungoverned, synaptically—according to no rule—without rule—without crowns—without dictation—enter the Imaginary, enter language, enter the human. This is a call to myself to write. That *enter* is about permission, about begin-ning.

JKL So the unruly is also liberating.

MMK Absolutely.

JKL What strikes me is how you are talking about the synap-tic, you are talking about a kind of opening.

MMK Synapses may fire or misfire, connections can be con-stituted or dismantled; no conclusions are possible.

JKL Like language, brushing of two languages. Entering the synapse of language.

Myung Mi Kim

MMK Yes, there's perpetual motion toward beginning and not necessarily toward knowing.

JKL Why in your latest book do you move from the contracted space to something more fluid?

MMK I literally had more time—formal articulations are, for me, rooted in the conditions under which writing is taking place. I wrote much of *DURA* during a residency at the Djerassi Residential Arts Program in Woodside, California, where for the first time since my child's birth I had even two days of uninterrupted work time. This particular "real time," this extended time, clearly figures into the more fluid, meditative, expansive lines in parts of *DURA*. If the writing act, as I've been trying to suggest in our conversation, is an ongoing, always shifting, always arriving state, then form, prosody, the very diction, imagery, etc. will also be constantly unfolding, figured as response and attention.

JKL Besides form, are there certain themes you're working on?

MMK I want to answer the question by first observing that in some intrinsic way there can be no separation between form and theme—that these conversations must coincide in the service of the urgencies that bring one to writing. Having said that, I'd add to my earlier comments about my reading (and what this suggests about themes I may be working on). I mentioned reading with a concentration on the history of scientific knowledge; anatomy has been a particular focus for me, given the ways it lends itself to thinking about the site of the female body, especially as it is linked with acts of colonialism. Of course, and this is not a new "theme" by any means, more an enduring one—as a writer arrived at an uncanny familiarity with another language (and having Korean as a tenuous *and* fierce spectral language), as a poet attentive to acts of living between and among borders, interstices, I am practicing questions of national narratives, transcultural narratives, narratives of cultural and political diasporas, and the attendant concepts, or, more accurately perhaps, *hybridizations* of human community. The wish here is something more akin to naming the world.

JKL But not to destroy it.

MMK Exactly. To register the world, to use language as an instrument for gauging, approximating, and rendering the world.

JKL How is your writing shifting now?

MMK I don't know if it's a shift or an intensification—but I am more and more aware that to participate in writing is to recognize the complicated interarticulation between language and historical condition. More and more, I am thinking of the poem, and of writing, as an experiment—an experiment that evokes the possibility of speaking at all and how this might be connected to notions of the liberatory.

Note

1. Site of the massacre of civilians protesting martial law in South Korea in May 1980.
2. See Maurice Blanchot, *The Infinite Conversation,* trans. Susan Hanson (Minneapolis: University of Minnesota Press, 1993); Edmond Jabes, *From the Desert to the Book: Dialogues with Marcel Cohen,* trans. Pierre Joris (Barrytown, N.Y.: Station Hill, 1990).
3. *Sa-I-Gu* (1993) was directed by Christine Choy, Elaine Kim, and Dai Sil Kim-Gibson and is distributed by Cross Current Media.

Selected Works by Myung Mi Kim

"The Days She Came To" and "Pleasure as Steadfast." *Antioch Review* 44 (1986): 112-115.

Myung Mi Kim

"Father Hat." *Ironwood* 29 (1987): 145.

"Into Such Assembly" and "Rose of Sharon." In *Forbidden Stitch: An Asian American Women's Anthology*, ed. Shirley Geok-lin Lim and Mayumi Tsutagawa. Corvallis, Oreg.: Calyx, 1989.

"Food, Shelter, Clothing." *Zyzzyva* 7 (1991): 111–115.

Under Flag. Berkeley, Calif.: Kelsey Street, 1991.

"Field of Inquiry." In *Writing from the New Coast*, vol. 2, *Techniques*, ed. Peter Gizzi and Juliana Spahr. Stockbridge, Mass: Garlic, 1993.

From *The Bounty*. *Avec* 6 (1993): 133–135.

"Primer." *Conjunctions* 21 (1993): 52–60.

"Anna O Addendum." In *Premonitions: The Kaya Anthology of New Asian North American Poetry*, ed. Walter K. Lew. New York: Kaya, 1995.

From *DURA*. *Sulfur* 36 (1995): 72–80.

The Bounty. Minneapolis: Chax, 1996.

"Exordium." *Positions: East Asia Cultures Critique* 4, no. 3 (1996): 417–419.

From *The Bounty*. In *Primary Trouble: An Anthology of Contemporary American Poetry*, ed. Leonard Schwartz. Jersey City, N.J.: Talisman, 1996.

From "Thirty and Five Books" in *DURA*. In *Making More Waves: New Writing by Asian American Women*, ed. Elaine H. Kim, Lilia V. Villaneuva, and Asian Women United of California. Boston: Beacon, 1997.

DURA. Los Angeles: Sun & Moon, 1998.

6

Le Ly Hayslip

Interview by
KHANH HO

Le Ly Hayslip's house is a mess. A jumble of brochures, books, and videotapes lies strewn across her coffee table. A map of Vietnam dangles precariously from the Navajo-white wall. A scribbled thank-you note from Oliver Stone floats among old newspapers and fading photographs. Red ants scramble across the tile of her linoleum kitchen counter toward the dried remains of a half-eaten orange.

Hayslip shuffles into the living room wearing a fuchsia satin pajama top and frayed, fuzzy slippers. She self-consciously touches her bushy hair, apologizes for the untamable mess, and slides onto the leather couch. She has only recently returned home after a period of aggressive campaigning for her humanitarian East Meets West Foundation, which administers humanitarian aid to impoverished Vietnamese in Central Vietnam.

She appears jaded yet simultaneously innocent. Tiny wrinkles form a semicircle around her pursed lips. Her long nails are painted a combination of crimson and saffron. Her blue-veined hands—bony and delicate—bear telltale liver spots.

Yet, despite her haggard appearance, despite the fact that she has experienced war, poverty, rape, and prostitution, Hayslip manages to maintain an appearance of spiritual purity. When she speaks, her body assumes the animated posture of a child who desperately wants to capture the essence of adventure and discovery. Her luminescent eyes sparkle with mockery as she defends her beliefs against the barbs and snares of critics. Her voice seems to move with its own jagged, halting rhythm as she traverses the confusing geography of English—her second language.

Hayslip insists that she must write fifteen books before she dies in order that she may be reborn as a man. While she acknowledges the fact that her limited English often frustrates this goal, she is nevertheless undaunted and imperious in the pursuit of her desired incarnation. To date, she has published two books: *When Heaven and Earth Changed Places* (1989) and *Child of War, Woman of Peace* (1993). She has also written an untitled children's book that has yet to see print. Currently, she is working on a book about village wisdom and spiritualism that she hopes will rival the works of Shirley MacLaine.

Yet none of these biographical tidbits can truly capture the eccentric and unaffected Hayslip. Her speech is vivid—teeming with life, abundant with grammatical slips. Above all, this charismatic woman is an unabashed creator who thumbs her nose at propriety, stringing bits and pieces of run-on sentences, a collage of Vietnamese phrases, a bountiful catalog of anecdotes, and a personal philosophy of human understanding. Her mission is the honest articulation of basic human values—a task she performs with pragmatism and gusto.

KH Tell us something about how you became a writer.

LLH To be honest, I have never considered myself a writer. I consider myself as one who has to tell the other side of the story. I don't know what it takes to become a writer. But I know what it takes to make things done. If I were to write good like you do, I would write one book a year.

When I came to United States, my in-laws asked me, "Have you seen a TV before?" Honestly, if I had to stay in a village and never came to the city, I would never have seen a TV. I've been to the city. But my American relatives asked stupid things like that. Did they think we are monkeys? They insulted me so much that I wanted to say something. At the time, the Vietnam War was still happening. In the evening, we sat and watched TV. Vietnamese people ran out from their homes. Homes were burning; bombs were dropped. I had to sit there and watch that and say to myself, "God, that could be my people, my village." And yet the Americans around me think I'm stupid because "the Vietnamese are our enemy." This put me in the spotlight. Who am I? What am I doing here? When Americans were killed, they felt so bad. "Why did Viet Cong Communists do this?" I just sat there and said, I am not Viet Cong, not Communist; I am just Vietnamese.

To me it's just very misunderstood that representations of the war are only one-sided. It takes people who carry two cultures like us to see both sides. The people around wouldn't understand the other side. That is what I want to write about. Even if nothing gets published, at least it's out of my system. At least I am doing something for people dying and telling how Vietnam was. I am lucky enough to have the book published. But I am not really looking for pay. I don't want to become rich and famous because I don't even know what being rich and famous has to do with the book. My story is meant to address myself and the people who fought in the war and were badly wounded. That is why I write.

KH Who encouraged you to write?

LLH It's in me, inside of me. The inside of me saw injustice. The inside of me saw lots of pain. For instance, I met

Le Ly Hayslip

American GIs. They talked about prostitution—Vietnamese prostitutes. How did they become prostitutes? I was a prostitute. How did I become a prostitute? Because of the war. Because all of those young girls came from the village. No education, nothing. How did they survive in the city? The best thing to do was to come to the city to get a boss and get a job. But they came to the city and got trapped by officers. There is an inside channel that the Americans don't see. They think everybody was a prostitute. It's not what we are born for. Do you know what it's like to be a prostitute in Vietnam? Our country and customs do not allow it. But we had no other choice. If you happen to talk to any Vietnamese person, you'd know that a girl like myself had no way to be married to another Vietnamese. I was only sixteen years old. No way would I have had a normal family life. I could either be a second, third, fifth wife or be a toy for somebody to use. It would be better that I did for an American. Then I would have a home for my mother, a home for my son. I would have a better life. That was how we saw our situation.

It's not an easy subject to talk about. But for me that's how I felt. If they condemned us about how bad, loose, and fierce we are, let me tell my side of the story. That is what inside me told me to write. Nobody thought that I can write. They also thought so because of my English. I didn't even have third-grade schooling in Vietnam. I came here, and all I did was housecleaning, be a housewife and a mother. I told people that I wanted to become a writer. They said, "What?" I had never taken any course. Just something inside me did not stop me from trying.

KH While you were writing the book, did you have any people or other writers who influenced you?

LLH I read only one or two books that had to do with spiritualism. I was influenced by any book that made my soul happy—made the inside of me happy. Those are the types of books that I like. The second book is not as good as the first because I was too busy with the [East Meets West] Foundation and the movie. So my energy was not there, and I regret it deeply. But the type of book that I want to write, I have no other book to guide me. All books are very dry to me. They have no connection with the inner feelings. All the books I want to write come right from the heart—directly *to* the heart.

KH How comfortable are you with the label *Asian American* writer?

LLH I am proud to be an Asian American writer because our culture is locked inside a little ball. People like us not only add to American society but offer different cultures, different points of view, different looks inside and out. When Americans write about Vietnam, it's just like outside looking in. It just scratches the surface. As for me, I start from the inside and [work] out. Especially when we live over here, we already know what people want, need to know, and what people should know about us. We offer something that they would not understand even though they may have lived there. They lived there as servicemen, journalists, politicians, and scientists.

My writing is based on human experience. I can never write about people going to the moon. I cannot offer anything other than a perspective based on old traditional Vietnamese thinking. I cannot offer anything about politics or about the war and its politics. What I do know is our culture. Our culture has held us strong for four thousand years. Now I have to write more and more about women, about our heroes, about everything that has to do with our culture. That is what I like to write about. When I come over here and talk about how I see myself as a writer, I feel privileged. I feel proud to offer another side because East and West are 180 degrees opposite. If we live here and we see what is needed to

Le Ly Hayslip

be done, the only way we can do that is to offer another point of view.

KH Do you think that, being an Asian American writer, you have certain obstacles or opportunities?

LLH My obstacle is that I can't write and read well. I have no schooling background. That's why I always have to have a coauthor, which is unfortunate for me. When I go to writers' conferences or a lecture or a seminar, the American audience is offered something totally different from what I need. But we are connected to a land of opportunity. I think we have much more to offer. If you have something good enough to offer, you can succeed, and that is an opportunity for Asian American writers.

KH What kind of audience do you have in mind when you write?

LLH An audience that understands Vietnam—understands Asian culture, the war. Yesterday I was interviewed. I won't give you the name of the newspaper. I was so upset. [The interviewer] was educated. She was fifty years old and worked in a major, major newspaper for eighteen years. I sat down, and she said, "I heard you wrote two books. What are they about?" I told her I worked for South Vietnamese during the day and I worked for Viet Cong during the night. She said, "Oh, so you prostituted yourself at night." Then she said, "So you are our enemy. Yes, we Americans call you enemy." She went on, on, on, and on. After we finished, I gave her the books. I just started to cry. If only she would read the book, she would understand. That is also the audience I want. The audience that—I don't want to call them stupid—but what do you know if you have everything? You don't know survival. You don't know what is out there. The word to describe her is not *stupid,* but it's something like *naive* and *simple-minded.* I want to offer something about human survival—

the pain and suffering—so that other people get to know.

KH A lot of Asian American writers feel they are split between a white audience and an Asian audience. Who are you directing your writing toward?

LLH I never would say I have two audiences. But I have to be careful about what I am saying. An American audience would accept me easier, understand me easier than the Vietnamese audience, who kept saying that I am uneducated. I have to write in a way so my Vietnamese audience doesn't say, "She lied." I do not lie. I know what I feel, especially about the war. My point of view is that the Vietnamese should not have had the war—should not have brought that sadness to our people. Our leaders at that time should have protected us—should have given us freedom and food. They should not have put us in that kind of painful harm. But I can't say that directly. So I have to say something in between. But, with an American audience, I can say it. And they'll understand.

KH Do you sometimes feel that you have to censor yourself, or do you feel that you have to alter your message in any way?

LLH Yes, I have to censor myself. And deliver my message straight to the heart without politics. Just human being feelings. Go with the feelings. Make people cry. Make people feel the pain. Make people read the book, read something different than before.

KH A lot of people in the Vietnamese community have reacted badly to the book. How does this affect you? Does the criticism affect your ego, or do you try to block it out?

LLH I have no ego. I would like for them to go back to Ky La, my village, and see for themselves. Most people never fought in a battle zone. They never understood about country life. If you tell the truth, it will always remain the truth.

Le Ly Hayslip

They misunderstand me because they never lived in the countryside. And they wouldn't like it because Vietnamese, we have a saying, "Chuyen that mat long." That means, The truth will always deceive you. And so, if they don't like it, I accept that, too. I don't expect everybody to like what I am saying. If they agreed with me, I wouldn't need to say anything. I need to address the people who don't like it. The reason they don't like it is because they have a different point of view. That point of view leads to debate.

KH What do you see is the relationship between Asia and Asian America? How does that relationship affect your work?

LLH The younger generation, I love them. The whole world depends on them. They could conquer the world if they wanted. And that is why I want to nurture them—help them spiritually. The older generation, we are old. We want things a certain way. My children have no pressure. They can just "be." And I am happy I can relate with the younger generation. They love me, and I love them. It's a lot of fun to work with them because they have a lot of energy, like I do. And they have a different point of view. I can call them *Vietnamese,* or I can call them *Asian.* I do not see them as American at all. I see them as Vietnamese—especially the ones who can speak Vietnamese. They have everything around offered for them. But they are not going to be successful if they totally lose their Vietnamese identity. They have to have that strong culture to carry them.

I consider Vietnamese or Asian cultures to be the master of the world. I've been back and forth working in Vietnam for the last ten years, and I can see the difference in how they live their life—how they talk about family. It's totally different. There is no way we can educate Americans to become Easterners. My goal is to bring Vietnamese and Americans down to a common level so that we are not so far apart, so that we're definitely communicating in a common culture.

The young generation can do that. Like in Los Angeles, Mike Woo was running for mayor. He would represent a different outlook. Somehow, we must form our culture into something bigger. I offer to the world something that is different. In *When Heaven and Earth Changed Places,* I deliver speeches by ghosts. They use my body to tell their dead stories. I am between East and West because I do not belong here and do not belong there.

KH How do you think you can bridge the East and the West?

LLH It's hard to raise money for the program. Racism and sexism are also problems. People don't take me seriously because I am a woman. I am a single woman. I am uneducated. People did not treat me like I would be treated if I were white. At the same time, I am not demanding too much. I don't think I have too much to complain about because I accept things as they are. I know if people did not accept me on some level, I wouldn't be here. I know that racism is very heavy-duty. So I offer them something so that they know better than to shut me off.

KH In what ways does being a woman shape your writing?

LLH I want to be honest with you. I am an old-fashioned woman. I don't accept women's rights. A proverb in our culture says, "When you put on a shirt, you must put it on head first." Therefore, a woman is always underneath a man. I accept that.

KH Do you think that there is an Asian American literary tradition for you to write from?

LLH I write in line with tradition—a line that runs with what I'm feeling. But I don't have any books that I can say, "That's good." I am reading a third book right now—no author, no title. This book has to do with the soul—how to become a human being. That's what I am interested in, and that is the

113

type of book that I read so that I can use that energy to write. But I don't have any other book that I can say, "Hey! I like her style, and I want to write like her or him."

KH Do you think there is a special language that only Asian Americans or Vietnamese Americans have access to when we write about our experiences?

LLH A very special language. The language is very special for me—it is the culture. How do I see these bizarre things in the West. To give you an example, the movie *From Hollywood to Hanoi* presents a dog killing.[1] The whole audience screamed, "Oh, my God!" when they got to that part. The Americans were upset. They remarked, "It's cruel. It's gross. It's unkind." But nobody reacted when the bombs dropped. Do you see what I mean? One bomb is dropped. You know how many dogs are going to get killed? How many cows? How many water buffaloes? How many kids? How many human beings? And it means nothing. But just one dog.

KH Frank Chin says writers should write from a heroic Chinese tradition. He has problems with feminism and wants to write a heroic version of truth. What do you think of his ideas?

LLH First of all, that is his truth. I have my own truth. You have your own truth. If he really thinks that is what he wants to write, he ought to stay with that writing. I tend to talk about man and woman a lot. I would like somehow to bring the people up to a higher level of consciousness. That is what I am really interested in doing. That is why art is very special. Four thousand years of culture. We can use that as a base. In my writing, Eastern and Western culture offer different kinds of things. For instance, I pay very high insurance. I hate it. But you live in this society you have to have it. In my body, I know Western medicine does no good for me. It's no good. Because I know what my body may get from wind, water, fire, and earth. Take those four elements from my body, and Westerner's medicine cannot heal it. But why did I bring the medicine from the West to the East? Because it alleviates somebody's pain. It takes care of it right now. Here and now. And so I accept it. For myself, I wouldn't take everything. But I know it is needed by the Vietnamese. That's why I bring a lot of medicine over there. Each individual has their own way of living. I am concentrating on uplifting people's consciousness. How to be a higher human being with different values, with different kinds of medicine.

I'll give you an example. I've talked to some Vietnamese right-wingers who are very much against communism. I think they should say "thank you" to the Communists. In 1975 a lot of people came to the United States because of the Communist takeover. Now they have cars. Some are very, very rich. Some have children who are becoming doctors and lawyers. Very successful. So why don't we take the opportunities and say, "Thank God Communists made it happen." Change negative to positive. Yes, some of them were in the camps for fifteen, twenty years, but I believe in karma. Perhaps the Vietnamese refugee also put someone in camp for twenty years. Perhaps, because of his karma, he has to give back his due. Accept it. Now he comes over here. He's sixty years old. He has hard time. That is his choice to come, too. I came here when I was twenty. I've been widowed twice. I also had a very hard time. But that's me. I am not condemning Americans. I am not condemning Vietnamese. I have to deal with it, do you see what I mean? It's a totally different point of view. I want to change the negative to positive.

I read a poem in some Vietnamese newspaper from San Francisco last night in bed. It's very painful for me to read— all the hatred in the poem. It's all about hatred, hatred, hatred. I ask myself, How can I write opposite from this? I try to find a message that is loving, compassionate, forgiving, understanding of a beautiful country. But who will print that?

Le Ly Hayslip

Who will print my writing if I send that to them? If I have a chance to write more, that's what I'll base my writing on. Just human feelings. I honestly don't think the hatred would solve anything. The resentment wouldn't solve anything.

KH How do you write? What role does the ghostwriter or coauthor play in your writing?

LLH The first book, I wrote it up just the way I talk. I cried a lot. And my son Jimmy put it in computer just the way I talked. Then we sent it to Jay Wurts. The first time we met I gave him everything we had—about three hundred pages. Then he went home and read through it and put in question marks for me and questionnaires for me. Then he sent it back. Either I wrote up a response, or I recorded it in the cassette tape just like what we are doing now. He would take it home and pick what he liked or leave out what was too bold. Yes, I lost a lot of things that I wanted to say. But the message still came out the same. Then he sent it back to me. I either approved it or disapproved it. I added on or took off what I wanted, and then I sent it back to him. He would work on it again until it was finalized. Then we sent it to the editor.

In the second book written by me and my son, we spent more time working in a real style. Dialogue and all that stuff. But we still sent it to Jay Wurts to edit a little bit. Because he was not there, the book did not have the kind of mood that I would have liked it to have. I am working on a third book now. It has to do with the spiritual side of my experience. I am looking for different cowriters now. I want to do it myself. I'll try that first. If not, I want to have someone more like Shirley MacLaine. People like her can deal with this kind of subject.

KH You write to inspire social change. What do you feel about people who just write for art's sake?

LLH That is their right. We need those, too. It's just like going into a restaurant and the waiter gives you a menu. You take one. I take one. We end up with the same table. We need all kinds of dishes. We need all kinds of colors. We need all kinds of tastes. We need all kinds of thinking to make the world go around. The choice is not up to me. It's up to the reader. What book should he or she pick up? If he or she is on a certain level of consciousness, that is the type of book they'll like to read. If someone has a higher mind, they'll pick up a higher-level book. That is what we have to offer. Everybody has something different to offer. But, if one person can write and inspire others to work for social change, that is the best kind of writing.

KH What is the role of memory or history in your writing?

LLH A big role, big role. I have the head of many. If I can just sit here and sing all the songs for you that I remember. Remember, I left my village in 1965. I was only sixteen years old. I left my country when I was twenty. But, because of those twenty years of experience, for some reason I can write and write and write and sing and sing and talk about this culture and talk about things that will educate Vietnamese, Americans, and others as well.

I am an old soul. I am an old soul coming here, now in this Vietnamese American body, so that I can share. And I haven't had my chance. Two books are only a scratch on the surface. They reveal nothing yet. The memories in my mind, I don't want to die with them. I want to tell stories. But I am handicapped in two ways. My English and Vietnamese are not very good because I don't have an education. That is one handicap. The second handicap is I am all alone to do everything from A to Z. I don't have help; I don't have people and opportunities to find help. But I will get there. Now the movie is out, people may come to know me more. I hope that all my memories will be left on earth before I go.

Le Ly Hayslip

KH You mention educating the Vietnamese. Do you plan to write in Vietnamese?

LLH I want to write in Vietnamese. But the second generation can't read or write Vietnamese. So my writing would only reach the first generation. If I were to write in Vietnamese to people in Vietnam, it would be helpful. But then I would write of a different kind of life in America. You see, the first book and second book should be translated into Vietnamese so that people who cannot read and write English can read it in Vietnamese. That is what I really want to do.

KH Tell us something more about your work in progress right now.

LLH The third book? I am just working on an outline, and I am just working on a couple of chapters so my agent can prepare negotiations. The book has to deal with many different angles, especially how they made my life into a movie. How to work with Oliver Stone. Who is he? It would discuss how this is the first woman's point of view that he has taken seriously. It would talk about how I worked side by side with him. I helped him not only with the difficult work but the visual work. To me, both of us have been together on the universe for many, many lifetimes. To me, it is a very giving process for us to be working together. That is a summary of the project right now.

But I have fifteen books to write in this lifetime. I have all the titles and all the ideas. The first two books you see here. And I have two children's books out there. One is almost just in contract, and another one I am still polishing and working on. I would like to produce a couple films about women in the Vietnam War. Not really a mainstream big movie but one based on culture—based on documentary. And I'd like to work on a lot of humanitarian work. To keep everything going, you have to work on all sides. In Vietnam or in

Vietnamese culture, I am still trying to let people everywhere know that nothing can succeed unless you have *dao duc*.[2] When you have *dao duc*, you have basic things to go by. And you cannot have *dao duc* unless you do your humanitarian work. That is why it is called *nhan dao*. *Nhan* is human being. *Dao* is virtue. If we have that and we are working on that, then everything will fall in its place. That is what I believe. That is what I am working hard for.

Notes

1. Hayslip refers to *From Hollywood to Hanoi* (San Francisco: Indochina Film Arts Foundation), the documentary by Tiana Thi Thanh Nga that recounts her return to Vietnam, specifically to a bloody dog-butchering scene, later juxtaposed with newsreel footage of dropping bombs.

2. The expression suggests compassion, caring, and charity. According to Nguyên Van Khôn, *Viet-Anh tu-dien: Vietnamese English Dictionary* (Glendale, Calif.: Dainam, 1987), it means "virtue, morals, morality."

Selected Works by Le Ly Hayslip

When Heaven and Earth Changed Places. New York: Doubleday, 1989.

"Sisters and Brothers." In *One World Many Cultures,* ed. Stuart Hirschberg. New York: Macmillan, 1992.

Child of War, Woman of Peace. New York: Doubleday, 1993.

"Commentary." With Hiep Thi Le. In *The Making of Oliver Stone's "Heaven and Earth."* Boston: Tuttle, 1993.

East-West: The Landscape Within. New York: Icarus, 1995.

Heaven and Earth. Burbank, Calif.: Warner Brothers/Warner Home Video, 1995. Videorecording.

Epilogue to *A Portrait of Viet Nam,* by Lou Dematteis. New York: Norton, 1996.

Foreword to *Vietnam: A Portrait of Its People at War,* by David Charnoff. New York: Tauris, 1996.

Le Ly Hayslip

"We came into the circle of recovery"

7

Janice Mirikitani

Interview by

GRACE KYUNGWON HONG

I first met Janice Mirikitani fifteen minutes before one of Glide Church's Sunday Celebrations. Earlier that morning, the church's choir director, who had been a close friend of Mirikitani and her husband, the Reverend Cecil Williams, had died of a sudden heart attack. Despite the terrible loss, Mirikitani graciously consented to do the interview as planned. She spoke candidly about her poetry, her activism, and how both contribute to her coming to terms with the sexual abuse she experienced as a child.

An acclaimed poet, activist, and choreographer, president of the Glide Foundation and the director of programs at Glide Church/Urban, Mirikitani is known both for her gripping, politically charged poetry and for her activism in communities all over the Bay Area. She has published three books of poetry: *Awake in the River* (1978), *Shedding Silence* (1987), and *We the Dangerous* (1995). She has also been anthologized extensively. I was interested in interviewing Mirikitani because of the unique trajectory of her activism—from her involvement with the San Francisco State Third World

Students' Strike in 1968–1969 to her current work with Glide Church—which has informed her poetry.

GKH Earlier, you showed me an article that dealt with the themes of sex and violence in your work. How does it affect you when a literary scholar writes on your poetry?

JM It is very interesting to see somebody else's impression of sex and violence as themes because you don't know what the effect of your poetry is. Being a woman, and being a sexually abused woman in childhood, I think the issue of sexuality and the abuse of women sexually is an unspoken, uncharted area in many ways, especially among Asian Americans; it is a taboo issue. I was brought up to believe that, whenever you bring disgrace upon yourself, you disgrace your family. And so it's kind of a triple, quadruple burden. For me as an Asian American woman, sexuality has been that arena in which we have been exploited. Whether it's my own personal experience with my own sexuality as a young female being exploited by the adult males in my family, or whether it's the (s)exploitation of women, specifically the exoticized stereotypes of Asian women in film and media, I would have to struggle against them all. That has been very much a part of my struggling to come to some form of authenticity and healing. That's why sex and violence have such linkage in my poetry and my work.

GKH Could you talk about how Glide affects your work, about how your role as an activist influences your role as a poet?

JM Because I'm dealing with my own recovery issues related to sexual abuse in childhood, when I helped create the recovery programs for women, the emotional and transformational effect it had on me was quite phenomenal. No matter how much I tried, I could not escape behind the arrogance and the position of supremacy that we all at some time or another put ourselves into because we think that's the way to escape our pain. And I couldn't escape the pain. All my life, I've been trying to escape the pain, and I've found superficial ways to do it—building walls, going to school and being perfect and excelling in grades, and being the typical Asian model minority person, yet feeling terribly inauthentic, terribly unacceptable, terribly ugly, and not worthy at all. So half of my life, which was spent trying to be white and be accepted by white society, was such a futile act. I went through my revolt period, which was the affirmation of myself as an Asian American, and that was a landmark situation for me. But, in the last three to five years, I've been dealing with my own recovery. When I say *recovery*, I'm not talking about substances or chemicals as much as I am talking about that addiction to my pain and to my powerlessness and my search constantly to control those factors that would not allow me to experience life fully.

Cecil started the recovery programs five years ago for men and women. I started working with women's programs specifically, and we came into the circle of recovery. The women came into the circle and faced each other and told each other what had happened in their lives. And I could see myself suddenly mirrored in the faces of these women who had been through the most atrocious, horrible experiences: being homeless, being addicted to crack cocaine, being alcoholic, being abused and battered and beaten and sexually molested by every single member of their family and fifteen stepparents, and on and on and on. They told about selling their babies for sex and drugs. I looked at them and said, "This is not me," and yet I couldn't deny that, yes, this is indeed my life. Not in those specific terms, not in the horrific terms they are talking about. But I felt that, if they can talk about the truth of their lives, which are so painful and so steeped in the darkness of cruelty, why can't I face mine? This realization slammed me up against a wall and shook my mask

Janice Mirikitani

off. It made me say, "OK, all this stuff you think you've got—I mean, here I am, married to the minister, I've got my degrees, I've got some books published—big deal." The bottom line was that I still felt unworthy. I still felt unacceptable.

GKH Until?

JM Until I spoke the truth of what had happened to me to other people. Prior to that time, it had been behind the psychiatrist's door, and I'd told close friends and my husband, but never a group of total strangers—not exactly strangers, but people I didn't know very well. One Sunday, Cecil asked if he could talk about how it felt to be a partner of a person who was sexually abused, and I said, "Would it help you if I said it myself?" Before I knew it, I'd offered to do it, and the words just flew out of my mouth. He said, "Yes, that would really be helpful." I had to face telling an entire congregation of people who were complete strangers as well as people I've known through the years. I didn't know how they were going to take this. But I talked about what it felt like, and the symbol that I used was that of the insect—that I always felt like an insect stuck in paraffin, and my wings were torn off, and my legs would just wiggle in the air, and I didn't have any power to release myself. I could see that the whole congregation was just weeping—hundreds of people. Afterward, hundreds of women came forward and talked about their own experiences with molestation, and we started groups around that, but I wouldn't have been able to do that had it not been for that circle of recovery.

What happens with my poetry—I don't know. I wrote my last book in 1987, and so now I have a whole new alliance with writing, a whole new area I'm exploring. I'm always concerned with self-indulgence and self-pity and being a victim and all that, so I'm walking carefully with that, not letting that be the effect of my poetry. I know that I cannot yet separate what has happened to me personally from what's hap-

Words Matter

pening in the world. So, if you talk about my activism not being separated from the poetry, that's true.

I really believe that we have to define and carve a place for ourselves as individual Asian Americans with our own sense of responsibility to whatever aesthetic we have. I can't force anybody to think like me, and I don't want to be approved or disapproved of according to somebody's rules of what is good Asian American literature. We've gone through enough of that with white standards. To hell with that stuff. To me, a good poem is a good poem if it works. And it requires discipline, it requires skill, it requires a gift, it requires depth, it requires perception, it requires vision. Those, to me, are the standards of good poetry. One's commitment is one's own lonely battle, one's own determination, to make.

To deny what is real for me is to deny me. So I have to authentically say who I am and not worry that I'm going to be approved and disapproved. I've done that too much my whole life. I've written shit: stuff that's not me, not good, not real, not honest, not the truth. I've tried so hard to be Dylan Thomas or William Carlos Williams or tried so hard to sound like Keats or Wordsworth; it didn't work. It was not me; it was irrelevant. I didn't even know what I was saying. I was a puppet, an imitation. So what is the purpose of writing if you're not going to be you? The issue of authenticity and self-definition, therefore, in terms of my work at Glide, is certainly an alignment that I have to have with my poetry. But my work as an activist at Glide is inextricable from what I write.

If I felt chosen, that would be total arrogance. It only takes a turn of the economy, the turn of a funder, and I can be on the street, too. I can be without a job, too, in an instant, at a moment's notice. So I have to be grateful each day for what I do have and be grateful for the strength and the ability to work, to be able, I hope, to be useful. That's a line that I use—"to be useful"—in one of my poems. I know that sounds so Christian—ugh. And I don't mean it to be because

Janice Mirikitani

I'm not that. If you don't open your mouth to right something that's wrong, and if you don't do something to help other people—not help in the sense of from up here to down there, but rather on a mutual basis—then you're not being useful.

GKH Your poetry isn't particularly religious.

JM No, it's not religious. I don't feel religious. I'm not religious. In fact, I'm antireligion.

GKH Really? So would you call yourself Christian?

JM I am attempting to seek spirituality in my life. I'm antidogma. I'm antiestablishment or anti–institutional religion because to me religion has done so much damage to our society. It's not that I'm anti-Bible, or anti-Scriptures, or anti-Commandments, but I believe that religion has to be humanized. For me, *humanization* means spirituality because God is not removed from the people. If you don't live your life in a way that is *useful,* then that's hypocrisy. And if you say, "No, you can't come into my church because you're this color or because you have AIDS," that's hypocrisy. You're not being Christian, not in the way I define *Christian.*

But a lot of Christians define themselves as Christian and act totally un-Christian. That's why I'm against religion as defined by certain institutional churches that practice a tremendous amount of bigotry, that don't accept people who have different sexual orientations. That's the kind of religion I reject. That's the kind of religion that is *not* practiced at Glide. It's very difficult for me to call God's name, to talk about Jesus Christ, talk about the Bible. I talk about being moved, feeling blessed, having a gift, gratitude, and grace. It's still hard for me to freely talk about God as someone who is a familiar factor in my life because I'm still struggling with it.

I came to Glide as an atheist. I was trying to be a radical, join the Red Guard, and do the whole nine yards. I began to understand what Glide is all about when Cecil made the commitment to be my friend, and we were friends for a long time before we became partners in a relationship. We were friends, very good friends, for almost fifteen years. He was going to unconditionally accept me, and that is very hard to receive. And, when Maya Angelou began to mentor me and help me see the kind of commitment and vision that one has to have as a writer—not that I have it, but she does—her mentoring certainly is an example for me. When Maya and Cecil began to say that I was worth something, it made me realize that I could maybe give up on the secrets. I know that sounds so abstract, like New Age babble, but I don't quite know how else to say it.

GKH So you feel that that kind of spirituality is something you get at Glide?

JM I think so. But most of all, this spirituality comes from the human beings who touch my life: Cecil, of course, but other people, other friends, just through their humanity, nothing spectacular, just through their honesty. These gestures, to me, were the spiritual acts.

I want to say something about my development because it was the Asian community that opened me up first. The black power movement, the civil rights movement, all of that had to slam me up against the wall because I was struggling to be white. So, when the Ethnic Studies Strike [of 1969 at San Francisco State University] occurred, there was a cause, there was a collective voice, and there were individual voices that were being heard, being shouted and being manifest in the books, the poems and the speeches that now are a legacy. Without that, there wouldn't be the advances that perhaps a lot of the students now take for granted. I must acknowledge my Asian American community first for forcing me to take hold of myself and realize that I had to find my authentic voice. That's when I first started coming to Glide, too. So it

Janice Mirikitani

was like the personal, the political, the social, the activist all came to a point, to a head.

GKH Can you talk about the choices you make in your literary work, whether to use prose or poetry, and the various styles you use in your poetry?

JM I choose to write certain things in prose instead of poetry when I feel there's a story that will take different voices, internal voices. Sometimes I try internal voices in poems: I separate the two voices into two sides of a poem, and often that dialogue is one's own dialogue with oneself. But, when I feel there is more flexibility required in regard to narrative or in regard to inner relationships, that's when I choose prose. A lot of times the poetry will grow out of the prose. In the play *Shedding Silence,* the opera star speaks about her GI lover and her death—she's speaking as a ghost. But I also created a poem for her in life and a prose poem for her about her relationship with her father. So the characters live still.

The characters have a perpetual ongoing relationship with me, I think. Some of them are autobiographical; some of them I fictionalize out of a point of reality. For instance, Chieko is an opera star, and she really was an aunt who really did die in the war, and there were these unusual circumstances around her death. But I elaborated on the life of a woman who under the worst circumstances—a time of war, the height of anti-Japanese sentiment—was performing in an artistic medium that was almost completely inaccessible to her. I thought, "How great!" Complete despair—that's my forte. She also had an incredible relationship with her father, which aroused jealousy among other sisters because her father so believed in her and took such great pride in her ability to sing. So she had tremendous support, and yet she had the conflict of dependency upon the father. The father-daughter relationship was so fascinating to me because I myself, who have never felt like I've had a father, wondered what it would be like to have someone who was so supportive of you that you were almost chained by that relationship.

I'm playing one example through to show you that there are various dynamics and psychological networks that I go through with characters. I like the poems that have characters as the focal point much more than the abstract poems. For example, I like poems like "Generations of Women," "Jade," "Jade Junkies." For me, a good poem is a poem that is very focused and very tight, and I find that I personally can write a tighter poem when I have a focal figure in it. "Healthy Choices" is what I mean by more abstract. I like it, but I don't think it's as emotionally compelling.[1]

I really like the poems about my mother. What I do with my mother is that she becomes me. I feel so intimate with her character that I can fly into her body, and fly into her mind, and become her motivation. So the dialogue that is created with her feels very real and very right.

GKH Does that have anything to do with you being a mother yourself? Or is it something personal to you and your mother?

JM It's both. I certainly have much more empathy for my mother now. I didn't feel like a mother for a long time in my daughter's life, I think. And she probably has a lot of feelings about me, and thank God she's not a poet, or else she might be writing terrible things about me! She's going to wreak revenge soon, I'm sure. I think it's because my mother and I have had such a chasm of silence between us. I almost had to create a mother in her that I could imagine as opposed to what she really was to me. I created a good mother because I think she is a really good person, but I think she had to make certain choices that perhaps made her more absent than I would have liked or she had herself been in situations that were not happy and therefore her priorities had to be else-where. For example, she was a single mother, right after the

Janice Mirikitani

war. My father left us, and she had to work two or three jobs, and I was home a lot by myself. She'd put me in a movie theater to be my baby-sitter. It was because she was poor. She had to feed us. We had to survive. So I can look back and admire that, and I can create dialogue about my mother ironing and making paper flowers. It feels very right to me. I don't feel I'm violating her.

A lot of poems came out of *having* to write a new poem. I do a lot of readings, and I get bored with myself if I don't read something new. I usually set myself an assignment, like you have to write a poem about war and peace, or bridging walls, or silly, trite stuff like that. For example, for the Wales trip [the Hay-on-Wye Literary Festival] I was absolutely determined that I was going to write something new because it felt like a very important event in my life. And the theme they gave us was "war and peace," which is absurdly huge. I sat there for three days—sixteen hours a day, a complete waste of time, just sitting there.

Finally, this poem came to me because Cecil was speaking and he quoted a line from Isaiah. I'm not a religious person, but I listen; the line was something like, The rain does not return to the sky until it comes to the earth and does something useful. And I thought of the war of my own body and how I have been so paralyzed by my dysfunction and by my own sense of powerlessness that I have not been useful. So I used the imagery—the metaphor of war—to talk about how my body was untouchable, how it was unable to be fully sexual in the positive sense of the word, to be truly feminine and giving and loving as a human being, as a woman in my relationship with my husband, until he began to help me heal. And the metaphors were all war, like Scud missiles and invasions in the night and assaults. And my assaulter had come to the village of my body and demolished it because he had to show the power that he had over life. And how healing had occurred in my relationship with Cecil because he had said that this is a demilitarized zone—our marriage is a place where nothing is too shameful. When I read that poem at Wales, everybody started crying. Maya Angelou came to the reading, and she said she wept. And I was gratified that the audience was so with me and so affirming.

GKH What is that poem called?

JM It's called "The War of the Body." It's not published anywhere. I was so terrified going into that reading—I mean this struggle with myself and performing is just horrible. Oh, I hate it. I'm nervous all the time. Cecil was just weeping, and all the women and men came up to me, and they hugged me, and they said, "We were so moved," and I realized that human beings all over the world, we're all the same. Now, why would I think that nobody would be interested in what I have to say?

You're asking how the poem is created. It's created in many different ways. After I have the idea, and after I have the skeleton of the poem, the story line of the poem—and I love the stories of the poem—then I work. Maybe I revise a poem about fifteen times, twenty times, with regards to the language, to the selection of the metaphor and the image, and tightening, and reworking, making sure that I have the right word for the metaphor that I'm seeking. And I can spend an hour looking up in my thesaurus one adjective because I get obsessed.

GKH So each poem in your books went through that process?

JM No. Some poems come fairly easily, but they're not as satisfying as the ones I work and rework. I worked and worked on the poem I read for the Davis Hall event, before Barbara Boxer and Diane Feinstein were elected. The main speaker was Ann Richards, the governor of Texas. I was so goddamn nervous. Three thousand people, Davis Symphony Hall, Bonnie Raitt, all these important political women. And I was

Janice Mirikitani

going to read this poem. So I worked two weeks on it. And it was great—I mean, they gave me a wonderful reception. That poem is not one of the better crafted poems, but it is a rousing poem. There is a difference between a publicly delivered poem and a poem that you read on the page. The poem I read at Davis Hall is a poem to be heard. But on the page it's repetitious, not poetically crafted. There is a difference between performance poetry and poetry on the page. Performance is a whole other art form. I've seen wonderful, beautiful, masterful poets just die, speaking publicly, just because their delivery is not as magnificent as the work. I look at some people's writing, and I really marvel.

GKH Like who?

JM Garrett Hongo writes beautifully. Alan Lau is just an incredible poet. And Russell Leong has some beautiful, beautiful lines, especially in *The Country of Dreams and Dust*. I love Pablo Neruda. I don't know how he does it; he's such a massive poet. Marilyn Chin is very good. A lot of the writers are in *The Open Boat*, Garrett's anthology. Chitra Divakaruni. I love Monica Sone's prose. And I love Wakako Yamauchi and Hisaye Yamamoto. Hisaye is a treasure. There're many more. Maya—I don't know how Maya comes up with some of the stuff Maya comes up with. It's a gift. She's a drop-dead presenter. The inaugural poem was wonderful, magnificent, and the occasion was momentous as hell, but you should see her when she's got an hour to do her thing. She has you absolutely weeping in the aisles and guffawing in laughter the next second. When she reads it out to the audience, there are thousands of people there, but it's you, you're it, you're that single individual. Cecil has that ability, too.

GKH I was reading some interviews and newspaper articles that implied that many people think that you're in Cecil's shadow, or, "Janice Mirikitani, she's Cecil's wife." Do you still get that attitude?

JM   Yes, it's absolutely the way it is. He's a very visible man, he's been out there for thirty years, he's nationally known. He's created programs that are nationally known. He's written two books. He's been involved in hundreds and hundreds of controversies that are public, media controversies. In a society that is very racist (that's a given), there are a few among us who are selected. When people talk about African Americans, who do they defer to? You know you have this standard list about ten people long. And, let's face it, in the mainstream literary arena, I am not known as a writer. Hey, how many books of poems do I have out? Five thousand?

But I must not allow myself to expect his life to reach me and therefore illuminate me. I must create my own. And small as that may be—and I'm not being self-deprecating—or as limited in scope as that light may go, it's still mine. I can't live in his shadow, nor can I hide in the minister's wife role and play it safe. Sure, I can be, if that's who I am. But that's not who I want to be. I have that baggage that goes with minister's wife plus the baggage that goes with Asian Americans or Japanese women. So, when I have an opportunity to speak, I have to make sure that I do it as authentically, as strongly, and as self-definingly as I can. It's interesting. Women will come up to me and say to me, "Oh, you're so lucky." We are not the lottery. It's a lot of hard work to create this relationship.

GKH   You also mentioned the things you had to deal with because you are in an interracial relationship.

JM   The way I dealt with the interracial relationship situation with my family was to simply inform them that this was my choice, and I wanted them to participate in my life, and I wanted them to know that it didn't change my feelings about them, but they were certainly not going to run my life. And now my family love Cecil much more—they really enjoy him. But I cannot honestly say that they do not have racism. My marriage didn't fix anything; it just simply changed their out-

Janice Mirikitani

look and their feelings about a particular individual. I've heard more flak from the African American community. I don't hear the flak from the Asian community because maybe I don't think the Asian community is as openly vocal; they're a little more behind your back about it. I have heard negative comments from the African American community, especially from the women, but that was when we were first entering the relationship. People have come to the point where they accept the fact that Cecil and I really are partners, not only in marriage, but in work.

I'm more reluctant to talk about the interracial part of us because I don't want to sound Pollyanna-ish about it. I don't want to sound like there aren't any problems. Cecil and I work so hard—and I don't want to, ugh, sound like I'm tooting our own horn—to break down the divisions among communities. For example, you saw the church today. Cecil does not have a black church, even though people who don't know him think that, because he's African American, he has an all-black church. In the nine o'clock celebration, there were about 150 Asians, and we have Asian American members in our church. We really try to break down the racial barriers. You do it step by step, you don't do it in one fell swoop. I think our kids are ready to do that. One hopes so.

GKH In one of your interviews, you said that you're not comfortable with the word *feminist* as defined by white women, and I know a lot of women of color struggle with that, too. Your poem "Ms." [in *Awake in the River*] talks about how white feminism tends to get picky and not see the greater picture. Alice Walker coined a term—

JM *Womanist.*

GKH Right. Is that something that you've had to think about?

JM The labels have become less important to me as I get older. I don't need to be called an activist for me to feel like

I'm an activist. I don't need to be called a feminist or a womanist in order to feel like I'm a woman of color who is struggling for women's causes and for the equality and the parity of women. The labels to me become dangerous because, to me, feminism can become as institutionalized as any other institution if indeed it becomes so structured that the access is not there for everybody. The very principles that you're struggling for like equality, parity, access, nonexclusiveness, etc. should be for everybody. But that's not reality. I don't see feminism in the trenches with poor women. I see the feminist movement taking on some of the qualities that I see in the old white establishment. The bottom line question is, Who makes the decisions? Who has the power? If the power is not being shared equally by women of color, it's bullshit. To me you cannot ignore a population that is growing faster than any population in the state of California. Not having those women helping make the decisions about that movement, or that organization, or that structure, or whatever—it's absolute hypocrisy.

I've been labeled many things, and not all *ism* words, either. I've been labeled a nonartist because I won't separate myself from politics. I've been called things that end in *i-t-c-h*. I can't control that. What I want people to do is look at what I do. I think that working for getting free mammograms for poor women is a feminist act. You don't have to talk about it. But, if I can get fifty women to get free mammograms, I feel like I've been an activist. If I can help poor women get child care so that they can go out and look for a job and get out of that damn welfare system, then I feel like that is being a feminist. So that's how I define my life. And I believe we need the alliance of men. Women of color more than ever must embrace the alliance that has to be made with brothers, whether they are gay, straight, black, Asian, Hispanic. We're too small a population, we have too few numbers, and we have too little power to be able to afford to separate ourselves

Janice Mirikitani

from each other. And that's how I've felt in the past, and that's how I feel today, more strongly than ever.

Note

1. All the poems mentioned in this paragraph can be found in *Shedding Silence.*

Selected Works by Janice Mirikitani

Time to Greez! Incantations from the Third World/Third World Communications. Edited by Janice Mirikitani et al. San Francisco: Glide, 1975.

Awake in the River: Poetry and Prose. San Francisco: Isthmus, 1978.

"Attack the Water" and "Sing with Your Body." In *The Third Woman: Writers of the US,* ed. Dexter Fisher. Boston: Houghton Mifflin, 1980.

"Desert Flower," "For My Father," "Loving from Vietnam to Zimbabwe," "The Question Is," "We the Dangerous," and "The Woman and the Hawk." In *Ayumi: A Japanese American Anthology.* San Francisco: Japanese American Anthology Committee, 1980.

"Breaking Silence." *Amerasia Journal* 8, no. 2 (1981): 107–110.

"Breaking Silence" and "Breaking Tradition." In *Breaking Silence: An Anthology of Contemporary Asian American Poets.* Greenfield Center, N.Y.: *Greenfield Review* Press, 1983.

"Assaults and Invasions" and "What's a Girl to Do?" *Bamboo Ridge* 30 (Spring 1986): 46–47, 43–45.

Shedding Silence: Poetry and Prose. Berkeley, Calif.: Celestial Arts, 1987.

"Assaults and Invasions," "A Certain Kind of Madness," and "Shadow in Stone." *Feminist Studies* 14, no. 3 (Fall 1988): 417–427.

"In Remembrance." In *Making Waves: An Anthology of Writings by and about Asian American Women,* ed. Asian Women United of California. Boston: Beacon Press, 1989.

"The Fisherman," "Shadow in Stone," and "Soul Food." In *The Open*

Boat: Poems from Asian America, ed. Garrett Hongo. New York: Anchor/Doubleday, 1993.

"Spoils of War." In *Asian-American Literature: A Brief Introduction and Anthology,* ed. Shawn Wong. New York: HarperCollins, 1995. Prose poem.

We the Dangerous: New and Selected Poems. London: Virago, 1995. Reprint, Berkeley, Calif.: Celestial Arts, 1995.

8

Chitra Banerjee Divakaruni

Interview by

DHARINI RASIAH

Chitra Divakaruni and I met five years ago when we were both involved in organizations that addressed the concerns of South Asian American and South Asian immigrant women. She contributed to an anthology I coedited, *Our Feet Walk the Sky,* and we were both involved in Maitri and Narika, domestic violence help lines for South Asian women in the Bay Area. As cofounder and current president of Maitri, Divakaruni often re-creates many of the powerful testimonials of the women she encounters. Her earlier work is primarily poetry, and her first three books, *Dark like the River, The Reason for Nasturtiums,* and *Black Candle,* vividly capture the emotions her South Asian women subjects experience with domestic violence, marriage, family, immigration, and death. Her short stories and poetry have been featured in a number of anthologies, and she is the recipient of several awards. *Arranged Marriage* is her first book of short stories; it received the 1996 American Book Award, the PEN Oakland, Josephine Miles Award, and the Bay Area Book Reviewers Award for Fiction.

I interviewed Divakaruni on 31 July 1995, shortly after *Arranged Marriage* was released and her first novel, *The Mistress of Spices*, was completed. I was able to interview her over the phone despite her busy schedule of teaching, raising her children, and touring with her two new books. After speaking with her, I went to a number of readings and discussions of *Arranged Marriage* and *The Mistress of Spices* in Los Angeles and the Bay Area. Divakaruni reaches a very wide audience, from students who are familiar with her writings and are well versed in Asian American literature to people who are curious about a book with a title like *Arranged Marriage*, which almost necessarily invites questions that revolve around issues of marriage and questions of "choice" that divide cultural/ethnic experiences. But Divakaruni deftly reworks questions that assume a polarized East/West cultural conflict that all South Asian Americans/immigrants uniformly encounter to address a more complicated reality that recalls histories of colonialism, geographic dislocation, and racism, and she often draws parallels to the experiences of other ethnic and racial groups.

DR I had read *The Reason for Nasturtiums* in 1991, and it was a major influence on the work I was doing at the time with our anthology and with the Asian Women's Shelter. So maybe we can start by speaking chronologically about your books of poetry.

CBD *The Reason for Nasturtiums* came out shortly before *Black Candle*, but the poems were written around the same time. I just divided them into two books with different focuses. *Black Candle* is very much a women's book. It focused totally on women's experiences, and a lot of it is the darker side of South Asian women's experience. So those are poems of oppression and empowerment, moving from oppression to empowerment. Being a writer yourself, you know that, when writing, one doesn't do this consciously; poems come out of the subconscious. But, when I was putting the book together, I wanted to show different stages of oppression and empowerment. Some of the women are victims because they are in a society that is too powerfully oppressive for them to overcome. They have no models; they have no inspiration. But that doesn't mean that their inner life is any less vibrant or any less human or any less powerful or painful.

DR How did you come to write about this?

CBD At that time in my life I was doing a lot of remembering. A lot of the poems in *Black Candle* are based on women I had come across when I was living in India—though of course transformed through writing and the imagination—women who were important in my life, in my family. I thought their lives in many ways were tragic and in many ways heroic because they were fighting against very difficult things (for example, being childless in a society that values children). I felt that no one gave them credit. They just lived out their lives, and it was no big deal to anyone. Of course you do that; you continue taking care of the family even when your heart is breaking. I wanted to give them their special moments through the poems in which they were the center and their pain was the most important element.

DR Much of your work deals with the problems of immigration, specifically the experiences of South Asian women immigrants.

CBD Yes, that was the next stage. But first I had to deal with the past. In some ways one is never done with that. I keep going back to it. But the women I see nowadays, the women I have come to know through my work with Maitri, the help line—their stories are also very moving and inspiring for me.

DR Can you speak about Maitri and your work on domestic violence?

CBD We started Maitri in 1991. I was one of the founders, and I've remained very involved with it; I'm still the president. We are a help line where South Asian women in distress can call, and, depending on what the problem is, we try to figure out what are the best options for the woman, and we offer her these options. We are a referral line, so we can connect her up with other agencies that can help her. We can talk to her, provide peer counseling to give her a sense that she's not alone in whatever it is that is happening to her.

It is so difficult for many of our women, especially those who come as wives, who don't come in their own right, as it were. They don't have family here. Their main identity is that of being someone's wife. A lot of times, they don't have a job, and they don't have a visa for work. They're terribly, terribly isolated. If things go well, they begin to adjust and make their own connections and develop their own identity; when things go badly, it's very hard for them. A good number of times they can't even call back and tell their families because their families put a lot of effort into this marriage and a lot of times the family won't be supportive anyway. They'll say, "Well, try to work it out," or, "Maybe you're not doing the right things." You know how it is sometimes in the culture where, no matter what happens, it's the woman's fault. It's the woman's job to make sure everything works out, including the marriage. That's why we have the line, to tell women it's OK. Not all marriages work out, and not always is it the woman's fault if they don't. In fact, a good number of times it isn't. So we're there to give her support and courage and tell her some of the things she can do and, if the situation is dangerous, help move her out of that situation. It's touched my life in many ways.

DR Do you participate in other social work?

143

Chitra Banerjee Divakaruni

CBD As part of Maitri, I'm in touch with the mainstream shelters. I've volunteered a long time with the mainstream shelters, and that helps us move our women into those shelters.

DR What are some of the differences in domestic violence for South Asian women as opposed to other groups?

CBD On one level, there are many similarities. They undergo something we call *a cycle of violence.* You might know this because of your work with the Asian Women's Shelter. They all have that hope, that belief that maybe this time it will work out. I think that the culture makes our Asian and South Asian women even more reluctant to leave, but mainstream women, white women, black women, Hispanic women, are also reluctant to leave. It's very hard for a woman to take that first step and say, "OK, I'm going to cut off this relationship and go out into the middle of nowhere." It is very frightening. So they have that in common. Our women have the added stress of family shame, community shame, because everyone knows everyone else in the community. They think, "What will happen if I leave the house and am never able to come back?" They have a stronger identity tie to being a wife and mother. Each woman is different, but these are some trends that we see: they are very concerned about their families back home in India. A lot of times they'll say, "Just get me out of this marriage and get me a ticket to go back to India." A lot of times we'll say, "Before you go, at least explore your other options here; don't make a hasty decision. It's easy to go back, but, if you go back, what will you do then? What will your situation be there?"

DR You also write about problems other people in the community face—immigrant men, children.

CBD Oh, yes, it's all interconnected. I write a lot about women because, being a woman, I am very sensitive to that area and I empathize more. But anything that's a woman's problem is bound to have resonance and reverberate in the entire community. You can't oppress women and expect that no one else is going to feel the results of that oppression. Not only do men oppress women, but women oppress themselves for various reasons. The result is that the role of the man becomes hardened and you can't move out of that role either. Because all these are connected, every once in a while I will write about what I see as those connections.

DR In a recent interview in *India West,* you spoke about Swami Chinmayananda. Could you discuss his influence on your life and work?

CBD What I have been most influenced by in terms of Indian spirituality, much more than conventional religion, is the teachings of Vedanta, which is what Swami Chinmayananda always focuses on, which is to say that everyone is the divine self and that we are all connected as part of the divine self and therefore we must try to see each other as not "other" or different but as parts of the same divine being. This thinking has had a big influence on my life. It has been very helpful to me as a writer because then you feel the pain of others, you see their situation imaginatively, not just from a social context or an activist context. You just empathize more with people. You're more aware of their being, and you don't think of yourself as different from them or as a separate entity from them. That has helped me immensely in "becoming" other people, becoming other characters.

DR How do you feel about the label *Asian American?*

CBD I have no problem with the Asian American identity. As a writer, I have many identities, and I'm relatively comfortable with all of them. Overall, I think of myself as a writer, beyond all other categories. That is our most important identity. The other identities of course influence us and make us

Chitra Banerjee Divakaruni

who we are. One must be a writer on some universal level beyond all these labels, which, after all, we put on ourselves. I feel happy about being a part of the Asian American community. I've learned a great deal from Asian American writers. We share many of the same concerns.

DR Do you ever feel that there are any obstacles with this term for a South Asian writer?

CBD No, I don't because each term is a different facet and one is a more specialized facet. I'm a writer, I'm an American writer, and then, when I think of it in more special terms, I'm an Asian American writer, then I'm a South Asian American writer, and I'm also a Bengali writer writing in the United States, and each of these is true to my identity. It's wonderful that more people are recognizing that we, the Indian American writers, are part of the Asian experience. Because otherwise, when people think *Asian American,* they forget about us. So it's a really positive step that recently I've been included in several Asian American anthologies.

DR Which anthologies specifically?

CBD Garrett Hongo's *Open Boat,* Geraldine Kudaka's *On a Bed of Rice,* and an anthology of memoirs called *Under Western Eyes,* also edited by Garrett Hongo; Calyx Books brought one out called *The Forbidden Stitch,* and the *Greenfield Review* Press brought out a prose collection called *Home to Stay.* I've been very happy. Otherwise, people pick up Asian American books, and they get an incomplete picture because, in some specific ways, our cultures are very different but, in some larger ways, we have many of the same values, problems, concerns. So I feel strongly positive about that.

DR When you write, who do you have in mind as your audience?

CBD Again, just as I think of myself as a writer at those many levels, my audience is on different levels, and they're just different people. Ultimately, when I write, I try not to think of an audience at all. I just think of the work itself because the idea of audience constrains you. But, at some point, in your subconscious mind, it is there. I write for people like myself, people who are interested, open, and careful readers. That's who I think of in terms of my audience at the most important and most embracive level. Some time back there was an article, a scathing review of *Black Candle,* and one of the things the critic said was, "Oh, this writer writes for white people," and she meant it as a real put-down. When I read it, I was really angry for a while, and then I thought, Why not? I live in America; America is a part of my life; should I not write for white people also? It's a defeatist and hypocritical attitude to say that I will live in America and write only for other Indians. I don't think writers anywhere think, "I will write only for this community, and nobody else should have access to my work." That goes against the whole impulse of what makes us write, which is to reach out and communicate across barriers and to create and improve understanding between people. Why else are we writing?

DR I find it strange that this critic would say that because, knowing the history of our community and the problems the community faces, I think that your work really speaks to other people in the community, other South Asians, very powerfully.

CBD That's what I thought, too. This book is very much for us. So, on one level, I hope I'm writing for that general audience, but, in my heart, I hope that the people who will feel it most strongly because it comes closest to their lives are other South Asians, other Asian Americans. I think I'm writing very much for my people and perhaps for other minority people, not in being a spokesperson, but in sharing with them an experience that they will be able to relate to.

Chitra Banerjee Divakaruni

DR Are you ever put in the position of a spokesperson, or do you ever feel that you are speaking for the community?

CBD When I give readings, people are always asking me questions about the Indian culture, and I always say that this is just one person's impression, that this is my understanding. I hope I have a good understanding, but there are many realities; there are many Indias, and each person carries one inside her head. That's the real bind about being a writer from a particular ethnic background living in a culture that is not of that ethnic background. There's a kind of subconscious assumption that, "if I read this book, I will find out all about that culture." And that of course is not true. One hopes people will find out something, though.

DR What other responses have you gotten from the community?

CBD This negative review is the one that got stuck in my mind, but all the other reviews have been very positive. The ones on *Arranged Marriage,* since it's come out, have been very positive.

DR Can you speak about your new books, *Arranged Marriage* and *The Mistress of Spices?*

CBD *Arranged Marriage* is very much a book that is set in this country. The stories go back and forth, but the present of the stories, all except one, the present life of the central characters is set here. So it's very much an immigrant book; I'm more and more involved with the reality of people right here at this time. The *Mistress of Spices* deals with a past that is set in a mythical India, but the present is very much set in Oakland, California.

DR Have you gotten responses from the Indian community yet?

CBD Yes, *India West, India Today,* the *India Post,* and *India Currents* have all done reviews. I was really concerned because some of these papers are very traditional; the reviewers are male, but everyone (touch wood) has been very positive. One of the things I wanted to focus on in this book is the women who come here: how their lives have changed. And you can't say for the better or for the worse; they gain certain things, and they lose certain things. It's a very poignant and often painful process but also a very exhilarating, energetic process, and for many women it is an opportunity for new empowerment and freedom. So I was concerned about how the community would react to that. But so far they have been very positive.

DR I know from my work on our anthology that, at times, some South Asian men are unwilling to acknowledge some of the issues women deal with.

CBD Yes, they feel that, if you say something that is critical of the community, that means you hate India or Indian values, and that's not true at all. One criticizes because one loves, because one cares. People lose sight of that very important point. If I didn't care about the community, why would I write about it at all?

DR Which writers have influenced your work?

CBD A lot of writers have influenced me in various ways. Starting with the South Asian canon, Anita Desai and Bharati Mukherjee have been big influences. It's been very interesting to me to read people like Meena Alexander. I've read everyone I could get my hands on, and I've learned a great deal. I've also read the works of several men that I like, Ved Mehta, some of Vikram Seth's work; I am immensely impressed by Rohinton Mistry. I also like Shashi Tharoor, Bapsi Sidwha, Vikram Chandra, and many others. Among Asian Americans, I've really been influenced by Maxine Hong Kingston. I like

Amy Tan's work also greatly. I've learned a lot about voice and character from Amy Tan, especially from *The Joy Luck Club*. But I also like women writers from other ethnic backgrounds writing in America. I like Sandra Cisneros, especially *The House on Mango Street*. I have that in my office and read it every once in a while. I love Louise Erdrich's work; *Love Medicine* and *Tracks* have been especially inspiring to me as I was writing *Mistress of Spices* because they contain an element of magic and mystery.

DR Could you describe *The Mistress of Spices*?

CBD Yes. It's about a woman who comes to Oakland and opens a spice store. Only it's not an ordinary spice store. It's magical because she has studied on a spice island off in the Indian Ocean; she studied the secret power of spices, and she knows how to use them to help people. And so the story is about all the people who come to her store, and their stories, and how she tries to help, and sometimes it works, and sometimes it doesn't.

DR This is interesting to me because my latest work is on South Asian women's small business enterprises and economic independence. A lot of women do start small businesses in the Bay Area and in Los Angeles and New York, particularly within the ethnic enclave. What is your observation on this?

CBD One of the big concerns in *Arranged Marriage* is the importance of financial independence for women. I have felt this in my own life as well as in my observations of society. The characters in *Arranged Marriage* often realize that, unless they are economically independent, they can't push for psychological independence. And so many of the women in those stories will try various ways of achieving this, some within the ethnic enclosure, so to speak, but some venturing out into mainstream America. In *Spices,* the main character will start very much within the Indian community, and there is a sense that she should work within only it and help only her own people. But then she will begin more and more to become interested in the larger world outside and get involved with Americans of other racial backgrounds. There's a real sense of breaking out of the Indian community and how, although our own community is important for us, it's really important also to relate across the barriers.

DR We still haven't talked about one of your books of poetry, *Dark like the River.*

CBD That was my very first book. I'm fond of it because it was my first. I've come a long way from that. That was very much based in India. I was more interested at that point in the emotion of those pieces. Since then, I've become much more concerned about craft—the use of language, the use of imagery, how one says things. In *Arranged Marriage,* I moved into the prose field. In *Mistress,* I'm trying to combine poetry and prose more closely, enough to dissolve the boundaries or at least to experiment and see if the boundaries can be dissolved between poetry and prose.

DR Are there any other writers who you believe accomplish this?

CBD I've been attracted to Sandra Cisneros's work for that reason, and also Louise Erdrich's work is very emotionally powerful in a poetic sense; that's why those two writers have influenced me so much.

DR Why did you move in the prose direction?

CBD Because I had all these stories that were battling to be told, and my poetry was becoming more and more narrative, and yet I felt I wasn't able to tell the story just because of the poetic form and the way it focuses on the intense moment. I wanted to show characters growing, changing, developing,

Chitra Banerjee Divakaruni

their reaction to certain events, and also how they interact. I wanted to show those things much more. I will always love poetry, but I'm very happy right now writing prose.

DR You teach creative writing at Foothill College, right?

CBD I teach creative writing and also English, so I teach various things. I love teaching. It's a very important part of my life. Foothill, being a community college, has an open door policy, which I really believe in. Education should be available to everyone who wants it, not just the elite, not just the financially able. It goes along with what I believe for my own writing, which is that writing or books should be accessible to everyone. That's what I try to do in my teaching and in my writing: make literature accessible to everybody. It sure takes away a lot of creative energy, though. That's why I'm taking the rest of the year off to write. Otherwise, being a mother and a wife and being a teacher and working in the community leaves very little time to write. It's such a struggle.

DR Any last words?

CBD Yes, I think that for Asian American and especially South Asian writers, but then again I'm speaking for myself, one of the things that sets our writing apart is—for those of us who know them—our native languages. And the rhythms of our native languages are very important in our own writing. It's certainly been that way for me. Bengali is always in the back of my mind, and I think it really does influence the rhythm of my writing.

DR Do you write in Bengali at all?

CBD I do, but not in my literary writing. I do a lot of translations from Bengali, though. I've translated a lot of work—men's work, women's work, poetry, prose. I hope to continue doing that in between writing my own work. So I'm very aware of literary writing in my language.

Selected Works by Chitra Banerjee Divakaruni

Dark like the River. Calcutta: Writers Workshop, 1987. Poetry.

"Doors." In *Home to Stay,* ed. Sylvia Watanabe and Carol Bruchac. Greenfield Center, N.Y.: *Greenfield Review* Press, 1989. Story.

"At Muktinath." In *The Forbidden Stitch,* ed. Shirley Geok-lin Lim and   **153**
Mayumi Tsutagawa. Corvallis, Oreg.: Calyx, 1989. Poem.

The Reason for Nasturtiums. Berkeley: Berkeley Poets, 1990. Poetry.

Black Candle. Corvallis, Oreg.: Calyx, 1991. Poetry.

"Childhood" and other poems. In *The Open Boat: Poems from Asian America,* ed. Garrett Hongo. New York: Anchor/Doubleday, 1993.

"Indigo." *Quarry West* 29/30 (1992): 104–105. Poem appearing in the special issue *Dissident Song: A Contemporary Asian American Anthology,* ed. Marilyn Chin and David Wong Louie.

"Leaving Yuba City." In *Our Feet Walk the Sky: Writings from Women of the South Asian Diaspora,* ed. Women of the South Asian Diaspora Collective. San Francisco: Aunt Lute, 1993. Story.

Arranged Marriage. New York: Doubleday, 1995. Stories.

"Lalita Mashi." In *Under Western Eyes,* ed. Garrett Hongo. New York: Anchor-Doubleday, 1995. Poem.

"The Word Love." In *On a Bed of Rice: An Asian American Erotic Feast,* ed. Geraldine Kudaka. New York: Anchor/Doubleday, 1995.

"We the Indian Women in America." In *Contours of the Heart,* ed. Sunaina Maira and Rajini Srikanth. Berkeley, Calif.: Asian American Writers Workshop, 1996. Poem.

Leaving Yuba City: New and Selected Poems. New York: Doubleday, 1997.

The Mistress of Spices. New York: Doubleday, 1997. Novel.

Sister of My Heart. New York: Doubleday, 1999.

Chitra Banerjee Divakaruni

9

Al Robles

Interview by

DARLENE RODRIGUES

Nothing escapes Al Robles, neither the mundane nor the banal, neither the poor nor the rich. Not even nature. Robles' first published collection of poetry, *Rappin' with Ten Thousand Carabaos in the Dark* (1996), is the result of a life effused with this gift of observation and sensitivity to the surrounding world. Consequently, Robles' poetry not only reflects the diversity of the people, cultures, and religious influences found in the Fillmore district of San Francisco, his neighborhood since childhood, but also includes a spiritual connection to the environment. Manongs and other Asian immigrants, prostitutes, and the homeless emerge from his work as complex beings who struggle daily in a society that has readily cast them aside.

However, Robles is more than a documentarian of the past and collector of stories. As reflected in his poetic vision, he cares deeply about how we are to live in a morally and spiritually bankrupt society. At times, the manner in which he conveys this vision may border on the absurd and the bawdy and may belie the seriousness of his struggles as a poet. This seriousness can be found in the questions that underlie his work: How can we capture what we observe instantaneously in a given moment with what we experience in a lifetime? How do we connect the immediacy of our suffering with the profound? How do we negotiate the middle ground between the future and the past? Ultimately, Robles shows us that the separation between people and places in his poetry and in our own lives is illusory.

DR When did you start writing, and why did you choose poetry?

AR You know the saying, "Writing away from writing." Through my whole life I create without knowing. You know all these things you collect from a book and you tuck away, right? A kind of unfinishedness of a poem. The writing becomes something where you actually lay out all that you know, all the people whom you touched. It comes about, not only through the people, but through every event that you can remember. A lot of the things that happened in the past sit in some part of your mind. It can be twenty or thirty years or even longer, and things still continue to write themselves. It's that kind of writing, a poetical feeling of the Manongs and the place. There has to be a place with the Manongs, the Issei, or the blacks, and out of that place there are places that you can move, down from Watsonville to Stockton, Stockton to Alaska, Chinatown to Nihonmachi: the places of these people, the places of the heart and soul, songs that are woven into the faces of these people. That actually goes back, beyond what your memory can capture. It is depicted in some of the faces and some of the songs that people sing. The Issei have Japanese poems that come from deep inside, like the song that tells the whole life of these people. You can say that it describes the entire life of those Issei. There's a thing like that for Manongs, too, that is like a Buddhist poem. You cry it out.

Al Robles

You sing. You chant. Like the songs, the poetry, the writings are all interwoven. So how do I write? I was listening, smelling, feeling, walking. All woven. The poetry, the writing became part of the smells, the sounds, the songs, and the people.

DR So when did you start? It sounds like it was very much a part of your life.

AR I was paying attention to myself in relation to my surroundings, so that everyone else who was involved with me and who touched me was sacred and important. For example, I lived in a community of blacks, some Chicanos, Japanese, Filipinos; besides we had Buddhists. They had nature. They had poetry. All that was like *halo-halo*.[1] You can't have a *halo-halo* without all that mixture. At the same time you get the purity because you get the Manongs who want the rice a certain way and the Issei who want the rice a certain way.

As with the Japanese, the stories of the Manongs are sacred. I started gathering these things. Huge things like rocks, stones, half the size of this table, wood, and sometimes trees. Watching and relating to how these people—the Issei, the Manongs, the elderly Chinese, and the blacks—were able to live in these little tiny alcoves, I wondered what we as a people had that enabled us to survive. The Japanese, the Filipinos—they came, and they came. Hey, they didn't come to no Fairmont Hotel; they came into a hole. They came into these little spaces. So these spaces became bigger for me. I saw where the outside became the inside. The barbershop became the Manong's room, the Manong's room became the pool hall, the pool hall became the café of the Manongs, the café became the dance hall, the dance hall became the bar. It was well woven together. I felt this whole thing moving around. It was a part of my daily living, gathering with the people and paying attention to them.

For example, I saw this elderly Japanese lady who was claiming that there was a leak coming through her ceiling down to her floor into my room. She was close to a hundred. So I went upstairs and saw her little room, and I saw the rain coming through the ceiling. I said, "OK, I'll fix that for you. We'll fix it." But she says, "No, look." I was wondering, "Look at what?" As I stopped and looked, I saw the water running through the ceiling, trickling like a stream, so it was cool to have it because it was beautiful.

I'm just saying that all these things came together in the relationship of the poverty of our people to isolation, exploitation, oppression. Some said there was no loneliness in these little rooms. See, from beginning to end, they came and stayed in all these hotels, but at the same time they were in Watsonville, Salinas, Alaska, and so forth. What happened was they were living from moment to moment but they finally came to that end right here—eighty, ninety-five years old in one room. I guess the greatest thing I saw in coming together with all these people was the tragic sense of life or the poetical sense of life, however you wanna call it. What I saw was like the birth of our people and the community; the poetry, the celebration were all woven together. It was music, and it was music when we celebrated someone's death, some event, but always trying to get together. It was real. These people were doing it because that was their life. The little rice that they got, they celebrated.

I guess the Filipinos, the Chinese, the Japanese were all together in this one way of thinking. We became one in thinking of finding multiculturalism. The beautiful thing about multiculturalism is finding your own way. I have a poem about something that's the same and it's different; and it's different and it's the same. The Manong is the same, but he's different; he's different, and he's the same. He came, and you see him in Alaska. You see him in the Stockton asparagus fields, and you see him doing all kinds of things. But he wasn't only a laborer. It wasn't only the portrait of the Manong or the Issei, the portrait of the poor. They always lived close to water. You

Al Robles

find Manongs close to water—whether it's New York, Seattle, Stockton. Maybe there's something about being from the islands. I was talking to someone about the lowlands and highlands in the islands, which are wet and dry.

DR It sounds like you are talking about finding the beauty in your life and then singing about it so that it's not forgotten. Why do you think it's important to listen and tell?

AR You remember the things that move you. You go from here to there and say, "I remember." What's the good of remembering? What's the big thing about these tales and these ancestral stories and epics and poems? What's the point? The point is that, as a people, we still hear our songs, and the songs just continue to live no matter what. You could be in Oxford, Cambridge, sitting around with some white folks, and somebody is going to look at your brown face and say, "Are you from the islands?" or, "Could you tell me about so and so?" In other words, you never get away from your skin, the skin of your face. I once wrote, "You cannot hide the fish smell." The fish smell is there no matter where you go. Somebody's gonna say, "There're some Filipinos around here." When you get up in the morning and look at your face, it's gonna be your own face. Like this guy Tagatac when he thought he was gonna be a six footer like John Wayne. Well, he wasn't John Wayne, and so he kept on looking in the mirror and said, "Oh, this is me. This is reality."

DR Tell me about where you grew up.

AR Oh, I grew up in a state of confusion where everything was actually happening—jazz, Manongs, blacks, Chicanos, Chinese, and Japanese. When I say everything was happening, we had every conceivable thing you can imagine. You had the music and the poetry. You had the jazz, the poverty, the children, the rice, the homeless, the prostitutes. I grew up with prostitutes.

DR   Where was this?

AR   In the Fillmore. We knew every single prostitute, but they weren't ordinarily the way you think of prostitutes now. It was like, "Oh, how's your mama?" It's not like today's "yo mama."[2] They say, "Oh, my mother's fine. Have you seen so and so?" They're talking about my sister and my nephews, and I say, "Oh, OK." I know what it was like because the Filipinos who were there lived alongside the prostitutes. And the prostitutes were on both sides of the street. Hundreds of them. No matter what we did in the neighborhood, they knew. When we saw them being taken away, it was kinda sad. We said, "Oh, God, Jean is being taken away by the cops." It was like a family situation; everybody was tight and close together. And that's where the poetry comes in.

You walk through there, and you say, "Gee somebody's roasting pig. Where is it at, man?" And you say, "Oh, man, I don't know; maybe there's a party somewhere." Maybe by the afternoon or around evening somebody knows where the party is, and we'd crash the party—a Filipino party with all this food. People knew each other. I link this up to tribal places. A study I read says that these people always shared. They were always celebrating. I have this thing about celebrating. Sometimes the celebrating became overly celebrating. "OK, where's the fish, more fish, more fish, more rice." We didn't have any money. But we still cooked all this food, and the food was just passing like a poem over to the person. And out of this all these other people came. Jessica Hagedorn flew in. Frank Chin flew in. Shawn Wong flew in. Sam Tagatac flew in.

What draws the soul and heart of the artist or the poet together? The people. The food. The food is the damn thing. What do we have in place of what that all means? Do we have something that belongs to us? Do we have something that we can call our own? That's what the I-Hotel[3] means. The I-

Al Robles

Hotel is saying that this belongs to you and your children. It belongs to everyone who has a heart, like the people who can sing songs, who can dance for the community.

DR And that's why poetry was so important.

AR It wasn't only celebrating. It wasn't just talking about social change. Like the leak, right? It was beautiful, and at the same time we wanted to get it fixed. Change the structure. It was not only the I-Hotel and the plight of the Filipinos in these little rooms but also the plight of the poor. You came with your poetry, your art, or your music, and you saw they were wearing rags and said, "We will sing a song after we bring down the rent. We will sing a song to get you a better place." It was always like that at the Kearny Street Workshop, where they had every kind of form that was integrated into one. They had silk-screening, poetry, and photography, and it all was connected to the community. On hearing that someone was trying to demolish a building, the artists, the poets, the people who were into film converged, whether in a park or in a sewing factory.

I see the feeling and the poetry of it, but I don't feel the poetry of it now. The question is, How do we find our own community? Here we were in this community—Filipinos from Fillmore to Kearny and the blacks over there.

I was the last one out of that building with the Filipinos. And the developers had come with the iron ball. When I got home, it was a little before five. I saw where the side of the building was opened up and the upstairs floor sunk in. To the people from the housing authority it was condemned. They said, "Move out." I had all my things in this house, and I had to get out because they were going to tear it down right there. Now that was a trip. How do you move all your things from the place you and all those Filipinos there and the Chinese and the blacks grew up in? They said, "You've got to leave."

Words Matter

The I-Hotel was a tragedy, and that tragedy was felt all over. It said that we will not step back. The awareness of tenants' rights came about through the I-Hotel. You will not treat people like this. So what came about was the protection of the Manongs and the elderly. Before, the poor had no rights. Tenants had no rights. But, after the I-Hotel, the city created all these amendments for the rights of the elderly and the rights of the tenants. Now the tenant has more rights than the landlord or just as many. Why? In fact, the landlord is making a living out of where the tenant is living. So social change matters, but not only social change. If we didn't have our songs and our music or poetry, I don't know where we would be. I'd say we would go down.

DR Go down?

AR Yeah, we would go down if we didn't have this spirit. Even when we chanted, there was a continuance, a feeling to build up this spirit. Then you had all this organizing. How do you organize? How do you advocate? You have passivity with some Filipinos; you get off the row, and you are overly comfortable. The more comfortable you get, the less you wanna be involved. During those periods, you had the Filipinos who were involved, the ones you would call Communists, radicals, revolutionaries, hippies, beatniks, and so on. Other Filipinos often felt and thought that this was too radical even though they saw the I-Hotel go down on TV and read about it in the paper. There was this great fear because four hundred police officers came down where three thousand people surrounded the I-Hotel. They were scared that the Filipinos had machine guns. Then there was the time when we got a call from the Weathermen, a revolutionary group that bombed a building near the city hall, and they got it out over the radio that they bombed this for the International Hotel.

So we had a lot of people involved in helping the community, all kinds of groups that were interested in social change.

Al Robles

We always talked about going beyond the community. You have the Manongs here; then we say, What about all those out there? Actually, all these Filipinos are part of this whole thing; all the Asians are part of this whole entity. But the wound is still there for the very people who do not want to be involved. They still carry the wound. Say a little child walks by the I-Hotel and asks, "What is this?" She is told, "Oh, Filipinos used to live here," and she goes home. When we come back and meet in this place called SOMA, South of Market Avenue, she says, "My grandfather used to live here." What is the significance of this? It tells the story. Like the legacy of black people, it is the legacy of the spirit of community and history.

DR You said that you don't feel the spirit of the poetry of today. Where is it, then?

AR It's not there. It's not visual, so how do we pass this feeling over? You can talk about it. It's all history, which means that you are talking about your people, right? It's not to say, "What do these five-year-olds, ten-year-olds know?" The question is, "Do they have just as much right to write about the I-Hotel if they were never there?" Yeah, because that's the sound that I was talking about; the smell is there. But, for someone who plays music, that person will never hear the sound of the guitar and then picture it in a barbershop in Manilatown or Kearny Street and the old-timers singing these old songs. Sometimes, if you explain too much, you explain nothing. And, if you say less, you say more, but you can say less and say nothing. Say you are just eating and someone says, "Back here in the I-Hotel, did they ever have this?" "Yeah, they had food just like this." And they say, "Ooh, that's good." That's enough. It hits. Not only is that good; it's interesting because it comes from the heart of things. The taste of the Manong, the taste of the fish. The writing is all linked up to smell and taste.

White architects and developers are always asking, "What is this barbershop? What is this pool hall?" I say, "It's really not like a barbershop." It gets more confusing to say what this means. "Well, if you can see all these people in there, just sitting, playing music." And they say, "Who's cutting hair?" I say, "Well, it's like their home."

DR That's not there for the generation of today.

AR Here's my little niece. She's ten years old, and she writes. She hears me read and talk about the past and no past. "Uncle, look what I wrote." I read these things, and she talked about the past and about getting back. It's a ten-year-old writing this. You know, it's so deep, so heavy. She's doing an ancestral thing on me. This poem she wrote is related to the Manongs, Manangs, the tribal ashes, the I-Hotel, the Issei, everything. She writes, "My grandma, I see her walking in the river. And she's catching fish with her hands. I like to eat with my hands from a crab shell. Already I'm riding a crab shell. I wonder who came before and before and before and before." So I say, "Oh, man. This is really heavy." The last line she says, "I like the taste of the *pancit*. I still can taste the *pancit*." I think that this taste called *poetical taste* goes beyond. In other words, there are some who can lay out a poem or a play or music. And, when you hear that music, you will go out to eat some rice because, you say, "Oh, man, that piece was so beautiful. It was like a meal."

Back to the cooking. In Manilatown and home wherever, they have a certain way they cook. Everyone has their own style of cooking *adobo*. Or fish, or what have you. So what's the difference? What's all this big fuss about cooking? You know the I-Hotel. How do we get together? When we talk about the heart of it, you can't forget these Manongs, you can't forget how they cooked the rice. "Where did they cook their rice? Did they eat in their rooms? What kind of rice?" The developers were asking these questions, but the problem went deeper than what the architects understood because we wanted them to give back Manilatown. To do our own cooking. "Give it back."

Right now, that is the stage of how we are dealing with the I-Hotel. When I say we want to do our own cooking, this is what we want. We want a cultural center and museum where we could dance, perform, play music, read poetry, have somebody from the Bontoc.[4] And then we wanted a community space, and we wanted it inside the I-Hotel. We are saying, "Give us back our spirit, our soul."

How do the architects get this picture? You have the TransAmerica, a billion-dollar corporation that doesn't like to see Asians too close. And some millionaire folks up on Telegraph Hill feel that the new housing project will obstruct their view. And then we got the Russians, the refugees who have demonstrated because they want housing. And if we get more blacks in there so we can have a balance, it would be cool.

DR You don't think that, if you gave your book of poetry to these architects, they'd get the picture?

AR Oh, yeah. See, in the book of poetry, there is a poem dealing with the church. I wrote this sometime back, but it's a heavy indictment against the church. You think that, if the church gets hold of the poem, then the negotiations will stop? I named the archbishop, and I named the church that was actually going up against us, but I wrote that before the I-Hotel evictions. And I called the archbishop of San Francisco the pimp of all these horrors. Now we are having negotiations with the archdiocese. They had two black altar boys holding his cape. The reason for that was the black community was going down and this billion-dollar church was going up. Isn't that ironic that you have the church going up and the I-Hotel going down? What goes around comes around. And the archdiocese is strong.

DR Let's go back to those days of your earlier writing.

AR There's so much stuff it would fill up this whole room. How do you lay things out? You know, like the writer keeps diaries, notebooks, and so on. And you have things that you are still working on. We have a lot of black stuff because we grew up with the black stuff. It was just there. So I guess you gotta be where you have your things. You gotta weave them together. When I go to read in a Japanese place, I have Japanese poems. I have poems in Japanese.

DR Where did you pick that up?

AR I didn't just pick it up. I studied. I did everything that was not "normal." In other words, I lived in the Fillmore with poets and artists, Filipinos—a mixture of other folks. Say they do the *lechon* [roasted pig]. They do the pig, the kalding, or the roasted goat, and at the same time nearby there's fish, raw fish. All together. You had the Manongs, and you had the Issei, and it was part of the daily life. I ate rice, drank tea, ate fish, drank tea. Just going back and forth. I have a poem where I say I am black. See, I am black because I'm Chinese. And the reason I'm Chinese is because I am Chicano. The reason why I'm Chicano is because I'm Filipino. And so on. I think I gotta say that, in the communities, when we're all writing, we're all together.

Alejandro Murguia, this la Raza poet, wrote a canto like the rap that kids have. They have the rhythm and the song, and it was like the rap of the rap. As he was doing this, I stumbled across the *ako* [Pilipino for "I"]. "Oh, *ako*," Alejandro says, "I got an *ako*, too." The Chicano poet says he also has an *ako*. We all got *akos*. We all got epics. He got his epic; I got my epic, this "*ako* canto." So he did his canto, his epic, and he saw it was very close to mine. We're singing our songs all together. One voice.

Al Robles

DR You were referring to "Ako ay Pilipino: A Thousand Pilipino Songs"?[5]

AR Yeah, how that came about was when folks were saying "I am, I am."

DR Like "Yo soy Chicano"?

AR Yeah, but I always write with no I. No I. No me. No who. No what. So they don't know who is writing.

DR Why don't you want to write the I or me?

AR I wrote this poem called "Soon the White Snow Will Melt." I was thinking about snow, and I was thinking of oppression and white people. And I was thinking of this one guy whose name is Richard Oaks. One day I saw him sitting at the Precita Bar, where all of us guys were just waiting to go up to Sacramento to read. He was just sitting there alone, drinking beer. He saw us and said, "What are you guys going to do?" We said, "We are gonna read." He was a Mohawk Indian who later died near the Eel River. He felt deeply about the plight of his people as they were taking over Alcatraz. He said, "You guys are poets? What do you guys do?" I said, "We read." He said, "You guys organize?" Cause he had some problems up north. He later got killed up there. We said, "Well, we gonna read. Would you like to?" He said, "Could I?" At that moment he became a poet. In one of his lines he was talking about oppression, and 99 percent of the people there were white. And he said, "Oppression, you know who you are." And he wasn't looking at us, right. He just kept on repeating that. He was very strong, very heavy. So I wrote these lines, "Soon the white snow will melt and underneath the black, brown, yellow, red earth will come to life." And at the end—affirmative action. Finally, you will see the brown faces and the yellow faces and so on and so forth. That was written way back when we believed that the layers of oppression would melt away only if we. . . .

Words Matter

DR Are patient?

AR Oh, no, not patient. 'Cause the thing is that you always hear these protest songs. It's not waiting. Your mind's gonna want to do it now. "Soon the white snow will melt. . . . " I turned the peace pipe into a gun. I was saying that enough is enough. If you create all the bad karma or the bad trips, they will in fact come back. But there is another thing besides karma, besides the Manongs and black power, yellow, and red, when you go beyond that realm and see the need of the community where you just help. The term is *bodhi*, short for *bodhisattva*. That means there is no one particular group, that you are not confined to one space. You embrace everyone.

DR Buddhist principles show up in your work a lot, right?

AR Birth is interesting. You have the birth of the Manongs, the birth of the Issei, the birth of the gold mountain. You have the birth, the growth, and then the end. Death. But you have that little thing called *rebirth*, which is the bringing back to life of all the things like the Issei, the communities, the poetry. You are creating. You're creating bagoong.[6] Oh, delicious, very good, very good. You are creating these things that are real. Out of nothing. It's not avant-garde.

DR So whom do you write for? Who is your audience?

AR There was this one woman poet who said, "Al, I got up and read in front of four hundred people. But you know who I read to? One girl, out there." I said. "Ooh. This is too heavy for me." Yeah, there's a thing called *performance*, but the audience can be whomever. When we have a Filipino celebration, we have the veterans and the Asians. I look out there, and I see the Manangs, the Filipino women, so I don't have any dirty words. I looked through all my poems. Maybe I'll take the water buffalo out. In a Japanese setting, I also make sure I don't have any dirty words. The young ones don't care.

Al Robles

So the audience is important, and it's not important. All of us read to our own selves. We would have this big celebration, and we see the same faces, the same poets.

We had this big reading of "Third World poets." We asked, "Why don't people come?" We had a celebrated poet, Genny Lim, who said, "I think we don't dress right." But she was dressed pretty nice. Actually, everyone else didn't dress right. And then one guy said, "Well, I think we're called *Asian American* or *Third World Poets*. So the audience was afraid of us."

We read to the blacks and Chicanos. They liked to hear "yo mama." Filipinos like that, but not the white audience. We did some heavy Filipino things, and a white member of the audience would come up and say, "Are you guys on TV?" "No, we're not on TV." "You guys should be on TV." These are, I wanna say, typical white folks who think this is like a comedy. We have a Manong playing a little guitar. They say, "Gee, it's kind of cute. Who's that little guy?" And I say, "Oh, that's Joe Lomanta." "Gee, that's very nice." It's a different trip, you know.

That's the trip: how you read the audience. Like church, too, if you are invited to a church. Or when you go off talking to the elderly in Chinatown or Japantown. It's a matter of respect. My brother in San Francisco used to go out to the beach, and he'd just take off all his clothes. Just lay there with his girlfriend, who stripped naked. They did a lot of Filipino performances at the Glide Memorial Church where Cecil Williams was pastor. During a memorial for Joaquin Legaspi, my brother performed at the church. Some folks came up to me and said, "Is your brother going to wear clothes? He can't strip in the church." "Well, then, what will he do?" "OK, he can go downstairs and dance." So he did his dance downstairs, but what happened was he still had nothing on there. Someone fixed a little tiny loincloth trying to hide his testicles. And they [the Filipinos] said, "What's happening is racist. Someone is trying to put a leaf there to hide his testicles." So you have the Filipino thing and the Catholic thing. Heavy, right?

Then you got Carlos Villa, who invited all the Manangs to this performance of painting with his body. He had paint all over his body, and he rolled and crawled on the canvas. And all the elderly women looked and said, "Nah, he has no good physique." They dug it because it was like a ritual or a procession. That's the first time I saw a Filipino strip right in front of all the Manangs. And all the roosters were running around. So how do you perform in front of the audience? You choose with respect.

DR Be respectful.

AR You must be alert so somebody doesn't say, "You goddamm revolutionaries." There's always somebody in the audience who says something like that. I don't know if you can say, "I don't want to hurt the white people by reading this or that." But, if you're invited to a poetry reading, you can't just read any poems. Sometimes, if you're reading some poems and then you see in the front of the audience all blondes, you can see the hurt in their eyes when you are talking about the Manongs chasing "blondies." You gotta choose.

DR What's the difference between a poem in performance and a poem in a book?

AR Performance includes the language of the body and the eyes and the hands. It's what you capture at that moment. When an audience reacts to the performer, the performer feels he is performing for the audience. Now in the No play you have performers who have been performing for twenty years. Someone says, "You've been doing the same thing for twenty years." How does the performance become alive? They have a thing called a *child's mind,* unfinished, fresh. So it doesn't make any difference if it's twenty years. When the actor gets

Al Robles

on that stage, it's the first time; each performance or each poem is new.

So how do you perform your writing? I would connect it to the way they prepare tea. What happens is that the performer who has been performing for twenty or thirty years becomes invisible. He becomes invisible after studying twenty or thirty years just drinking tea because his presence is already there. The performer on the stage becomes the audience. He becomes one with the audience, just like the nonperformer.

How do you become one with the poem, one with the audience, one with yourself? A lot of the mountain tribes have these beautiful vignettes—two or three lines. And these three lines are actually like a performance. How do you work toward brevity? How do you say everything in an encyclopedia in three lines? The Japanese say, "The lightning flashes, and you visualize the flash of lightning." How can you when light is fleeting? And the moment you write that poem down the poem and the mind become one. The poet is always working toward becoming the poem.

I have to tell you this story. Maybe this will give you the gist of what the poem is.

I had these Filipino children—about eight years old. I told them, "There was somebody drinking tea, and someone came up behind the person and drew his sword. The person who was drinking tea turned around with his tea bowl, and the guy who was going to chop off his neck put the sword back in its case and walked away." I asked, "Now, why did he put the sword back and walk away?" And little Malani—she was ten— said, "I know, I know! He got the thing." Sounds beautiful. And then I said, "OK. Now we have this man, this poet on the bridge, and underneath the bridge is the river. The sky is moving. It's raining, and he's holding on to the bridge. What is moving?" They said, "The sky, the river, the heavy rain, the little bridge, the birds." Then one goes, "Oh, no, I know, I know, I know what. His mind." How do you catch this in a flash? These kids caught it in a flash because they were not thinking.

Back to the performance. You gotta have that playfulness with the audience. You gotta become like that child. The state of poetry and art is always childlike. There's that moment when kids strike out; it's full and pure. They just strike out, and you say, "I wish I could be like that." One time, we did this reading, and somebody said, "We have Al's younger brother, right there." And then my brother Ray went down, trying to hide. And they kept saying, "We have Al's younger brother, right there." So he came up. And the people called out, "Where is the poem, Ray? Read the poem." He got up and gave these three lines. They were the heaviest lines: "I'm bamboo, I'm brown. I rise, I die. I cry." You know what he did? He cried. He got out there and just cried. The whole audience was sitting there, and they didn't know what to do. The playfulness, the beauty of it. So that's it. Letting yourself go.

Notes

1. A Filipino shaved-iced dessert with preserved tropical fruits and condensed milk.

2. An insult with reference to one's mother.

3. The International Hotel, housing poor and elderly Asian immigrants, was one of the last remaining buildings in an area formerly known as Manila Town in San Francisco. The struggle to save the "I-Hotel" became a rallying point during the late sixties and early seventies around the issue of affordable low-income housing. The I-Hotel provided low-income housing for primarily retired single Filipino and Chinese men and served as a economic and social support network for its tenants. In the late sixties, developers wished to exploit the hotel's prime location near the expanding financial district of San Francisco by demolishing the three-story, 155-room hotel. Tenants refused to move and, along with other activists in northern California, regularly demonstrated against the planned demolition. On 4 August 1977, nine years after the first eviction, four hundred police and sheriff's deputies armed

Al Robles

in riot gear broke through the human barricade around the hotel and forcibly evicted the remaining tenants.

4. An ethnic tribe in the Philippines from northern Luzon.

5. An epic poem first published in *Liwanag: Literary and Graphic Expressions by Filipinos in America* (San Francisco: Liwanag, 1975).

6. Fermented shrimp/fish paste used as a condiment.

Selected Works by Al Robles

Looking for Ifugao Mountain. Illustrated by Jim Dong. San Francisco: Children's Book Press, 1977.

"The Fall of the I Hotel." San Francisco: CrossCurrent Media/National Asian American Telecommunications Association, 1983. Videorecording.

"Hanging on a Carabao's Tale." *Amerasia Journal* 15, no. 1 (1989): 195–218.

Rappin' with Ten Thousand Carabaos in the Dark. Los Angeles: UCLA Asian American Studies Center, 1996.

10

Philip Kan Gotanda

Interview by
ROBERT B. ITO

Philip Kan Gotanda began his career as a playwright in 1979 with *The Avocado Kid*, a rock musical adaptation of the Japanese fairy tale *Momotaro*. Since then he has written numerous plays dealing with the Japanese American experience, including *A Song for a Nisei Fisherman*, *The Dream of Kitamura*, *Yankee Dawg You Die*, and *The Wash*. He has received a National Endowment for the Arts fellowship, three Rockefeller Playwriting Awards, a McKnight Fellowship, and the 1989 Will Glickman Playwriting Award. In addition to his busy schedule as a playwright and director, Gotanda also wrote, directed, and starred in the short film *The Kiss* and recently finished production on a jazzy film noirish spoken-word piece, *in the dominion of night*.

I met with Gotanda on three occasions, and he generously supplied me with production copies of almost all his plays, including works that were either out of print or currently in production. When I met with him in 1993, he was overseeing theatrical productions in both Los Angeles and New York. He spoke about how he had "fallen into" writing plays and about his desire to return to two of his former loves, film and music. After discussing his early career playing in a rock band with fellow Asian American artists David Henry Hwang and Sam Takamoto, he talked about small-town racism, his Nisei parents, and growing up Sansei in Stockton, all topics that led into a discussion about "the camps."

RBI Many of your plays deal with the Japanese American internment experience. Did your parents talk much about the camps?

PKG When I was growing up, they didn't talk about it; they were rather traditional in that way. They would talk a little about the good times, every now and then refer to the positive stuff—my father would talk about fishing—but beyond that not very much conversation about it. But, when these organizations like the Daughters of the American Revolution, Native Sons, would come by asking for donations, my mother would lecture them. As a kid I remember wondering, Why is my mom doing this? She was rather fearless. She would lecture them, saying, "It's because of you people we were put in the camps; why should I give you money?"

RBI Were you ever confused about what your parents were talking about, when they would talk about camp and you would think "summer camp"?

PKG No, I never thought that. I know other friends have said that they thought they were talking about some big summer camp that everyone went to, one summer, and they just stayed for a long time. People always ask each other when they meet, "What camp were you in?" or, "What camp was your father in?" No, I always thought that it was a peculiar event that had a certain aspect of being not so good, but, beyond that, I just let it go. As you get older, you figure out certain things, so, by the time I was about twelve, I already kind of knew what it was.

RBI How has the camp experience affected your sense of self-identity as a Japanese American and a playwright?

PKG My parents' camp experience continues to inform my work and life both on a conscious and on an unconscious level. I've exploited themes of its psychic scar in *American Tattoo* (1982), the subsequent internalized racism being passed on from generation to generation in *Fish Head Soup* (1986), and its immediate psychological aftermath in *Sisters Matsumoto* (1999).

RBI Was there any resistance from your family when you decided to become a playwright?

PKG Yes and no. On one hand, I was raised with a lot of exposure to the arts—took a lot of piano lessons, violin lessons, painting lessons—and I played in bands all my life as I was growing up, all through junior high and high school and college. And there was never an active discouragement of that, but there was this expectation that, at some point, when I got down to a career, I was going to be a doctor. Even though it wasn't mentioned, it just was assumed that I was going to be a doctor because they assumed everyone in my family was going to be a doctor. So, once I began to move away from that, there was a certain sense of disappointment from my father, strong disappointment. And what I began to realize was that he was never going to understand and that's simply him looking at me through his world. He grew up on the island of Kaua'i, a huge family struggling to find a career, to find the American dream. To him, the idea of becoming an artist made no sense (how does one feed oneself?). That's a luxury that, in his lifetime, he didn't have. And that's a luxury he afforded me because he went through what he went through, but, at some point, as I got older, I realized that it

Philip Kan Gotanda

was unfair of me to expect him to give up his world to understand mine.

He passed away a couple of years ago. He had started to accept my career as a playwright even though I think on some level he never fully understood it. And that was fine. I think that, when you're younger, it's important that your parents totally understand what you're doing, and for me, at least in my relationship with my father, I finally realized on some level that he just couldn't. He would come to see my plays, and that's more than I could ever ask of him. If I ever have a child, that might be more than I might be able to do. To make the jump from where he came from and what he went through to survive and accomplish to showing up at one of my plays around a lot of young Asian Americans watching this thing called theater, which was never a part of his life, never a part of his vocabulary. And yet he would show up. My mother, on the other hand, was much more comfortable with a lot of these notions of art and its pursuit.

RBI Do you think you would discourage your own kids from going into the arts?

PKG Well, you know, I can sort of understand why parents say that to kids now because, having tried to make a living at this for almost twenty years, I know it's simply not easy, and, quite frankly, the majority of those people who set out to make a living as an artist don't make a living. The majority are not able to pursue their work full-time; it's a very rough life. There are certainly rewards that one gets, but it's a very, very tough life. What Mom and Dad said was true: It's gonna be really hard. How are you going to feed your family, your children? How are you going to feed yourself? You're used to a certain lifestyle, it's fine now, but what about when you're thirty, forty, struggling, and it's not gonna be much fun? And, you know, it's true; it's not fun.

RBI Do you ever worry that people might mistake the parent-son conflicts in many of your plays with your own relationship with your parents?

PKG Actually, I know people do because, after *The Wash* came out, they were surprised my mother was still alive. They'd meet my mom and go, "You're still alive!" and she'd answer, "Yes. For a long, long time now." No, I don't actually. Maybe early on I used to, but now, as a working writer, I don't think about that too much. I do know people within the Japanese American community get upset sometimes when I talk about certain things.

RBI Dirty laundry.

PKG Yeah, dirty laundry stuff, the fact that these characters are not necessarily . . . healthy people. In *Fish Head Soup* it's a very dysfunctional family. I think they're really interesting families, but they're not your role models. But that to me doesn't matter as much as that they're interesting people. I think they're interesting families *and* dysfunctional. As are a lot of people in our community.

RBI Do you write with the Japanese American community in mind?

PKG I used to answer this differently. I used to say, No, I don't have any particular audience in mind, but, at least right now, I always do sort of think it's an Asian audience. It's not conscious, although I think my feeling is always that there are Asian Americans who will be looking at this and responding to it. But maybe it's because of the characters that I write about; I always see the world filled with Asian characters. In my newest play, there are no specific Asian American themes per se, but all the characters are Asians; it's just filled with all these people who are Asians.

So I guess that, in terms of an audience, I'm not sure. But

Philip Kan Gotanda

I do know that I don't try to write for an audience. Ultimately, I'm just trying to tell the story, and, as I'm trying to tell the story, in the back of my mind, I think I see Asian American faces out there. But it's more what I see as opposed to what I'm writing. I absolutely think that you should not try to write for an audience. I think that's dangerous for a writer. Tell the truth of what you're trying to tell, and that'll take care of it.

I'm always worried about writers who feel they have to change their work to accommodate people outside their Asian American group. I find that sad, that people would ever consider that. Stop writing if you're going to do that, you know; go write for television. Because you just should not in any way change it for that reason. You can change it for other reasons, but not that.

My sense is just to write as specific to the world as possible, and, at some level, the audience has to come to you. And, in terms of the work you've been doing and the body of work you've created, part of the exchange is that you learn from each other. It's like the whole idea that there exist these Asian American communities in America, all so different and varied, but they exist, and they're whole worlds unto themselves, and, as you walk down the street, you may look and think and not realize that this person walking up the street returns home, to a family, to a relationship to food and his or her god, to his or her cousins and his mother's mother that extends back and back and back, to a whole world of psychology, philosophy, politics. And it isn't just this one person walking down the street. And, on some level, it's your responsibility to figure out that world. If that story bends over backward to accommodate and reduce that world to the lowest common denominator, then everyone's lost in terms of being able to enter into other people's worlds and understand them. What happens when you change it to accommodate things or allow other people to change your work? You end up with what you see in films or on television: stick figures, creations that have nothing to do with us but rather a national need for a scapegoat, or a sophisticated racist cartoon that walks and talks a little more in the nineties, but ultimately has little to do with us.

RBI *Yankee Dawg You Die* is a play you did about the expe-
riences of two Asian American actors in Hollywood, and it deals with these same issues of artistic integrity. When you wrote Vincent's defense of the demeaning "Charlie Chop Suey" roles that many veteran actors played, did you have any particular actor in mind?

RBI *Yankee Dawg You Die* is a play you did about the experiences of two Asian American actors in Hollywood, and it deals with these same issues of artistic integrity. When you wrote Vincent's defense of the demeaning "Charlie Chop Suey" roles that many veteran actors played, did you have any particular actor in mind?

PKG The play actually draws from a lot of people; there's no one person in any reference. People continue to come up to me and say, That's so and so. Guy Lee came up to me, "That's about so and so, isn't it?" and I said, Well, not really. It's drawn from a lot of different actors.

RBI How did you come up with the idea for the play?

PKG The play comes out of my first experiences doing theater with the Asian American Theater Company and the East West Players, companies that had come out of the Asian American movement. The plays were supposed to be political expressions, cultural expressions, trying to find the language, theatrical language, to say what we were and are. And, as a writer, you're put in the middle. I'd be sitting with these older actors, and they'd always go on and on about the young actors, and how they just don't know what it's like to be a professional and to work in the industry and what it was like before, and it's so easy to point fingers, but wait, wait until they start to work in the industry, they'll find how hard it is. And then to hear the younger actors go on and on about how, I can't believe it, did you see so and so, the role that he did, I can't believe how these guys can do that. So this play was supposed to be a tribute to Asian American actors and the

Philip Kan Gotanda

situation that I felt they were all placed in. Put them in a room, and let them talk to each other, and see what happens.

RBI In the play, Vincent defends his participation in racist movies to his younger colleague by saying that he and other veteran Asian American actors "built the mountain, as small as it may be, that you stand on so proudly looking down at me" [p. 98]. Do you think Vincent's defense is a valid excuse?

PKG Personally, I don't think it is an excuse. If an actor knows he or she is doing a role that is, on some level, demeaning to Asians or is helping contribute to a climate of anti-Asian sentiment in the country but willingly takes the role—that's not good. Because [the racists] are going after us. And not only are they going after us—they're consciously trying to make us disappear or misrepresenting us in the media, thereby making us disappear by being other than what we really are. That makes us easy targets and also affects how we perceive ourselves and how we deal with racist acts. And it's no longer a matter of just being called a name: it's a matter of being shut out of everything. Shut out of all political and cultural systems in the most basic ways—even being killed. And so for somebody to say now, "I'm sorry, I can't worry about how Asians are being perceived, I can't worry about issues that deal with anti-Asian violence, hate crimes, I can't worry about that, I just have to make a living"—that's no longer a position one can hold. People have to be held accountable.

RBI How do you react when you see some of these obviously talented Asian American actors—actors who have done strong work in your own plays—being forced to take some pretty weak film roles?

PKG That's something that you should ask the actors about. I talk to them, and I think I know their work well, but it's sort of tragic that you have someone like Nobu McCarthy, who's an extraordinary actress, and yet, in film and television, she's offered very, very little. There are a lot of wonderful actors running around—all ages, all shapes, all sizes—who just are never afforded the opportunity. And this sets up all sorts of peculiar situations where, if you're never afforded the opportunity and you're wonderfully talented, when you get that one shot, you're all nervous. You have one little window, you have one little audition to show exactly what you can do for this one role that's come along that everyone wants, and you may not be able to relax enough to put your best foot forward, in terms of both a moment on screen or in the audition. You don't get enough opportunities to continually go up because that's all part of the game, too. Or enough opportunities so that, when you're in front of the camera, you know how to work it. Or you aren't given a shot by a director who won't allow you to take your moment.

It's sort of the Vincent thing: you take your moment. That's a big deal, you know. Talk to someone like Sab [Shimono]. He talks about taking your moment. So you're on there for just a short time playing a North Vietnamese general. They're trying to get you on and off real quick, and you're thinking, "Gee, you know, thirty years doing this, and I have this one shot. There are a lot of things I've thought about in terms of what this character should do, so let me take my moment. It may be a small thing to everyone else, but I'm an actor, in a drama, and people don't get that."

RBI An audience member at an Asian American film conference that you attended at UCLA referred to a lot of these same kinds of concerns for Asian artists and actors as "whining." How would you respond?

PKG I think the idea of whining is sort of a subjective comment; it depends on your point of view, right? What he perceives as whininess I might perceive simply as an honest appraisal of the situation and pointing to the problems so we can go about rectifying them. How can you talk about Asian

Philip Kan Gotanda

Americans involved in filmmaking without talking about the idea that we either don't exist or aren't given the opportunities to succeed? And, when given opportunities as actors, we're given roles that are shitty, roles that force you into a position where you either make a living doing what you've studied all your life for and risk angering your community or just don't work. That's what *Yankee Dawg* is about, although in the play the decisions are never that clear-cut. You have to own up and be responsible for what you do; that I feel absolutely. But it's not that clear-cut.

RBI What do you think of the current state of Asian American theater?

PKG As far as the institutions themselves, they're having a hard time. No monies, and an identity crisis over who they are and what they're supposed to be saying as we hit the year 2000. When you have bigger, better-funded white institutions doing the programming you used to do and are still trying to do with only a fraction of those theaters' budgets, you've got to be fiscally creative and philosophically rigorous to survive and to justify your existence to a society that is becoming increasingly sophisticated and balkanized in matters of race and culture. It will be interesting to see where everything lands in the next few years.

RBI What do you think of the segregation of American theater into mainstream and "other"?

PKG As it represents only what America thinks as a cultural nation, why should that seem surprising? The same issues that need to be addressed in the country are the same ones that American theater is trying to cope with.

RBI *Fish Head Soup* is about a Sansei son who returns to his family to make a film about their lives. In addition to standard Hollywood roadblocks, the son even faces opposition to the film from his mother, who tries to talk him into doing a more

"normal" story, one "not just about Japanese Americans."
Do you think this is a fairly common feeling within the
Japanese American community, that there just isn't an audi-
ence for Japanese American films?

PKG The play explores internalized racism, so obviously she
is buying into the idea that no one would be interested in a
story just about Japanese Americans; you have to include one
white character because that's what makes it interesting to
other people. Dorothy's a very interesting character in that
she is proud of being Japanese and Japanese American and at
the same time she also buys into the idea of being a second-
class citizen. She believes something is happening beyond
them in white culture that is perhaps . . . better and that any
kind of alignment with it gives you a certain stamp of credibility. It's a very complicated psychological mind-set but one
that I've certainly come across a lot in the Japanese American
community, where there's a strong love-hate relationship
with the dominant white culture. This would be an expression
of it in concrete terms that I've found among a lot of Asian
American artists. They say to the community, "We've been
slogging around here trying to do our work, and no one sup-
ports us. The moment we have some success out in 'white
culture' and the press acknowledges it, then in the community everyone goes, Oh, you're a big artist, you're a big celeb,
you're a star, we want to come see your work." It's only once
you get the stamp of approval from 'the white press and white
culture,' outside the community, that you are ever given any
credibility and are ever seen in the eyes of the community as
being truly an artist. So it's that kind of thing that I've certainly felt and that a lot of other artists have complained
about.

RBI With the amount of publicity that *Miss Saigon* and
Rising Sun received, do you think that white audiences are at
least a little more aware of some of these issues?

PKG Yes, I think more people are aware of them. Everyone says that now the upside is that people are going to be a little more careful in the future. And it is true, now, when all the critics talk about *Rising Sun,* they all talk about the Asian Americans who are protesting and offer some kind of opinion on it. And I'm sure their opinions also take into consideration the whole *Miss Saigon* struggle. But, for me, I think the more things change, the more they stay the same. So many people just don't get it. Asian Americans still remain very fringe. There are ways we're treated and perceived, particularly in my field, in entertainment and in films, that just make me so angry; they just lack so much knowledge and sensitivity to who and what we are.

RBI How do you think Asian Americans should respond?

PKG For me, the only way to deal with this is to speak out, to say what you have to say. You cannot be silent. And to create new works—put your own works out there, and don't wait for anyone to come to you and offer anything to you. Don't wait for anyone to say, "We're going to help you," because I'd say, in the grand scheme of things, they won't because, ultimately, they don't know how to. They really just don't know how to.

Selected Works by Philip Kan Gotanda

A Song for a Nisei Fisherman. Directed by David Henry Hwang and presented at the Fort Mason Center, San Francisco, 15 August–21 September 1980. Included in the collection *Fish Head Soup.*

The Avocado Kid. A musical directed by Dee K. Carmack and presented at the Chinese Cultural Center, San Francisco, 16 May–28 June 1981.

The Dream of Kitamura. Directed by David Henry Hwang and presented in San Francisco 19 June–25 July 1982.

Fish Head Soup. Directed by Oskar Eustis and presented at the Berkeley Repertory Theatre, Berkeley, Calif., in 1991. Also presented in Los

Angeles by the East West Players in association with the Mark Taper Forum in January 1993. Reprinted in the collection *Fish Head Soup*.

Yankee Dawg You Die. New York: Dramatists Play Service, 1991. Included in the collection *Fish Head Soup*.

The Wash. Portsmouth, N.H.: Heinemann, 1992. Included in the collection *Fish Head Soup*.

Day Standing on Its Head. New York: Dramatists Play Service, 1994.

The Kiss. 1994. A short film presented at the Sundance and Edinburgh International Film Festivals and available through the National Asian American Telecommunications Association; it won the Golden Gate Award at Edinburgh.

Fish Head Soup. Seattle: University of Washington Press, 1995. A collection including *Fish Head Soup, A Song for a Nisei Fisherman, The Wash,* and *Yankee Dawg You Die*.

The Ballad of Yachiyo. New York: Dramatists Play Service, 1996.

Drinking Tea. 1996. A short film presented at the Sundance Film Festival and available through the National Asian American Telecommunications Association.

Sisters Matsumoto. Directed by Sharon Ott and presented at the Seattle Repertory Company in 1999.

Yohen. Directed by Anne Bowen and presented in Los Angeles by the East West Players at the Robey Theater in 1999.

Philip Kan Gotanda

"It's like putting us in the Chinese laundries"

11

David Wong Louie

Interview by
STACEY YUKARI HIROSE

Taking a sip of water from a plastic bottle, David Wong Louie watched patiently as I set up my tape recording equipment in his office for the third time. My first two interviews with him—together over three hours long—were rendered virtually unusable owing to technical difficulties with the recorder. On hearing the news of the lost interviews, Louie good-naturedly joked with me about my recording equipment blues and, despite his busy schedule, agreed to sit with me for yet another interview.

Raised in New York, Louie is the eldest son of Toisanese immigrant parents. He received his B.A. from Vassar and M.F.A. from the University of Iowa and has taught at several universities, including Vassar and the University of California, Santa Cruz. Currently he is an assistant professor in the English Department at UCLA, where he teaches both creative writing and Asian American studies courses. Louie's work has appeared in several journals and anthologies, including *Ploughshares, The Big Aiiieeeee! An Anthology of Chinese American and Japanese American Literature,* and *The Best*

American Short Stories, 1989. Pangs of Love (1991), his highly
acclaimed collection of short stories, received the 1991 *Los
Angeles Times* Book Prize for First Fiction and the *Ploughshares* John C. Zacharis First Book Award. He is presently
completing his first novel, *The Barbarians Are Coming.*

190 As Louie's former student, I initially wanted to interview
him so that I could learn exactly how he crafted his short stories and find out who and what inspired his work—subjects he
curiously seemed to evade in his creative writing class. In the
three hours we spent together, he candidly spoke (and
laughed) about a wide range of subjects, including his childhood and family, his views on interracial dating and ethnic
identity, his politicization and growth as a writer, his upcoming novel, and even Chinese dinosaurs.

SYH What motivated you to write?

DWL I think it was in the fourth or fifth grade there was a
music teacher named Miss Lark who would come to our class
once a week. For some reason, she played us some movement
of Tchaikovsky's 1812 Overture. She kind of set it up and told
us what the overture was about, its historical context, and
then she played us the music and had us write essays on what
we thought was going on while the music was playing. So I
wrote this essay, and she read it to the class. I think that was
the first time I was kind of praised in that way, singled out and
praised. . . . I don't remember thinking much of the experience, but that memory stays with me, and I guess that's why
I've always associated this approval with writing. But, again,
there are other things that are going on along with approval
because there was a lot of time when nothing was ever being
taken, but there were friends who were believers. I guess
that's still another kind of approval, friends' approval.

SYH Did you always write short stories, or did you experiment with other forms of creative expression?

Words Matter

DWL   I was a high school poet, and I wrote very bad poetry about love and war—I even wrote Watergate poems. And I got a lot of approval out of that. I think I rode that through high school. I was deemed one of the literary stars. I did a poetry magazine, of course. I was an editor and one of the major contributors as well as an editor of the yearbook. I was identified as a writer type.

But I went off to Vassar as a science major; I thought I was going to major in science—geology in particular. The next year I just found myself going back to the poetry. I guess I never feel that the impulse to write is ever that pure. There is this other motive that operates, some kind of psychological thing at work. For me it's this need to get approval. I would like to think that I write because I have something to say, but that's not why I write. People have a need to make things, and this is what I make. . . . I think about my siblings. We all make things: my sister paints for a living, my brother went to art school, the other one is making things with his hands right now. I don't know where the impulse comes from. I know my grandmother did something with hemp. I think she made thread. Writing is as close as I could get to creating something out of raw material.

SYH   So you started writing short stories in college?

DWL   Right. I started writing short stories at Vassar. I took an independent study class.

SYH   What did you do after you graduated from Vassar?

DWL   I went to the University of Iowa—it was just luck that I got in. I wrote a bunch of stories in my senior year in college as part of my thesis, and I used one or two of them, and I got in. But the reason that I went to school was not that I had a desire to write or get a degree. At the time I was working in an advertising place, and, unfortunately, it was a very small firm. The upside of that was that I got a chance to do a

David Wong Louie

lot of things that I would not have done. I would have gotten pigeonholed at a larger firm, learning to do something on either the creative end or the business end. But, in this case, I got to do everything from copywriting and doing artwork to answering the phones. The downside of it was that my employers were a husband-and-wife team who were there all the time and they would squabble and get into marital problems. They were talking about business, but clearly what they were talking about was their marriage! It alienated me, and I really wanted to get out. I was tired of that.

I was also living with my mother, like the protagonist in "Pangs of Love." And I just wanted to get out, and I knew that the most comfortable way of leaving would be to go to school. She could appreciate that. It wouldn't be like I was just leaving her. So I went to Iowa.

I think the most important thing I learned there was that I really care about writing. Writing *mattered* to me. That's the experience of a lot of people who go there because there are so many writers there. You see so much other work, and a lot of it is quite good. Everybody takes it seriously. I think that's the great thing about a place like that. It's a fairly good-sized community, and everybody talks about it, cares about it, *believes* in it. So within this kind of ideal environment—at least for a writer—a lot of people had the chance to tell themselves, "Well, clearly, if I don't function well even in this ideal environment, then I'm not getting work done, and all of it is bad, or I don't believe in my work," then these people get their degrees, and they never write again.

What I found out was just the opposite. Particularly after about the first year, I realized that writing was something very important to me. And I guess proof of that is how much I struggled financially for years in order to be able to write. Not that anyone was extending full-time jobs to me, but I chose to work part-time in order to have more time to write. And I was putting myself on two-year plans, five-year plans, trying to get *x* number of stories to get a book out by a certain period of time or else give it up. These deadlines would always elapse. Of course I set new deadlines, and I could never just quit. I almost took a job driving a juice truck. I don't know how close I was, but I was seriously thinking about doing it, and I went for two trial days. It was so tedious, but that would have cut into writing time very seriously.

SYH Who has had the biggest influence on your writing?

DWL Well, I still go back to a teacher, Joanna Robbins, whom I did an independent study with at Vassar. She said to write in the first person. And I think that was really decent advice. My Shakespeare professor at Vassar was also very important because he taught me Shakespeare and he taught me how to read, really. Some fellow students of mine at Iowa were important. But I don't see any of these people as influences.

SYH Did other writers influence you?

DWL I can name some authors who really got me excited about writing. I did some reading after college. I read Kafka, Günter Grass. I read that French guy, Céline. A novel here, a novel there. And I actually read Flannery O'Connor in school. All those folks spoke to me in ways other writing just didn't. Günter Grass's *The Tin Drum* really made me want to write. Later on, I was definitely influenced by Raymond Carver when I was in graduate school.

These authors all articulated a certain kind of "otherness" to me. They spoke of and wrote from a marginalized place. People like Kafka and O'Connor, who was ill and a devout Catholic in the Protestant South—she's an odd character. On some unconscious level, this kind of strangeness and oddness tapped into my own sense of difference and alienation. Because I guess there is no one really more alienated than Franz Kafka. Those authors are really important to me. And I still go back to all of them from time to time. Carver is more of a stylistic thing. His people seem "out there." His characters always struck me as rednecks. And, if I met them in a room, they probably wouldn't give me the time of day. But I was really interested in him stylistically.

SYH Did any Asian American writers influence your writing?

DWL I don't feel influenced by them in the same way. I think I was influenced somewhat in the way I think about Asian America by *Aiiieeeee!* The introduction, I thought, was very good. I studied it! I tried to make sense of it 'cause I wasn't always sure what those folks were talking about. It was startling to me because I didn't know how to process it. Frank Chin talks about that dual personality, and he debunks it, and he's right. It's fascinating to think about this idea of how we are given this notion of dual personality. . . . And somehow it is unquestioned. Chin argues about this other identity, this Asian American or Chinese American identity. And I was like, "Wow!" That had an influence on the way I started viewing myself.

SYH Which Asian American writers do you like?

DWL Well, I like Yamamoto. I think clearly she'd been discovered. I mean, I'm not the only one. But she's written some great stories that stack up with anything. Who else? I like Marilyn Chin's poetry a lot. I like a lot of those poets. Li-Young Lee is pretty good, and so is Garrett Hongo. I like Jessica Hagedorn and Bharati Mukherjee. I know people have trouble with her politics, but I think she's an excellent writer. I like some of what Frank Chin has done and some of Maxine Hong Kingston's stuff. I have my problems with some aspects of *The Woman Warrior,* but I think there is a lot there to admire. Louis Chu's *Eat a Bowl of Tea* is a very wonderful novel. I guess I'm naming everything now.

SYH Where do you get the ideas for your stories?

DWL Things are going on in a writer's head that he is not even aware of that make him want to write. The best example of that is the title story, "Pangs of Love." It's about a lot of things, but it's about this guy who basically doesn't trust his mother to handle a certain piece of information. So it's about a form of deception, but another form of disrespect ultimately. And what was going on at the time was that I was having a difficult time in my marriage and I knew I was going to leave it. In the back of my mind one of the things I had trouble imagining was telling my mother. I mean this is like, it's ugly, it's bad stuff. It's like a loss of face that's hard to recover from. I wasn't thinking about that when I was writing the story, but it's the sort of anxiety that propelled the writing of that story. It informed a lot of the stuff that's going on there.

I think a writer has to be in what I call a *writing mode.* You've got to be on, receptive. I think I was in a good writing mode during the period when I was writing "Social Science." I just saw that "for sale" sign in front of a house. Paul Valéry said, "Seeing is forgetting the name of the thing one sees," meaning you've seen something really odd, in ways that you'd never seen it before. And I think that, when you're on, when you're in the writing mode, things strike you that way. That "for sale" sign is an image that opens up something in my head. In "Pangs of Love," I wasn't struggling with the story, but it wasn't working until I got the guy his job; and right then comes this metaphor, this masking, deception. In a way, the whole thematic structure of the story is there in the job, and it became very easy to write. Of course you can't force that image. I think the best thing to do is just to keep writing and hope that you discover it. If it never does appear, then you've just got to push through.

SYH Do you write for a particular audience?

DWL I remember in my younger days I thought I could write

David Wong Louie

any kind of bullshit. I could set something in China and write any kind of bullshit I wanted because who is going to know? And who is going to call me on it; who's gonna say I'm not accurate? And, clearly, I'm thinking of a white audience—maybe even an ABC [American-born Chinese] one.

When I wrote some of the stories, particularly the early ones, I wrote stories that didn't have identifiably Chinese American narrators, though in my own head I'd always visualized the speaker as someone not unlike me, going through his various acrobatics. I did that in the belief that the publishing world wasn't interested in hearing stories by folks like me. So I thought that, if I could just cheat a little bit, I might be able to get things published. I guess I came to that conclusion just by virtue of the sorry dearth of Chinese American/Asian American stuff being published, particularly by large presses. So it probably was wrongheaded, I suppose, but that's what I was thinking. . . . I was writing to get published. And, if that meant writing to a white audience, then that's what I was trying to do then.

I don't think about writing to get published anymore. That's the beauty of having done it. The hard thing is getting published the first time. My concern now is to write a good story. I do feel a little pressure because some people know what my work is, and I think I do have some fans—which is nice—and I just want to be able to deliver the goods. So, in that way, I am aware of an audience, but these fans generally have been Asian American. I see myself now as saying sometimes to myself that some people will get this, and other people won't, and I'm not going to bother to explain it to everyone; you get it, or you don't. So I'm aware that there might be at least two different sets of audiences: a white one and one that is Chinese American or maybe even Asian American.

SYH Is there a certain process you use to write your stories?

DWL I probably do my best thinking as I write. My actual

Words Matter

process used to be where I would get some idea, and, again, it's usually something very small, and it just kind of triggers something in the way "Social Science" was triggered by a "for sale" sign in front of a house. I just saw the sign. I could have walked by that sign a hundred different times and not have noticed it or not thought twice about it. Just for some reason it interested me that day, and I made this kind of connection about the sign and the house. I remember playing with the idea of what it would be like to live in that house. That's where that story comes from. . . . I think there are Chinese American/Asian American themes in that story about feeling dislocated. This guy pretending to be somebody else, trying to be someone he's not, or trying to transform himself— those themes surface because, on a certain level, that's what probably concerns me. But, if I were to go back and try to talk through all these stories, you'd find that, in terms of theme, I wasn't thinking of anything. Although I could carry on about the various Asian American or Chinese American themes that run throughout them, none of that stuff was even remotely on my mind during first draft to last draft.

I write a lot of drafts. . . . Part of the process was sending the stories out. Some of the stories I showed to friends from graduate school, and then I worked them up into whatever point I thought they were done at. Then I would send them out to these magazines, and they would be rejected, and then, by the time I absorbed enough rejections, enough time had passed that I took the rejections as a clear message that the story wasn't done, and I would go back, and I would start rewriting it. Because I'd had enough time away from it and had stopped being so much in love with it, I was able to really attack it. I think that's probably the right word. I really attack some of those drafts and overhaul them. . . . That's where the work is. One of my problems is that I fret about stories at the sentence level—the word-to-word level. It makes for a very slow unfolding of a first draft.

David Wong Louie

The second draft is when you really get to think about what it is you're trying to do. You try to start understanding what is going on in that first draft. Sometimes it takes somebody else to say to me, "I think the story really is about *x* instead of *y*." Or someone would say, "*This* is what interests me." So sometimes that would help, and I would move in that direction to see what happens. What I'm trying to say is that the final draft is a very different thing; it's in some way a different story. I've done things as radical as write the next draft without really looking at the first draft.

SYH Do you transfer things that happen in your life into your stories?

DWL Yeah, in two ways. One is that I grew up working for my parents; I did a lot of work in the laundry, and I grew up watching my mother and father working all the time, so everybody in the stories works, and the jobs that these characters hold says something about who they are as people. I'd like to think that none of the jobs that the characters hold in the stories are throwaway jobs. They work somehow in the story, metaphorically or otherwise.

The other is growing up in predominantly white towns. I don't think I really write about that experience, but I think that experience totally informs the way I have viewed myself as a Chinese American and how I've viewed my parents, my siblings, and other Chinese Americans. I mean, it's hard not to when you are someone so clearly different than your friends, and this is also a class thing.

Sometimes I don't know where to draw a line between race and class because my father's businesses never did very well and so we never had much money as kids. Consequently, we didn't have very many things as a family or as kids, toywise or going to camp, which was a common experience of all my friends growing up. That was a totally foreign notion, taking a class outside of school that you had to pay for, renting an instrument in order to be in the band, that kind of stuff. That was a very foreign idea, and, more than anything, it had to do with money.

A reviewer said that one of my stories was surrealistic. I guess she wasn't the only one who ever said that, and so I have been asked about dreams playing a part in my work. Of course, the answer is no because I don't remember my dreams. I think part of that quality that she's picking up on has something to do with being different, experiencing that difference and not really being able to articulate what the difference was all about, why I didn't feel confident about certain things, trying to understand why it is that I seemed like all my friends, but yet there was this real special difference. I think that's what I'm trying to get at; difference defines my whole way of seeing things. I think it's a way of internalizing stuff. I was just reading *Orientalism,* and Said was saying how the European sees himself as normal and the "Oriental" as somebody who is exotic, abnormal. I think I internalized that notion. How could I not, being in the position that I was in? And I think I saw my family as somehow abnormal. I don't remember thinking about it, but I know I experienced it, and I think it's from that place of internalizing the stuff that makes the stories surreal; it's where the edge comes from. Now that I'm able to articulate those feelings more, I feel sometimes the work has lost some of that kind of edge that it had before.

SYH How has the Asian American community's response to your writing differed from the mainstream's response?

DWL I think the mainstream critics latch onto stories like "Birthday" or "Displacement" or "Pangs of Love" or "Inheritance" where there are overtly Chinese American characters. They talk about generational clashes and culture clashes, but they don't give you the time of day as a writer. They don't talk about you as writing beautiful sentences or having a sense

David Wong Louie

of humor because, you know, what Asian has a sense of humor anyway? But, by the same token, I would be miffed if they read the book and didn't even acknowledge it as being Chinese American. That's problematic as well.

The Chinese American/Asian American response has been really good. I'm glad that a lot of people do identify with the characters. At readings, after I sign people's books, usually these guys come up and say, "Finally there's a book I can identify with by a Chinese American or by an Asian American." I'm not sure what they're identifying with, but it's certainly nice to hear. It's nice to know that it's read and it *means* something to people. My sense of it is that the people in my book seem very real to Asian American audiences, particularly Chinese Americans.

The mainstream literary world has managed to ghettoize me, and I find that a little troubling. I have no problems with being identified as a Chinese American or an Asian American author; it's just that I sense this kind of prevailing, underlying need to kind of see me—maybe it's just a convenient thing—as Asian American/Chinese American. I think that translates in some people's minds as African American does still for some people—as something less than, something not as good, something inferior. It's sociology; it's not fiction.

SYH Do you think that you have opportunities that other writers do not have because you are an Asian American writer?

DWL Well, I have friends who are white, who joke, but I think they mean it—that I've gotten as far as I've gotten because I'm Chinese. I don't know if they're right. I may have gotten published because of Amy Tan for all I know, in book form I mean. (I was publishing in magazines before anybody knew about Amy Tan.) Maybe that's the advantage.

The disadvantage is that whole argument about what is the real stuff and what is something else. What could be part of the canon, and what couldn't. You know, this power sharing, giving everyone else the economic power or not. It's like the intellectual pie: how are we going to divvy it up, how can we give him a little slice here, but not too much? There is something about that in the publishing world as well. . . . It goes back to what I said before about feeling ghettoized. I don't understand why my publishing house didn't do more to try to sell the book, why they haven't done more to sell me— market me. I know that there is something called *sexiness* or *glamour,* not that I'm saying I'm "sexy" or "glamorous" as a writer. . . . I understand that "sexiness" or "glamour" in publishing often equates with sales. Amy Tan is about the "sexiest" thing in the publishing world because she sells; she makes people money as well as money for herself. And good for her. But I know that, even within Knopf, my hardback house, there are writers whose sales don't seem to be that great; they're not celebrities. But somehow I think publishers regard them in a way that they don't regard me. I don't know what it is. I'm not going to say they're racist. But it's just that whole way of ghettoizing folks. I think it's hard for people to see this stuff just as writing.

There was a guy who introduced me and Marilyn Chin when she and I read together down in San Diego. He gave Marilyn a really nice introduction and kind of talked about us both. He talked about Chinese Americans, Asian Americans, but then he ended by saying, "They're both damn good writers." And I think that it's hard for publishers to see that Asian Americans are good writers and can write as well as other writers. As long as publishers label Asian American writing *their stuff,* Asian American writers are not competing with other writers. It's like putting us in the Chinese laundries.

SYH Do you feel that the *Asian American/Chinese American* label places limitations on your writing?

DWL That's a tricky question. I'd like to think that we should

David Wong Louie

be free—*we* meaning Asian American authors—to write about whatever we want to write about. And I guess in many ways we are. I also think that the publishing world does look for those types of subjects because they know what to do with them. What would happen if I wrote a courtroom drama? I don't know how that would wash.

With Cynthia Kadohata's *In the Heart of the Valley of Love* I felt the same way. At the end of it, I was complaining to some friends about the book. It has an interesting aspect to it, kind of spooky. I liked it, but I kept saying there's none of that Asian American, Japanese American stuff in there. Finally I asked myself, "What's your problem, boy? Why does she have to write about that?"

I'd like to feel like I can write anything I want the next time around. And nobody is making me write what I am writing now, either. I'm writing what I'm writing because I want to write it. It's not because I feel people are expecting me to write about a Chinese American family or these types of issues. Does that mean that you are free to write books that exploit stereotypes? Does that mean that you are free to pander to a white person's racist tastes? I don't know. I'm uncomfortable with that.

Toni Morrison said that, when a black woman writes, there's something political in that act of getting in people's faces and opening your mouth and raising your voice. There's something in that for people like me as well. That's where I think there's a responsibility; since there are so few of our voices out there being heard, we should be at the very least careful of what it is we say. Obviously, my work isn't overtly political, but I think that it does have its aspect. If nothing else, it may help reshape ideas of what it is to be a Chinese American of a certain generation.

SYH As an Asian American writer, do you think it's possible for you to separate into "Asian" and "American" components?

DWL No, I don't think so. Even if I wrote a fiction about China, it would be colored by my experiences as a Chinese American. Obviously, China plays a big part in my work. It shows up in the form of the characters. Mrs. Pang—at least in the eyes of her son—is a representation, almost a metaphor for China, but clearly she is Chinese American after being here and being the way she is and her Johnny Carson and wrestling. She's of this place. So she's not really Chinese Chinese, and she shouldn't be read that way. But *he* does, and he sees her as China. There's a lot of China in my novel right now in the form of the food, and then there is all this stuff about Mao. It's there, but it's very much Chinese Americanized—"I-zed"—version of China.

"Disturbing the Universe" takes place in China, but the characters are playing baseball. This is a case where I think it's very clear that I am appropriating China for my own uses. I'm not trying to represent China. And obviously it's East meets West. But the bottom line was that I was fascinated with the wall. I see these pictures of this damn wall, and it goes on for miles and miles! I just thought, God! What can I use this thing for?

SYH So what made you think of baseball?

DWL Because the wall is like the fence, the barrier you have to hit the ball over to get a home run. . . . That's how I made my start. I'd read Kafka's story about the wall, so I thought, Yeah, it would be fun to do something like that. So, you know, that's not *China*. It has more to do with the author's imagination about creating fiction.

SYH Which of your stories is your favorite?

DWL Well, my favorite story is probably "Bottles of Beaujolais." I like how visual it is. And I just like the otter. I guess it was animals. I remember writing that story and feeling like that guy when he was all drained of blood and he was sort of

David Wong Louie

hot and cold. I remember writing that story in almost that state and being really engaged in it. And I cannot begin to tell you how it came together at all. I had torn out of a *New York Times Sunday Magazine* an article about wines. There's a food page also. I don't know if there's always a wine page, but, anyway, there was an article on the food page about fish, sashimi, and stuff. At the time I wrote that story, I had never been to a restaurant that was like that, which is why it doesn't even sound like a sushi place. What I remember was being struck by the picture of the fish. There were these almost translucent blocks of fish that didn't look fish, but like lovely objects. They looked like jewels in some strange way or semiprecious stones, and that becomes almost a metaphor. That's what the story is *about*. It's like this *stuff* that is supposed to be fish but is no longer fish. And it's sort of like the wine that isn't wine but they call it this kind of wine, right? They call it Beaujolais, but it's really sake mixed with blood, and Luna is really not Luna because she's really Peg, but he sees her as Luna, constructs this idea about Luna; and the weather, of course, is not the real weather but made-up weather. There's a certain kind of togetherness, wholeness, cohesiveness to it all.

SYH How about "In a World Small Enough," published in *The Big Aiiieeeee?*

DWL I love that story. But my editors made me take it out of *Pangs of Love*. They thought it was too weird, too out there, had nothing to do with anything else in the book. That was a hard story. That story was a lot of fun to write because I did a lot of reading of physics books and I tried to piece together as much physics as I could. Quantum mechanics, boy oh boy! And then I was told by another lay reader of quantum mechanics that I got it all wrong.

Within the book, "One Man's Hysteria" was also a lot of fun to write, in part because the game the guy plays with identifying poems is something this friend of mine and I used to do. The guy used to do it over the phone. It was more like a "Name That Tune" kind of a thing, except that we would do it with poetry or fiction. That was fun because I spent a lot of time looking through poetry and trying to find good lines and look for specific words. That story is also an articulation of how so many of us were feeling when Reagan first took office. We were all so scared that something was going to happen, that Armageddon stuff.

SYH And "Pangs of Love"?

DWL I like the story, but I don't feel an attachment to it in the way I do to "Bottles of Beaujolais." It was easier to write, but the ease of its writing had to do with *(a)* not having written something in a while and having a block of time, *(b)* when I wrote that story, I was having serious problems with my marriage, and I knew that eventually I needed to make the break, and then of course after that I had to somehow tell my mother about it. What the story ended up being about is protecting her from certain information . . . along with that idea of seeing the mother as an infant who can't take certain news. I modeled that mother on my mother, so that presented me with a character. But, again, there was this underground stuff going on that I think really informed the writing and gave me energy to write it.

The story was inspired by a weekend I spent with my brother and some of his friends. It was a totally mundane weekend, except for the fact that everyone was gay except me. And I think that was actually the first time it was made clear to any of us in the family that my brother was gay. I mean, we all knew it, but it was never as explicit as it was. I was surprised, and I shouldn't have been. As I left his house, I remember throwing the car into reverse. Then I paused and said out loud, "Now that's a story!" And the weird thing about it—and I think that this is what writers do—you see a

David Wong Louie

story in places where there is no story at all because, as I said, nothing happened. We played tennis, and then we ate, we read the newspaper, we chatted, and that was it.

My brother liked the story. I was surprised. I was worried about what he would think, but he liked it. He thought I named the character Nino inappropriately because he's such a WASP.

SYH In what ways do you feel that gender shapes your writing?

DWL I think that my experience with being Asian or Chinese American has a greater effect on how I ultimately have come to see the world than gender. That's the privilege of being a male.

In stories like "Inheritance" and "Displacement," there is that quality about assuming different skins, assuming different guises. Writing it from the women's point of view was necessary for both those stories. "Inheritance" is in first person because the third person just wasn't working. So I switched it into the first person. The narration just wasn't working in the third person because I felt like somehow Edna needed to know more—or maybe she needed to know less, and in the first person she would know less because she'd know only what she knows. "Displacement" was much more the story about Mrs. Chow and her idea of having children in this country and her attitudes about raising a family in a place that seems uncomfortable at best, if not hostile.

Often I model after women I know. It's not like they're pure creations. Mrs. Chow is a combination of me and my Chinese-language professor in college and a little bit of my mother. And I think that Edna is largely me, but I kind of use my sister as a model, a very loose model. Some of the stuff obviously came from being around women, whether it's my sister or a girlfriend or my mother or my mother's friends.

SYH   Do you feel that your stories challenge stereotypes about Asian American men?

DWL   Yeah, sure. Of course I do, but I want to emphasize that I don't set out to do that. And I write about people who interest me, and the people don't normally conform to stereotypes. The stereotypes are imposed or perpetuated by people who see Chinese people not as people but as stereotypes, as foreign to their own experience. So, if in some way my male characters work against a stereotype, it's nothing intended; it's just that I obviously don't see these men in that way.

SYH   Why do many of your Asian American male characters date or have relationships with white women?

DWL   That's there. That's why it's political. Part of it has to do with my own experience up to that point when I was writing those stories. Most of my involvements were with white women. Now, I also think there are ways of reading that. Speaking as a student of my own work now, these are characters who are active sexually—and you've heard this crap before—that if you date white women, it's somehow empowering, particularly in the case of an Asian American. There's always talk about emasculation. Now, I guess you could say that these guys always get dumped, too. In a story like "Birthday," women come to signify this kind of desire to assimilate and to get lost in the mainstream. The narrator wants to be part of a family where he doesn't belong; he just doesn't fit, no matter how hard he tries by clinging to this boy as his son. Obviously, it's not his son. So the white woman comes to represent the desire to marry out or kind of lose oneself, to identify with that set family. But, at the end of the story, he wants to realign himself with his original family more.

These people in all the stories really live in some kind of

isolation—the same kind of isolation that I lived in as a Chinese American. The Chows lived in that little parcel of land. They're the only Chinese characters in that story except for the restaurant guy. Same thing with Edna. All the references are to the immediate family, and there's nobody else in that community except, I think, a Korean woman.

SYH Do you feel that your work has become more political?

DWL No, I don't. I think that the one way it's become more political, if that's the right word for it, is that now there are definitely more overtly Chinese American characters. That's important for me now to do in my work. I think that my writing is political in its own way, just by virtue of the act of writing, of getting our voices out there. It's demanding a piece of the pie in a sense.

I would like to think that some of the stories and the characters in the stories redefine images of Chinese American guys in particular. I think they broaden the pie in terms of the subjects and the themes that might be articulated by a Chinese American or Asian American writer. I think that they also do speak about race and racism, though these concerns are buried. They are in there in quiet ways, in little quips, remarks. I think my writing articulates some of the struggles of the Chinese Americans for the first and second generations.

SYH Why now more than before?

DWL Before, I was working under the idea that I was just writing and I was like any other writer. I have sort of come around to an understanding that I'm also of a particular background, and people perceive me in a particular way, and it is important to perhaps quietly address those concerns. If it just means writing about them honestly, I think that's valuable, and you can call that *political.*

SYH Was it anything that you read that made you get to this point?

DWL I came to this late in the game. Having my own son had something to do with it. When you have your own child, you think of yourself as a child, and you think of your own parents. I did. It's one way of looking at my parents and rehabilitating them in my own head. And they did some incredibly courageous things, things that I could never imagine doing, like going to China without knowing very much Chinese, *any* Chinese, but trying to make a go of it. I don't know if that's a reasonable comparison, but it's just that idea of kind of picking up your life and trying out something entirely different, and that's what they did. I think they did all right.

At the University of California, Santa Cruz, I taught a lot of authors of color: Morrison, Anna Castillo, Kingston, and some Frederick Douglass, and Cherríe Moraga. It was just interesting to teach that stuff and realize that it all spoke to me and helped me begin to articulate some of the things I had been experiencing as a kid. And it was a real eye-opener. I'd read the introduction to *Aiiieeeee!* even before that experience at Santa Cruz. I puzzled over it because I just was so out there. I just wasn't sure what Frank Chin was talking about half the time. *That* stuff started making sense after my teaching experience at Santa Cruz; things started to fall into place. So I began to revise the story of my life. I started seeing my life differently. I would go through things that happened in my past and see, "Oh, yeah, well, this is what it was really all about. It really had to do with race. It was not just an oversight on this person's part."

SYH In what way do you feel that your stories have changed over time?

DWL The obvious thing is that my subjects, my characters, have become increasingly Asian or Chinese American. That aspect of my personality went "underground" in my earlier stories—stories such as "One Man's Hysteria," "Bottles of Beaujolais," "Social Science"—in which the protagonists

David Wong Louie

were not overtly Chinese American. I still think—this is speaking as a student of my own work—that they express the same sense of what my experience of growing up Chinese American is all about, of growing up in a white suburb and feeling different because I was from a Chinese background and of a different class than most of the people I went to school with. In "One Man's Hysteria," what interested me back then was this whole thing about narrative structures, *ways* of telling a story, of constructing fiction. "Bottles of Beaujolais" works in the same way, where one character constructs another character, Luna. He constructs a fantasy about her just as he constructs the weather.

My sense is this: I was striving for a way of telling a different story, and I was not able at that time to talk about my *own* story of difference, so, instead of telling the story of difference, I told the story in a different way. I was also reading this kind of "unconventional" stuff like Robbe-Grillet, and to a lesser extent people like Robert Coover and Nathalie Sarraute, and some Faulkner with his screwed-up chronologies. In a lot of those stories there are recurring themes of people assuming other people's identities, becoming others, and wanting to pass or wanting to be something other than what they are. I think that speaks to various kinds of experiences of being different and wanting to fit in. And I could even go so far as to say that these ideas of transformation are also a way of making oneself a Chinese American, echoing this idea that Frank Chin first articulated, that we're not born but created.

SYH Has your writing changed since you've come to Los Angeles?

DWL You can almost know too much. I feel in some ways there's an aspect of writing that is not unlike childbirth in that, in childbirth, you want to let your instincts, your body kind of take over. You don't want to be too "thinky" about,

"Oh, I'm dilating now! Oh, I need to dilate!" You can't try to command your body to do things; you can't be overly self-conscious about what's going on; you've got to let your body do its thing. And I think there's something about that in writing as well. For me, the edge and the weirdness in some of those earlier stories grow out of the fact that I was actually articulating—through peculiar images—this notion of difference and anger and the insecurity of being who I am.

Now I'm too aware of the conversation that's out there. I'm too aware of some of the themes, and it's almost knowing too much. I think this is shutting me down a little bit because, yes, the characters in my novel are now largely Chinese American. I'm more aware of those characters and what they're supposed to be about, how people might be reading them, whereas initially I was just kind of doing it on automatic pilot.

SYH I remember reading an old story ["Growing Up West"] that you wrote in *Bridge* magazine as *David Louie*. When and why did you start using *Wong*?

DWL I don't remember when I started using the *Wong*. I would say I was using it in '84, but I don't know. It's a whole identity thing. Not that I'm saying that *Louie* is not a Chinese name, but I think that there are people who aren't Chinese who have the name *Louie*. And I had a belief that publishers didn't want to publish folks like us, so I used to just use *David Louie*. But that's what I used to always go by anyway. So it wasn't like I was trying to hide anything. That was my name. The *Wong* clearly is more ethnic sounding, and I think it is more of an aggressive way of asserting who I am. It's my middle name; I didn't make it up.

SYH What is the basic plot of your upcoming novel, *The Barbarians Are Coming*?

DWL It's about a guy who's a chef; he cooks French food;

David Wong Louie

he's a Chinese American guy. He has this kind of self-contempt, and it has to do with his parents; he has problems with his parents. But he really also has problems with his own sense of self. He's a cook who eventually comes around to cooking different types of cuisine, that is, Chinese. Now, how he gets there is the fun of the novel, and it has to do with various romantic relationships, which also lead him to reconciling with members of his family: the sister who was born in Hong Kong and the father, who actually dies during the course of the novel.

I like the idea of a cook because somehow he thinks he's moved away from what his parents do but, in fact, he's still a servant to other people. His parents work in a laundry, so he sees them as servants to the clients who are all white. He looks down on them for that kind of work, but, in a way, he's just another kind of servant, and he's also playing the other traditional Chinese American role, which is a restaurant cook.

SYH Has the novel made a progression since short stories like "Pangs" or "Inheritance"?

DWL It's basically the same cast of characters. I wrote a chapter of this book, actually, before I wrote "Pangs of Love," so maybe "Pangs of Love" really belongs in this book. And I've been trying to catch up with the chapter that I wrote earlier because what occurs in that chapter occurs probably somewhere in the next hundred pages.

SYH Do you have any other work in progress?

DWL I wish I did. I want to write some personal essays. I'm interested in writing about my experience of being my father's son, the experience of having a son. I'm also interested in writing about being an absentee parent. Half the things regarding my son always feel like something that should be written about. And I always see these moments where I compare what it was like for me as a child with what it is like for him, how differently I parent and my father parented. I'm moved to write about it, but then sometimes I start, and I know I won't get very far because I'm an extremely, extremely slow writer. So then I think, if I'm gonna struggle, I might as well struggle with the thing the publisher is waiting for, rather than struggle with something that will never see the light of day.

What I do next will probably be to try to write about my illness, about having Hodgkin's disease. And I have a second brother who is closest to me in age who has sort of kept himself apart from the rest of the family, so I find him kind of an interesting subject. I don't know if I really accomplished what I set out to do regarding one of those "search for the father" type of things. So that's something I want to do as well. I also want to do something really plot oriented. Away from this kind of character stuff. Maybe something with dinosaurs? Chinese dinosaurs?

Selected Works by David Wong Louie

"Growing Up West." *Bridge: An Asian American Perspective* 7, no. 1 (1979): 51–55.

"One Man's Hysteria—Real and Imagined—in the 20th Century." *Iowa Review* 12, no. 4 (1981): 69–85. Reprinted in *Pangs of Love* (1991).

"Bottles of Beaujolais." *Iowa Review* 13, nos. 3–4 (1982): 102–115. Reprinted in *Pangs of Love* (1991).

"Disturbing the Universe." *Colorado State Review* 10, no. 2 (1983): 66–79. Reprinted in *Pangs of Love* (1991).

"Love on the Rocks." *Quarry West* 18 (1983): 30–43. Reprinted in *Pangs of Love* (1991).

"Movers." *Mid-American Review* 5, no. 1 (Spring 1985): 45–53. Reprinted in *Pangs of Love* (1991) and in *On a Bed of Rice: An Asian American Erotic Feast,* ed. Geraldine Kudaka (New York: Anchor/Doubleday, 1995).

"Warming Trends." *Kansas Quarterly* 18, nos. 1–2 (1986): 149–160. Reprinted in *Pangs of Love* (1991).

"Birthday." *Agni Review* 24/25 (1987): 72–83. Reprinted in *Pangs of Love* (1991).

"In a World Small Enough." *Chicago Review* 35, no. 4 (1987): 90–102. Reprinted in *The Big Aiiieeeee! An Anthology of Chinese American and Japanese American Literature,* ed. Jeffery Paul Chan, Frank Chin, Lawson Fusao Inada, and Shawn Wong (New York: New American Library–Meridian, 1991).

"Displacement." *Ploughshares* 14, nos. 2–3 (1988): 77–91. Reprinted in *Best American Short Stories, 1989,* ed. Margaret Atwood and Shannon Ravenel (New York: Houghton Mifflin, 1989), in *Pangs of Love* (1991), in *Other Sides of Silence: New Fiction from Ploughshares,* ed. DeWitt Henry (Boston: Faber & Faber, 1992), and in *Kalifornien Erzhalt,* ed. Stefana Sabin (Frankfurt: Fischer Taschenbuch, 1993).

"Social Science." In *An Illuminated History of the Future,* ed. Curtis White. Urbana: Illinois State University Press, 1989. Reprinted in *Pangs of Love* (1991).

"'Is It Not That the Goats on the Boats Near Bikini Survived the Atomic Bomb?'" *Fiction International* 18, no. 2 (1990): 140–151.

"Inheritance." In *Pangs of Love* (1991).

Pangs of Love. New York: Knopf, 1991.

Dissident Song: A Contemporary Asian American Anthology. Santa Cruz, Calif.: Quarry West, 1992. Edited with Marilyn Chin.

"Cold Hearted." *Los Angeles Times Magazine,* 7 July 1994, 22–23, 28–29.

"Outer Space." *Los Angeles Times Magazine,* 2 June 1996, 20–21, 53–56.

The Barbarians Are Coming. New York: Henry Holt, forthcoming.

12

Gish Jen

Interview by
RACHEL LEE

Gish Jen won the respect of a wide audience with her first
novel, *Typical American* (1991), which was shortlisted for the
National Book Critics' Circle Award. In this novel, as in her
published short stories, Jen broadens the definition of Asian
American literature by writing beyond its "typical" themes of
cultural dislocation, generational conflict, and immigrant success. For instance, her short story "The Water-Faucet
Vision"—reprinted in *Best American Short Stories, 1988*—
probes the nuances of religious awakening. Though not
strictly about race, it features Asian American protagonists
whose ethnicity remains integral to the author's long-term
project of rendering Asian Americans a familiar part of
America's literary landscape.

As part of that mission, Jen crafts unexotic, "everyday"
characters such as the Changs, whose trials in Northeast suburban America provide the grist for several of the author's
published works (e.g., *Typical American, Mona in the
Promised Land,* "What Means Switch," "The Water-Faucet
Vision," "The White Umbrella," "Grover at the Wheel," and

"In the American Society"). Creating Asian American protagonists who are fallible, sympathetic, and even mundane remains one avenue through which Jen pursues her political goals. Another strategy involves writing about Asian Americans even in cases where ethnic identity is not crucial to the plot.

The interview first took place by telephone on the evening of 9 September 1993; it was updated on the publication of *Mona in the Promised Land*. Early in our conversation, Jen talked about switching from a "practical" profession to a career in writing. As a matter of record, her choice to "throw everything to the wind" has resulted in numerous publications and has garnered for her several fellowships, among them a 1992 Guggenheim Foundation Fellowship and a 1988 National Endowment for the Arts Fellowship.

I also asked Jen about her relationship to Asian American literature. As a writer who grew up on the East Coast in the sixties and seventies, Jen seems particularly attuned to the location and historicity of Asian America. She remarks that, when she was younger, "there was no Asian America . . . it hadn't been invented yet." While acknowledging the overwhelmingly supportive aspects of discovering an Asian American literary community, Jen also admitted to resisting a "ghettoized" identity as ethnic writer. We talked about the tensions within the Asian American literary community, particularly the ongoing debate spearheaded by Frank Chin over whether Asian American men ought to be portrayed in a blanket, positive light in order to counter the negative stereotypes of them in popular culture. Setting herself apart from writers who would argue for artistic freedom, Jen finds the political context in which she writes crucial to what she eventually publishes. One makes ethical choices when one edits, Jen seems to say, and her personal ethics decry misogyny and racism. We also discussed her engagement with various communities, her commitment to social responsibility in writing, and her opinions on the serendipitous receptivity of current readers to her kind of satiric female voice.

RL I saw from your résumé that you went to business school. Was writing on the back burner then?

GJ Business school was a particularly uninspired decision; the decision was just to go to professional school, meaning that, as an undergraduate, I had tried being premed and prelaw already. That left the one thing that I really had never had any interest in, which was business. A lot of that is being the daughter of immigrants. I did write poetry as an undergrad. I distinctly remember telling my roommate, "I love this, and, if I could, I would do this for the rest of my life." But it never even occurred to me for one second to try to become a poet. I didn't know anyone who was a poet. It just wasn't something that someone like me did.

I remember that, in a graduate seminar in prosody, Robert Fitzgerald, the translator, did ask, "Have you thought about doing something with words?" I told him I was premed. He said, "You should really think about writing." I told him that I simply couldn't imagine being a writer. So then he asked me, "Have you at least thought about publishing?" And, as professors at Harvard will, he got me a job in publishing. Once I was there, though, I distinctly understood that I had landed up in the middle ground between a world I was quite interested in and a world where you actually could make a living. I was making something like $5,000 a year. For awhile that was fine, but it couldn't go on forever. Meanwhile, my parents were hammering at me to do something practical. I realized that I was going to do one or the other. And I said to myself, If I can't decide which to do, let me try the more practical route first. So I applied to business school. It was a lark. Then, to my amazement, I got in—to Harvard and to Stanford. It just goes to show the power of the word.

Gish Jen

I met my husband during orientation. I remember pointing to a line in the course catalog and asking him, "What does this mean?" I didn't even understand what the courses were about. Meanwhile, he had exempted out of everything.

I read a hundred novels. I think it's safe to say that I was the only first-year business school student who read a hundred novels while she was at business school. I passed, amazingly. But, the next year, I found that I could not get myself to go to class. Literally, the first day I overslept; the second day I overslept; the third day I overslept. By the end of the week, I realized that I was never going to go to class. So I dropped out and never went back. It was difficult to drop out, but I've never regretted it.

RL What made you switch to writing fiction?

GJ When I was at Doubleday, there was an editorial assistant at the next desk, and we were always talking about fiction. She actually had an M.F.A. in poetry. Still, it was fiction we talked about, nonstop, instead of working. I had started writing some stories back then—it wasn't very serious. Then, at business school, I became more serious. Life works that way. You push the pendulum in one direction, and then you swing back. You're pushing it that way in order to see that. Going to business school was good in a way. One of the hardest things about being a writer is you flagellate yourself with the idea that you could have done something else more practical. I was lucky to know that I couldn't—that I hated business and didn't want to do that. When all my friends started thinking, "Maybe I'll go to law school now," I didn't. I'd already tried other things. I had to become a writer or die.

But to back up: I dropped out of business school, went to China, came back, and got my M.F.A. There's no question that I would probably not have written *Typical American* if I had not gone to China. When I went to China, I saw so much that I recognized. But you see it in a purer form. I really began to understand that certain trains of thought in my parents and also in myself were Chinese. In some ways, I didn't even know what my conflicts were until I went to China—what it means to be Chinese; what it means to be American; what it means to be Chinese American.

I was supposed to be working on my Chinese, to little avail. I spoke very well when I was there. Now I'm back, and I can't speak a word. Mostly, I was absorbing; I wasn't writing. But I began to get to a place where I understood what my concerns were.

RL What is that problem or way of thinking that drives your writing?

GJ Somebody said, In everything there's a dragon. What's the dragon? That's what you're asking, right? Probably in *Typical American,* in addition to this concern about how much you can do—whether the self has limits or not—is being poised between two visions; one is "You're lucky to be able to do anything," and the other is "You can do whatever you want to do." Which of these is true? Another thing driving the book was coming to terms with a kind of assimilation that had to do with economic success.

People always ask me whether I'm against assimilation or for it. I'm neither. It's simply a fact of life. It's like asking someone if they're for or against growing up. It just happens. So it's not like bad characters are assimilated, or vice versa. There are certainly different patterns of assimilation, though, better and worse patterns. A pattern of assimilation that appeals to me, for instance, abhors racism. Let's face it, you don't want to talk about all the Chinese, but, in general, China's a pretty racist place. They make no bones about it. They definitely say things about blacks, for instance, that are at least publicly unacceptable in America. If part of you assimilates and learns to say, "That's wrong," that's a great kind of assimilation. As for the kind of assimilation where you come

Gish Jen

here and learn all about American greed and take that as far as you can—I'm not so sure that's so great. I have seen a range of assimilation in my family, including some of the not so good.

I came to understand a lot about America by thinking about this book. A lot of what drives the action is the negative things about America. But I also came to understand a lot of the possibilities in America. When I wrote that opening line, "This is an American story," I was redefining an American tradition. That's one level of my book. As an Asian American, I understood that I was going to be ghettoized, and I wanted to get out.

RL So you were writing against a tradition that would pigeonhole you as an exotic Asian American?

GJ Absolutely. *Typical American* is extremely antiexotic, while it is still an Asian American book. I did not struggle against the pigeonholing by choosing to write a book with all white people in it. That would have been a strategy, but that wasn't my strategy.

RL You mentioned *assimilation*. In your *New York Times* article ["Challenging the Asian Illusion"], you talked about your family identifying with white America but realizing that wasn't quite the whole story. There was this feeling of not belonging—was that something you discovered later? From my own experience, I know I didn't wake up knowing this. It took a long time to discover that.

GJ That you weren't white?

RL That, as well as that there was something like Asian America.

GJ It's strictly an American invention. When we were younger, there was no Asian America. It wasn't as if we just didn't realize it was there—it hadn't been invented yet. In terms of that understanding, for me it came late, too. Not immediately knowing that you're Asian American is much more of an East Coast phenomenon. If you are in California, it's going to occur to you a lot earlier that you're not white. In San Francisco, you belong to a community. On the East Coast, there's no community.

RL Was it immediately something you wanted to write about, or did it only later feed into some things you were already concerned with?

GJ I had already been writing about isolation. So, at some level, the emotional truth was already there. I just had to learn to name it. Since naming it, I've written about it more explicitly.

RL So these feelings of isolation were disconnected from race at first?

GJ Feelings of isolation do not stem only from race. The part of myself that feels isolated is partly racially defined and partly not.

Discovering racial isolation was painful, although it was also reassuring. You know all along that something is the matter. Maybe you would have preferred that you didn't have those feelings. If you're going to have them, though, it's nice to know that you're not just loony. There's a sense of injustice that goes with it, of course. Why should you feel that way when other people wear green pants and pink shirts and get along fine? They also have problems, I realize. America is a lonely place. I think a lot of those people also have feelings of isolation, and they don't have race to fall back on as an explanation.

RL Is there an Asian American community of writers with which you identify?

GJ There is no question that we see each other as kindred. I

Gish Jen

was recently reading this interview with Cynthia Kadohata in which she talks about how she feels sisterhood with me. I met her once years ago. In this interview, she says that, whenever she sees me doing well, she always thinks, "Go Gish." How nice! Just today, David Wong Louie was in town and left a message on my machine.

RL You've had a positive experience with that Asian American writing community.

GJ I think more positive than negative.

RL What do you think about the tensions in the Asian American literary community, however you want to define it?

GJ I was waiting to get attacked by Frank Chin. It hasn't happened. Maybe he hasn't read my book. I don't know what to make of that. Either I haven't heard about it, or he hasn't read my book, or he couldn't figure out what to think about it.

RL Why did you think he would attack *Typical American?*

GJ I thought I would be attacked because of who I was. One could say that Ralph Chang is not exactly a role model for Asian American males. And the women are a lot more sympathetic in my book than Ralph is. Now, I personally find Ralph very sympathetic, but I understand that he's not as sympathetic as Theresa. I thought that, as an Asian American male, Frank Chin would be unhappy about that. And I could imagine being attacked because I'm East Coast, a woman writer, I'm married to a *haole* [a white]. I heard that he didn't like that, which is probably not even true—I don't know anything really because I haven't had any personal contact with him. It's all just this myth. From what I can tell, Frank Chin has a lot of valuable things to say, but he expresses himself in a very unfortunate manner.

To see this kind of polarization breaks my heart. There are

so few of us. The atmosphere's been so difficult for so long. While it's important that we all say what we have to say, I wish that everybody could say that in a clear manner without it turning into a bloodbath.

RL Does that inhibit your writing at all? Do you think twice about whether you're going to make a character a certain way, or do you ignore it all?

GJ It's not just with Frank Chin. The whole atmosphere now. . . . I support social responsibility in writing. I think I'm a rare writer in saying that. Most writers argue for artistic freedom. But to imagine that your images have no effect on what happens in society and the way people see themselves is completely naive. I think also that you are a better writer as you start considering questions like *representation*. I don't see how writing stereotypes about blacks or Asians or anybody else could possibly make you a better writer. The whole way of writing that used to be popular—in which there is a black and a white, a good guy and a bad guy, and certain people or races get to be the bad guys—is very unfortunate and stupid. We live in a much more complicated world.

There is a way in which you have to stand back before your work is published and ask yourself what it was in your unconscious that was triggering this. If you were in your heart of hearts anti-Semitic and there it is on the page—you have to think again before you send the story out.

RL Your published work is about Asian Americans. Is that a conscious decision? Have you written works not about Asian Americans that didn't get published?

GJ No, they did get published. Early on I wrote a number of stories about Caucasians. Then I started writing about Asian Americans, not necessarily with their Asian American–ness being the subject. For instance, "The Water-Faucet Vision" is about the religious impulse. These characters came to me.

Gish Jen

Writing is like dreaming: that I would dream about Asian Americans seems to me no surprise. Later on, when I realized I had a lot of Asian Americans in my work—that I didn't write things with all white characters—I kept on with it partly as a political thing. It didn't start as a political thing, but I did feel it was important that there be Asian American representation in literature. I didn't see that it limited my subject matter in any way. There's nothing I couldn't write about using Asian American characters, and I didn't see why I shouldn't just go on. I felt I had a social responsibility—it wasn't a big burden. I just did it.

RL So this next work of yours [*Mona in the Promised Land*]—is it on Asian Americans?

GJ Yes.

RL Are you keeping some of the same characters?

GJ I'm trying not to talk about my new work. Dorothy Parker said, "The goose that laid the golden egg died looking up its crotch. Would you lay as well? Don't watch." You can't have your whole creative process out there.

RL Has writing *Typical American* allowed you to get the issues resolved and go on to. . . .

GJ Yes, new issues, but related issues. I'll probably be writing more about race than I was. *Typical American* was about bigotry—the prejudice against the Changs. But that's not really the subject of the book. Society isn't really that present, except for pieces that they take down and put in their nest, if you will. It's much more about what they take of America and what they're making of it. The new book is probably more about actual social forces with which the characters have to contend. It is an angrier book . . . it's a funnier book. Those two things go together a lot.

Words Matter

RL You use humor, then, to diffuse anger or pain?

GJ There is for me a type of humor sometimes in my books, in my work, where that humor is a way to organize your anger. It's a way of being angry but telling a coherent story. It's not just pure rage. Maybe it's also a way of transcending it.

RL How has your family reacted to your work?

GJ My mom got to the end of *Typical American* in galleys, and she said, "Ahh! So well written!" And then she said, "And it's not about anybody!" My favorite quote so far. My family has been very happy about it, which I was sort of surprised about because they had been very against my becoming a writer. I cannot tell you how against it they were, even after I enrolled in the workshop. I would go home, there would be fights. Walking out in the snow with no coat on. They refused to pay for any part of my writing education. They were very against it, not necessarily for such bad reasons. They were immigrants. Here are these two people; they came to America only to see their home country collapse. That doesn't exactly give you a view of the world as a stable place. Of course they value security.

But they've accepted my decision, ever since there was an article about me in the *World Journal*. . . . You know how it is with these Chinese news articles: they're half article, half wedding announcement. The piece began: Gish Jen, daughter of Norman and Agnes Jen, and so on. All their friends called, and, after that, it was fine for me to be a writer. They've been supportive.

RL When you look back on your work, do you see an intention that you keep coming back to or that you work out in various ways?

GJ I can't see it across all my work exactly. It's very hard for

Gish Jen

a writer to see these things. But probably self and family is a big tension along which I write. And that's very Asian American. In America, one of the big themes is the individual in society—for me, the society that really matters is often the family.

RL You chose a male protagonist.

GJ There's a way in which you can see the whole story as being about a son coming to America and seeing this as an opportunity to break away from the family.

RL Earlier, you said that you could see how Theresa is a more sympathetic character. How did you play around with the gendered subtext of Ralph's and Theresa's interaction—the male younger son with the older sister? Are you going to be doing more with gender and sexual politics, which is an especially heated subject in the Asian American community?

GJ I just didn't see it that way. I saw it much more in a sibling-like way. I wasn't thinking so much about sexual politics—although obviously it's there. So much of both Theresa's and Ralph's problems has to do with social roles as prescribed.

RL Do you feel that you break the stereotypes? Ralph in the end says that there are limits to America, but, in your life, you've come to the opposite conclusion.

GJ Ralph says that on the worst day of his life. Also, it's followed by an image of incredible freedom and possibility, Theresa and Old Chao. The image is supposed to undercut the statement so that it's not only that. That's one truth, and there's also this other truth. Possibilities despite the limits.

My own story has mostly been about miraculous things happening. I don't think that I've made them all happen—a lot of them have happened to me. I've been lucky. Times happened to change in a very fruitful way for me.

RL Has being an Asian American writer helped you in this publishing atmosphere right now, or has it not made a difference?

GJ It hurt me early on, and now it helps and hurts me. When I was talking about this being a lucky time, I was talking less about publishing and more about the material that presented itself to me and a way of thinking about the material. This confluence of my life's experience, things in the air, a way of thinking, all came to a boil, and I got to that place of understanding where I could write my book. That's what I'm trying to say. There are writers who are not in the right time for them. I'm a writer in a time that can help me explore my preoccupations. Had I been writing in the fifties, I might not have been able to come to a point of clarity. I live in the right time for my sensibility, for this desire to play with stereotypes, for my kind of humor. I can have a satiric edge. We live in a time where that's fine for a woman, whereas, in other times, it would not have been such a great thing.

In terms of the publishing atmosphere, I think that, early on, it was an incredible disadvantage to be Asian American. Fifteen years ago—good luck. When I was at Iowa, the distinct understanding was that I would never be published in a commercial magazine. I certainly understood that; people around me understood that.

RL Unless you wrote about white characters?

GJ Yes. I think it was understood that nobody wanted to read about Asian Americans, even from the literary magazines. I got letters that said point blank, "We prefer your more exotic work." That was from the *Paris Review*. I still have the letter.

RL What did they think was your more exotic work?

GJ Things about China—stuff like that. They were more

Gish Jen

interested in stories about China than little Asian American girls running around in New York. Things have changed a lot. I have this story, "In the American Society," that has many problems but is clearly about something that can be discerned. I say this because it's been anthologized dozens of times. Today, I can look at the editor's questions at the end of the story, and I can see that people were able to read this story and figure out what it was about. Yet, when I sent that story out, I got these letters back that literally said, "Brilliant writing, but what's it about?" *Now* this story is said to be about being "between worlds." But editors didn't use to have this theme on their laundry list of things that a story could be about. So these well-meaning editors would come to the story and be baffled by it.

The present is different. As a result of multiculturalism, the list of possible themes is greatly expanded—not expanded enough probably. But it is expanded, and there's definitely a new receptivity. There is also quite a serious backlash against multiculturalism that writers like myself have definitely felt. It's very "in" to be an "independent thinker"—never mind that you're being an independent thinker in a very fashionable way. But one of the ways in which people are "independent thinkers" is to be anti-PC, whatever that means, in the publishing world and academic world. I get this feeling that Asian American writers in general are in the cross fire.

RL Have you had different or surprising responses to *Mona in the Promised Land* from the various ethnic communities— Jewish, Asian American, and African American?

GJ With *Typical American,* I was expecting a reaction like the one Philip Roth received in the fifties. I thought not everyone in the Asian American community would like it because Ralph Chang was so far from the model minority. But, by the time the book came out, the Asian American community was so much more sophisticated about fiction than the Jewish community had been. I was braced for being attacked. Instead, I was given awards by Chinese civic groups in Boston and New York.

By the time *Mona in the Promised Land* came out, there were so many books published by Asian Americans that I felt much freer. There was much less pressure to write something representative. Also, I was too exhausted by trying to juggle child rearing and writing to worry about other people's reactions.

RL Did you receive any civic awards from Jewish groups?

GJ I was offered an award from the Brandeis Library Association, but I couldn't travel to Los Angeles at the time to accept it. For the most part, Jewish American groups have been thrilled with *Mona*. Individuals come up to me and say, "Your book made me so happy and proud to be Jewish." My German publisher said, at first, that he was sure I must be Jewish, that no one could have written this book who wasn't. He was shocked and thrilled to discover I wasn't. In a way, I've tried to contribute to the process of boundary crossing, to painting pictures that are a little less black and white—a little more complicated.

There haven't been any negative reactions from black groups either. Individuals tell me that they were glad I had taken the time to portray different kinds of blacks instead of just one type.

RL I think of *Typical American* as a book about Asians adjusting to the United States, about national character and biculturalism; you've characterized the message of *Mona in the Promised Land* as dealing with ethnicity as an unstable quantity—I believe you referred to America as a place where "all the groups . . . have rubbed off on each other."[1] Is there a further development along these lines that you are pursuing in your current work?

Gish Jen

GJ My newest book [*Who's Irish? and Other Stories*] is a collection of stories that reflects a range of interests. Some of them are about ethnicity, but others about religion and art. Ethnicity is a great and big subject—I love it. Even though ethnicity is a truly large American subject—and it's a gift to have a subject that big to address—I found that, in my shorter work, I had other subjects to address. "Who's Irish?" is the title story of my newest book. It's already appeared in the *New Yorker* [in September 1998]. "Who's Irish?" is about cultural difference and cultural tension. The second story, "Birthmates," is about the price of racism, about its personal costs to a particular man. The third is about religion, and the fourth is about China—an Asian American man's romantic ideas about China.

RL So questions of race and ethnicity overlay these stories, which are also about larger issues of home and exile?

GJ That's right.

RL Are *Typical American* and *Mona in the Promised Land* part of a trilogy, the third part of which you haven't yet written?

GJ I have always thought that the Chang family would be a trilogy. I think there will be a third book, but it won't be my next book. Having just had a second child, my time is fragmented. So I'm on the fence between the long form and sticking to short stories for now. I hope, though, that within ten years there will be another Chang family book.

Note

1. From a question and answer session on the web sponsored by McDougal Littell Inc. The site address is www.mcdougallittell.com/lit/guest/garchive/jen.htm.

Selected Works by Gish Jen

"Bellying-Up." *Iowa Review* 12, no. 4 (Fall 1981): 93–94.

"The Small Concerns of Sparrows." *Fiction International* 14 (1982): 47–55. Published under the name Lillian Jen.

"The White Umbrella." *Yale Review* 73, no. 3 (April 1984): 401–409.
Reprinted in *Home to Stay: Asian American Women's Fiction,* ed. Sylvia Watanabe and Carol Bruchac (Greenfield Center, N.Y.: *Greenfield Review* Press, 1990), and in *My Mother's Daughter: Stories by Women,* ed. Irene Zahava (Freedom, Calif.: Crossing, 1991).

"Eating Crazy." *Yale Review* 74, no. 3 (April 1985): 425–433.

"In the American Society." *Southern Review* 22 (1986): 606–619. Reprinted in *New Worlds of Literature,* ed. Jerome Beaty and J. Paul Hunter (New York: Norton, 1989), and in *Imagining America: Stories from the Promised Land,* ed. Wesley Brown and Amy Ling (New York: Persea, 1991).

"The Water-Faucet Vision." *Nimrod* 31, no. 1 (1987): 25–33. Reprinted in *Best American Short Stories, 1988,* ed. Mark Halperin and Shannon Ravenel (Boston: Houghton Mifflin, 1988).

"Grover at the Wheel." *New Yorker,* 31 December 1990, 32–37.

"What Means Switch." *Atlantic Monthly,* May 1990, 76–84.

"Challenging the Asian Illusion." *New York Times,* 11 August 1991, B1, B12–B13.

"Our Luck: Chips, but No Breaks." *New York Times,* 28 November 1991, B4.

Typical American. Boston: Houghton Mifflin, 1991.

"Birthmates." *Ploughshares* 20, no. 4 (Winter 1994): 81–97. Reprinted in *Best American Short Stories, 1995,* ed. Jane Smiley and Katrina Kenison (Boston: Houghton Mifflin, 1995).

"An Ethnic Trump: They Always Said They Didn't Want Their Young Son to See Himself as More Chinese Than Irish. But Is That Possible?" *New York Times Magazine,* 7 July 1996, 50.

Mona in the Promised Land. New York: Knopf, 1996.

"Who's to Judge? Identity Politics v. Inner Lives." *New Republic,* 21 April 1997, 18–19.

"Who's Irish?" *New Yorker,* 14 September 1998, 80.

Who's Irish? and Other Stories. New York: Random House, 1999.

232

13

Russell Leong

Interview by
ROBERT B. ITO

Russell Leong was born in San Francisco's Chinatown in 1950. He began his writing career with "Threads," in Kai-yu Hsu's *Asian-American Authors* (1972), and "Rough Notes for Mantos," in *Aiiieeeee! An Anthology of Asian-American Writers* (1974). Since then, his criticism, fiction, and poetry have appeared in numerous anthologies and journals, including *Tricycle: The Buddhist Review*, the *Seattle Review*, *The Open Boat*, *Zyzzyva*, the *New England Review*, the *Los Angeles Times*, *Charlie Chan Is Dead: An Anthology of Contemporary Asian American Fiction*, and *Positions: East Asia Cultures Critique*. Leong has been the editor of UCLA's *Amerasia Journal* since 1977, and he has also edited *Asian American Sexualities* (1996). His first collection of poems, *The Country of Dreams and Dust* (1993), received the 1994 PEN Oakland Josephine Miles Literature Award. His first collection of short fiction, *Phoenix Eyes and Other Stories*, is forthcoming from University of Washington Press.

Although I have known Leong for three years, I was initially unsure about how an interview with him would go on account of his cutting wit, particularly in group settings (two days after the interview, he amused a group of students with an extended run about how certain Asian American authors could market their own lines of underwear). I was also aware of his "life is war" philosophy as well as his disdain for academics (Leong considers himself a cultural worker rather than an academician). Before the interview, Leong lent me his short story "The Painted Branch," which had recently been published in an issue of the *New England Review* entitled "Questions of Identity: Ethnicity, Apprenticeship, and the New American Writer."

RBI Here's that journal you lent me. I think I'll get a copy.

RL You should because there are other things in there. Other "apprentices."

RBI Yeah, what's that about? You've been publishing for about twenty years. How does it feel to have the *New England Review* call you a "new writer" or an "apprentice"?

RL Well, that's their point of view. Writers of color in America help validate American writing. Actually, the editors are the apprentices because they're learning from us.

RBI How are they using the term?

RL Oh, probably in the academic way, like we are traveling beyond our ethnicity and learning English, or learning how to write, and not relying on our politics or ethnicity. That's probably the implication, that real writing is "universal" and can get beyond the barrio and the ghetto. Very patronizing, but not unexpected.

RBI I thought there was an interesting parallel between that whole apprenticeship idea and the other article you lent me, "Litany" (republished as "Paper Houses"), where the white woman covets your friend's Thai pillow and says something like, "This would look good on my patio." After getting published in journals like the *New England Review,* do you ever worry about your work becoming commodified, becoming a kind of "Thai pillow"?

RL The Filipino writer N. V. M. Gonzalez put it well: For too long, Third World writers, and Third World people, have been furniture in the colonialist's house in the sense of being domestic servants—minor characters; if not furniture, then people who dust and move furniture around rather than the subjects or owners of the houses. So, while things have changed, many times we have been relegated to the furniture of literature.

RBI Why the pseudonym Wallace Lin in "Rough Notes for Mantos" in *Aiiieeeee!?*

RL Wallace Lin was a pseudonym based on Wallace Stevens, who was one of my writing icons. Lin was a Chinese surname. So I combined the two. The bio, I think, was written by Shawn Wong. Nothing is true. The reason I used the pseudonym was that the story dealt with some sensitive subjects, such as father and son relationships. Part of it was this diatribe against my father or against his questioning of a relationship, and I didn't want my father to read it. He read it anyway.

RBI Knowing that you wrote it.

RL I think so. The details were accurate: the steel cleaver, vegetables, mixed emotions between father and son. He probably recognized himself.

RBI Were you primarily concerned about your father reading it?

RL Maybe other people as well because I was young then, maybe eighteen, nineteen, when I wrote it, and these were unsettling issues about my own sexuality and about my relationship with my father, relationships with men or women. And, at that time, since I was also involved in the Asian American movement, issues of sexuality could not really be a primary concern for me. The main focuses of the movement were the reclamation of community and community history, so questions about sexuality were seen as bourgeois preoccupations. I actually wrote the story in Jeffery Chan's class, which was one of the first Asian American writing classes at San Francisco State College.

RBI What was that like?

RL It was a lot different in those days. We did our writing, and we had those little purple mimeographs that we'd hand around the room. A lot of Asian American writers—at least on the West Coast—came through either San Francisco State or the Kearny Street Workshop. I remember people like Shawn Wong, Alan Chong Lau, George Leong, Janice Mirikitani, Genny Lim, Merle Woo, Al Robles. A lot of artists and musicians, too—Paul Yamazaki, Jim Dong, Nancy Gee. San Francisco is a really small place, so artists, writers, and community activists all came together.

RBI *The Country of Dreams and Dust* was originally entitled *The Migrant Ideograms.* For the non-Buddhist readers—why "dreams and dust"?

RL Even though "dreams and dust" is a Buddhist or Taoist term, even non-Buddhist readers may get something out of it. Those are pretty common words, so I think you'll still be able to get some sense of your own dreams. "The Migrant Ideograms" sounded too sociological. What do you think?

RBI I thought that "migrant ideograms" made it sound like you would be completely focusing on the immigration experience in terms of a one-way, East to West move, when your poems seemed to be more concerned with prisons or bondage.

RL Originally, when I wrote *The Country of Dreams and Dust*, I utilized some historical material, but then, as I began writing, I realized that it was not a historical text or a reconstruction of history; I was just using certain historical reference points to talk about other things. So, even though it's been reviewed as a piece about Chinese migration, that's just the topmost level. Those historical reference points serve as props for other things that are occurring: prisons, bondage, liberation.

RBI The poems have these huge historical moments—you called them *props*—but then you pick out seemingly random smaller moments within them to focus on. For instance, the Tiananmen Square poem, "Name," deals almost exclusively with one student's escape.

RL Well, there's the view of history as grandiose, the "sweep of history," but most history is made up of the lives and actions of ordinary people and really not the "heroic" in the sense that it's even recorded. It could be just about something mundane that happens. I wanted to show the juxtapositions between larger historical moments like, say, the Opium War and a child growing up in a Chinatown barrio a century or more later and to try to find the connection, if any. The grand sweep of history is for traditional historians, and that presupposes that history is linear, and that it's going someplace, and that there's a beginning and an end, a goal located within a master narrative. But many times, when you're just living life, you're not sure of its end point, or its beginning, or its middle. Also, in Buddhism, history, karma, a lot of things become transformed; there's a constant process of transformation and transmutation.

RBI You were talking about the juxtapositions between larger historical moments and these smaller "histories," but you also juxtapose lines from an 1882 English/Chinese lesson book—the text of authority and domination—and Asian American "countertexts," for instance, the poems scrawled on the walls of Angel Island by imprisoned Chinese immigrants.

RL I was educated in both American schools, which taught English, and Chinese schools, which met after the American school, so I feel that what's not officially written is just as important, if not more important, than what is within the text. For instance, I remember that, in Chinese school, Chinese history would go up only to 1949, and then, afterward, we'd go into geography, the provinces of China, or something like that. The classes were held in a Methodist church that had connections with the KMT [Kuomintang]. So Christianity and the KMT were a sort of conglomerate. I talk about that in the poem "Ideograms"—that the lessons we learned in American school and in Chinese school were both official versions of history and that they neglected other parts of history or other perspectives, both here and in relation to modern Chinese history and politics.

RBI Does this poem reflect your take on Christianity as you now look back on your experiences in Christian schools, or were these problems you felt at the time?

RL Even though I don't think the poem is anti-Christian, it does subvert certain kinds of Christian and English texts. They were the official texts that I grew up with—English and Christianity—and they remained so throughout my education, even in college. English, the language of instruction, the language of learning, the language of opportunity—even the language of Asian American studies. We must question that and incorporate other languages in our art as much as possible: the language of film, theater, music, both Western and non-Western.

RBI But the poem is pretty harsh. You compare Christian missionaries to prostitutes and leeches, and one of the priests is a serial child molester. Does your critique go beyond just the fact that Christianity and English were the tools or voices of authority?

RL Yes. The line between the body and the spirit, in terms of sexuality and sexual mores, has been carved out by the church. Fragmented, and split: How do you reconcile these parts? What matters between my heart and my thigh?

RBI Is this part of the reason that you find Buddhism more applicable to your own life?

RL Yes, Buddhism is a more apt metaphor for my view about life, writing, relationships. It seems to be a very self-contained philosophy and yet expansive and inclusive. When you look at the spread of Buddhism in Asia, you can see how it has been adapted to local cultures, local languages. It is a very inclusive philosophy rather than a static or an oppressive one.

RBI You use a lot of fire and incense imagery in "Dreams and Dust," and also in "Unfolding Flowers," as symbols of purification and cleansing. In "Unfolding Flowers," you mix images of incense burning with the fires of the LA riots, and the poem ends with, "Americans bombed Baghdad, / now burn their own cities. / Always, what we do returns to us." Do you see the riots as part of a natural process?

RL If you allow too much scrub to grow underneath the trees, natural fires will occur. With the LA riots, we allowed things to deteriorate for too long: education, housing, city hall politicians, the infrastructure. Then one spark ignited a prairie fire, to paraphrase Mao.

RBI "Geography One," your short story in *Charlie Chan Is Dead,* is one of the few Asian American stories to deal with the problems of intraethnic relationships, an intraethnic gay relationship.

RL Even though the text deals with two Asian guys, and though it deals with an intraethnic relationship, those are just props, too, this ethnic stuff, and this sexuality stuff. People in Asian American studies or critical studies tend to focus on these catchy words: *intraethnic, interethnic*. To me, "Geography One" is about various terrains: The terrain of the floating world, of sexual and physical desire. Also the terrain of spiritual searching. And the other terrain, of course, is the very real terrain of LA and the different types of people one encounters, whether it's a man and a woman, a man and a man, a woman and a woman. Whatever race or sex or age, these encounters happen in LA: in the laundromat, in a bar, in a temple. So LA is just a metaphor that leads you into the other terrains: sensual, spiritual, physical.

But, in terms of the differences, or problems, in the intraethnic relationship, I built those differences in to show that, even among Asians, there are many differences and that these differences are based on subtle nuances around Orientalism and colonization. So one cannot always blame the Western colonizers. In Asia, you can't forget that many of the colonizers were also Asian—the Japanese in Korea and South Asia, the Chinese in other places—so the process of incursion and colonization is also intra-Asian. That carries over even now—certain prejudices and biases within our Asian American communities—and so I put it in the context of a personal relationship.

RBI Staying on the subject of colonialism, your essay "Litany" talks about the overlap between colonialism in Asia and in Asian America. Do you want to talk about that?

RL Yes, because that's partly the reason why *The Country of Dreams and Dust* turned out the way it did. It's ironic that a lot of the first Christian ministers in Chinatowns were missionaries who had originally served in China, in Canton, in Ningbo, in Shanghai, so they knew the languages. And so, in a sense, Chinese settlements here were the last outposts after China, "post-China."

RBI Do you see a connection between that type of dual colonization and the inability or refusal of many white Americans to distinguish between Asians and Asian Americans?

RL Probably, in the sense that colonization crosses oceans and national borders, so that you bring it to China, or you bring it to Hong Kong, and so there's a complex relationship. Also, besides colonization through education or through economics, there's the colonization of the body and sexual domination. Even now, it's common knowledge that images of whites and Asians in advertisements or in pornography—whether you're talking about straight or gay images—are usually of white men and Asian women or white men and Asian men. Richard Fung talks a lot about it in his work on film and sexuality.[1]

RBI It's also in "Geography One," where you talk about that fetishization. Can Asians have Asian fetishes?

RL Frantz Fanon talked about the fact that, even after the colonizers leave, they have already educated and developed a class of people who have internalized attitudes of the oppressors, so that they will be the ones who oppress their own people.[2] An African filmmaker, Sembene, did a satiric film called *Hala* where he talks about how, after the French colonizers leave, you still have this class of people left behind who will do the dirty work. And, yes, I think that Asian Americans also internalize a lot of these ideas. But what do you mean by *fetishization?*

RBI When you look at fetishization in terms of white male and Asian male or female, it's latching onto certain stereotypes about Asian sexuality, stereotypes that Asians presumably should know better than to believe. But, given the way

Russell Leong

that society works or that the media work, do you think that these assumptions also come into intraethnic Asian relationships?

RL Edward Said said it best, that Orientalism is so ingrained in Western culture that it affects all of us. And Orientalism is not just a matter of stereotypes; it's a whole system of dominance: educational, literary, cultural, political, economic, and so on, and includes racial and sexual stereotypes. It's very hard to even talk about it because you're faced with it at almost every turn. Winthrop Jordan wrote a book called *White over Black* where he talks about the origins of "blackness," European and Western attitudes about "blackness."[3] Before Africans were forcibly taken to the Americas, they had been contextualized by the Elizabethans. Certain perceptions of darkness and lightness became ingrained in literary and cultural imagery and became part of our cultural baggage. So I think we can recognize them, and we do our best, but I'm sure that I have certain fetishes. Colonized is colonized. But through language and through my writing—that's why it's a personal thing for me, language and writing—I'm trying to counter my own internal colonization.

RBI So what are some of these internal fetishes?

RL [*Long pause.*] I don't know whether you'd call them *fetishes,* but ideas about the dominance of the West, its technological superiority, its ability to conquer, to develop the nuclear bomb to destroy the world. So that's a certain amount of power and arrogance, and, like it or not, a lot of Third World countries are following the path, as a mark of sophistication, and trying to develop nuclear warheads, and basically polluting their countries with more industry. So you can see the dominance of Western technology.

I wouldn't call it *fetishization,* though I see and acknowledge that type of power. But I'm also a part of the West, so sometimes I do question whether going into metaphysics and looking at these things metaphorically could be an escape from direct political confrontation. Maybe I should join more political groups, ecology groups, to put my beliefs to the test. But, then again, I don't want to end up another groupie, either. There are various ways to effect change, and I'm trying to do it through the language I use and how I write. I also try to question certain tropes and assumptions about "great moments" in Asian American history. For instance, in my poem "Ideograms," I think the young schoolchildren are not scrawling poems like the Angel Island immigrants did; they scrawl cusswords and other kinds of graffiti on their desks.

RBI In your poem, one kid scrawls "your mama" on his desk.

RL Yeah, because they may be more influenced by African Americans than Asian American history or Chinese poetry. That's just a reality, unless you major in Asian American studies or something.

RBI In "Geography One" and "Rough Notes for Mantos," the protagonists are fairly unlucky in love. We talked about how you use certain tropes as "props": are these autobiographical incidents that you worked into stories?

RL Some of my fiction is based on my own experience, and some of it is based on observation. But, as a writer, I heighten, dramatize, or manipulate time, action, language, etc. to create a richer text, often different from "what happened" to me personally. Personal desire becomes public domain once you write about it. So writing is basically this dialogue between the personal body and the body politic.

RBI Here's the obligatory "emasculation of the Asian male" question. Defend Asian men as sexual beings.

RL Why? I never have any problems. Defend Asian men? Do they need a defense? That's sort of a defensive posture.

Russell Leong

RBI But I think that, any time you talk about emasculation in literature or the media or in films, it always is somewhat defensive.

RL I always thought that the ideal Asian man would be a combination of three things: a poet, a politician, and a warrior. And they're not necessarily mutually exclusive: you could be a politician in your daily life, a warrior when you have to defend your country or your family, and a poet when you create some distance from your day-to-day living and you're able to analyze it and express it. So I don't see flower arranging, let's say, as feminine. I enjoy it myself. I also took karate and judo—it didn't do me any good—when I was younger. But a lot of this emasculation bullshit is because we've become internally colonized and accepted certain kinds of images as the ideals. The new kinds of Asian American yuppie magazines like *Transpacific* are not providing very interesting alternative images of Asian males. For one thing, the Asian males usually all look like they stepped out of some shopping mall. They're usually a certain age, and they're very commodified. It's basically consumer commodification; even if they look hip, they also look highly commodified by current consumer cultural standards. It's not interesting at all. I'd rather look at Asian men and women in erotic pillow books, whether Chinese or Japanese, or eroticism in South Asian sculptures; it's much more sensual and, I think, much more authentic, although I guess this could be construed as Orientalist in some ways. But then I'm Asian myself.

RBI Loni Ding talks about an elderly Chinese man who watched English-language videotapes just to see Asian faces. You don't have a TV, right?

RL No. It broke. But I see Asians in my dreams. I touch them, talk with them. Make love with them. No barrier between them and me!

RBI But what about when you're awake? I think that a lot of Asians probably hate *Transpacific* for some of the reasons that you mentioned, but they might pick up an issue just to be able to look at Asian faces. Is that where you go—to the pillow books—to see beautiful Asians?

RL Let's see. Where do I see beautiful Asians? At Asian American conferences? No. Well, this may seem like a funny answer, but, when I go to the temple—it happens to be a Vietnamese temple—and I see the various types of Asians. Sometimes I see little children; they're beautiful in their kind of active way. Then I see elderly women—Vietnamese women and some Chinese women—who have another type of beauty that comes from experience, survival, a certain type of living in the world. That's what I would call beauty, beauty that's based on "living in the world." And I see my Sifu. He has a certain kind of gaze, a direct gaze, and he's also handsome, has a very stoic look.

There are various types of Asian imagery that I'm drawn to; it can range from the very young to the very old. But it's more the presence of mind that creates a certain type of beauty. And there's beauty only when it's juxtaposed against the corruption of the world. Also vegetarians; I'm not a pure vegetarian, but vegetarians tend to have better skin. And more luminous eyes. So I guess there are vegetarian beauties. Walking vegetables. No, I'm halfway joking. But, as I said, there's a certain kind of beauty that comes from living in the world and also through a certain amount of discipline, intellectual and spiritual discipline. As for sexual beauty, the Western kind of sexual beauty is to let everything hang out, wear as little as possible. But a lot of times, at least for East Asians, we're pretty clothed. Just the contrast of skin against cloth is very sensuous.

RBI Mishima had that whole thing about the kimono against the nape of the neck.

Russell Leong

RL Yeah, that's true. But Mishima had a lot of hang-ups about other things, and he also worshiped a certain Western type of beauty. As a child, he admired the image of Saint Sebastian being shot with arrows, as he said in his autobiographical *Confessions of a Mask*.

RBI Maybe more than admired.

RL Yeah, what do you call it, your favorite word . . . *fetishized?* Well, you guys are into that. Maybe academics are basically sort of repressed and horny.

RBI That's probably true. Shifting gears here, you're good friends with Frank Chin.

RL Yeah, I've known Frank Chin since I was eighteen. I've known the *Aiiieeeee!* people for a long time. They emerged at a crucial time in Asian American history. Warriors out of the Dawn? They played an important role in a number of ways. For one, I think, raising issues of racism in the reception of Asian American literature; you have to remember that this is in 1970. The *Aiiieeeee!* people acknowledged the alliance with African Americans in terms of publishing and certain types of sensibilities when it came to language. Ishmael Reed was a great influence, and *Aiiieeeee!* was published by Howard University Press when white publishers would not publish it. And they did try to draw attention to certain motifs in Asian American lit, like father and son relationships and the idea of autobiography as Christian confession. They were able to bring out some important ideas that had not been brought out before as well as to bring neglected works to light: *No-No Boy, Eat a Bowl of Tea, Yokohama, California,* etc. And so I think they should be looked at with a historical perspective.

RBI Do you think a lot of the criticism of *Aiiieeeee!* ignores this historical perspective?

RL A lot of times the *Aiiieeeee!* folks all get lumped together as rebellious voices from the sixties—a gross oversimplification. And the sixties themselves were rather complicated, so I think it's basically dismissive.

RBI What gets glossed over?

RL What's glossed over is that they're trying to grapple with certain issues: racism and the relationships between whites, blacks, and Asians. Frank Chin's *Chickencoop Chinaman* questions assimilation. I think that these were themes that the *Aiiieeeee!* editors talked about head-on.

RBI I think part of the reason that they all get lumped together is that they all signed their names to the somewhat famous—infamous?—editorial introduction to *Aiiieeeee!* But what are some of the differences between those four?

RL When you look at their writing, they're quite different. Lawson Inada is primarily a poet, and his writing is very epigrammatic. It draws heavily from jazz, the blues. He's a "dealer" of language; he deals language like somebody deals cards, fast, smooth, like one of those Asian dealers in casinos, where dealing cards almost becomes a part of your body. But Lawson takes on quite a number of themes: the camps, racism, the *ornamental Orientalist*, which is Frank's term for it. Lawson also gets around; his poems get carved on rocks. So Lawson is a real wordsman.

Shawn, I find, is not as fast with the words; his second novel is coming out after fifteen years. He's crafted, a poet also, and deliberate in the way he constructs his stories. But Shawn has gone into academe, heading the Asian American studies program at the University of Washington. And he's involved in a lot of publishing as well as teaching and supporting younger writers. He has a slightly different sensibility. A lot of times his protagonists are Asian and white. I think this reflects his coming to terms with being Asian in America and to what degree one can assimilate.

Russell Leong

Frank, of course, is the most prolific by far, and not just as a playwright, but also as a journalist. He's done a lot of journalistic work in both print and broadcasting, documentary work. He's done a piece that's been published in the San Diego paper on Chinese on both sides of the border, Mexico and California. So I think Frank's skills as a journalist and as an observer of Asian American life have been overshadowed by the polemics of the debates.[4] I think of the four, Frank is the most driven by his curiosity and his quest for history.

Jeff Chan. He's the most comfortable. Being a history teacher at San Francisco State, he hasn't written that much. But some of his works are classics of Chinese life. His middle-class suburbanites reflect his own lifestyle, too. He does live in Marin County. So I think they are quite different in terms of their language, their voice, their sensibilities.

RBI There's a perception that some of the ideas in the *Aiiieeeee!* introductions, particularly the distinction between "the real and the fake," are primarily Frank Chin's ideas that the rest of them signed their names to. Do you buy a lot of his distinctions?

RL Well, Frank is the most driven as far as "the real and the fake" goes, and he considers himself the most real and almost everything else fake, which is a pretty clear distinction that means you don't have to worry about the other stuff since it's all fake. I wouldn't necessarily apply these distinctions as consistently as he does because, being Buddhist, I can see that things could get transformed from one to another. Despite Frank's polemic, I think it's crucial to take a stand on literature, on history, on craft. So I'd agree with him there.

RBI I'm not sure what you mean by that.

RL Well, what appears real might turn out to be fake. Like in the story of the monkey, where there is a fake monkey running around, and they have this big fight, and they're trying to figure out which one is the real monkey and which one is the fake monkey. And so that's possible too: that what we're seeing as real may change or maybe it has changed.

RBI What are you working on now?

RL I'm working on a novel called *Oxidation,* which deals with the transformation of people, elements, energy, life, death, at different levels. *Oxidation* is the transfer of electrons from positive to negative, and it's a certain metaphor for things I'm interested in.

RBI So it will deal with some of the themes of transformation and change that you've been playing with in your poems?

RL Yes, a continuation of those themes, but more developed, because with a novel you can really develop a plotline that you can only hint at in short stories or in poetry. And it's going to be much broader; I'm not going to write another Chinatown novel. I think it was Heraclitus who said that you can't stand in the same river twice—water moves on, as do writing, time, and passion.

Notes

1. See Richard Fung, "Looking for My Penis: The Eroticized Gay Asian in Gay Video Porn," in *Asian American Sexualities: Dimensions of the Gay and Lesbian Experience,* ed. Russell Leong (New York: Routledge, 1996).

2. See Frantz Fanon, *Black Skin, White Masks* (1967), trans. Charles Lam Markmann (New York: Grove, 1982).

3. See Winthrop D. Jordan, *White over Black: American Attitudes towards the Negro, 1550–1812* (1968; Baltimore: Penguin, 1969).

4. See Frank Chin, *Bulletproof Buddhists and Other Essays* (Honolulu: University of Hawai'i Press, 1998). The essay on Mexico and California is "Lowe Hoy and the Strange Three-Legged Toad."

Russell Leong

Selected Works by Russell Leong

"Threads." In *Asian American Authors,* ed. Kai-yu Hsu. Boston: Houghton-Mifflin, 1972.

"Rough Notes for Mantos." In *Aiiieeeee! An Anthology of Asian American Writers,* ed. Frank Chin, Jeffery Paul Chan, Lawson Fusao Inada, and Shawn Wong. Washington, D.C.: Howard University Press, 1974. Published under the pseudonym Wallace Lin.

"Aerogrammes." *Seattle Review* 11, no. 1 (1988): 131–141. Reprinted in *The Open Boat: Poems from Asian America,* ed. Garrett Hongo (New York: Anchor/Doubleday, 1993), in *Invocation, L.A.,* ed. Sesshu Foster et al. (Albuquerque, N.M.: West End, 1993), and in *Image Magazine (San Francisco Examiner),* 14 November 1993, 16–19. Poem.

"Disarmed, San Francisco State, 1968–1988." In *Reflections in Shattered Windows,* ed. Shirley Hune et al. Pullman: Washington State University Press, 1988.

"Selected Poems." In *The Statement of Two Rivers: Selected Contemporary Chinese American Poets,* ed. and trans. Henry Zhao, L. Ling-chi Wang, and Sau-ling Wong. Shanghai: Shanghai Literature Publishing House; Seattle: University of Washington Press, 1990.

"Beware of the M Word." *High Performance Magazine,* Summer 1992, 30.

The Country of Dreams and Dust. Albuquerque, N.M.: West End, 1993.

"Geography One." In *Charlie Chan Is Dead: An Anthology of Contemporary Asian Fiction.* New York: Penguin, 1993.

"Ideograms." In *The Country of Dreams and Dust* (1993).

"In the Country of Dreams and Dust." *Positions: East Asia Cultures Critique* 1, no. 1 (1993): 131–159. A revised version appeared in *Asian-American Literature: A Brief Introduction and Anthology,* ed. Shawn Wong (New York: HarperCollins, 1995). Poem.

"The Painted Branch: A Parable." *New England Review* 15, no. 3 (Summer 1993): 93–98. Story.

"Unfolding Flowers, Matchless Flames." *Tricycle: The Buddhist Review* 2, no. 3 (Spring 1993): 49–51. Poem.

"Granite." *Los Angeles Times,* Sunday, 13 February 1994, 6. Poem.

"Litany: An Account." *Tricycle: The Buddhist Review* 4, no. 1 (Fall 1994): 58–63. A revised version, "Paper Houses," appeared in *Race: An Anthology in the First Person,* ed. Bart Schneider (New York: Crown, 1997), and another, "Litany," in *Q & A: Queer in Asian America,* ed. David L. Eng and Alice Hom (Philadelphia: Temple University Press, 1998).

"Fish Don't Wear No Hats." In *Remapping the Occident,* ed. Bryan Joachim Malessa and John Jason Mitchell. Berkeley: University of California Press, 1995. Story.

"A Yin and Her Man." In *On a Bed of Rice: An Asian American Erotic Feast,* ed. Geraldine Kudaka. New York: Anchor/Doubleday, 1995. Story.

Asian American Sexualities: Dimensions of the Gay and Lesbian Experience. With an introduction by Russell Leong. New York: Routledge, 1996. Editor.

"Eclipse." Featured in *The United States of Poetry,* directed by Mark Pellington, for national broadcast on PBS, February 1996. Printed later in *The United States of Poetry.* New York: Abrams, 1996. Poem.

"Phoenix Eyes." *Zyzzyva* 12, nos. 3/4 (Fall/Winter 1996): 128–143. Reprinted in *Best Gay American Fiction* 2, ed. Brian Bouldrey (Boston: Little Brown, 1997). Story.

"The Eclipse of Kwan-Yin and Rahu." In *Disciplining Asia,* ed. Karen Shimakawa and Kandice Chuh. Durham, N.C.: Duke University Press, 1997. One-act dialogue.

"What Does the Body Dream at Rest?" *Tricycle: The Buddhist Review* 7, no. 1 (Fall 1997): 50. Poem.

"In the Western Palace." *Disorient* 6 (1998): 81–86.

Phoenix Eyes and Other Stories. Seattle: University of Washington Press, forthcoming.

14

Amy Uyematsu

Interview by
SCOTT KURASHIGE

Amy Uyematsu's genesis as a writer can be traced to the early days of the Asian American movement. In the late sixties and early seventies, this Sansei author became widely known among activists for her biting polemic "The Emergence of Yellow Power in America." Drawing on both her experience with racism as a youth and the inspiration of the black power movement, Uyematsu produced a fiery, programmatic statement that crystallized simultaneously the anger and the aspiration of her generation. Her scathing indictment of systematic oppression in America and the psychological scars it left on Asian Americans quickly became a manifesto for the fledgling social movement.

While her direct involvement in political activism has receded to the background, Uyematsu has brought her sharp instincts and unwavering sense of social justice to a wider range of issues through her poetry. Whether addressing her resentment of American military involvement in Southeast Asia, the enduring scars of Japanese American internment, or her feelings toward interpersonal relationships, she continues to write with the same brutal honesty that initially drew the attention of movement activists. It is this ability to speak about intensely personal opinions, emotions, and events that has won Uyematsu a loyal following among both literary critics and Japanese American "common folk."

Winner of the 1992 Nicholas Roerich Poetry Prize, Uyematsu had her first collection of poems, *30 Miles from J-Town*, published in the same year by Story Line Press. Written over the course of a decade, the poems intersect with various points in her life, spanning her adolescence in the fifties and sixties, her radical coming of age in the movement, and her more recent experiences as a divorced, single mother. In an attempt to better understand these intersections, I asked Uyematsu to retrace the paths her life has taken, the issues and environments that influenced her consciousness, and the choices that she made along the way. I caught up with her in her modest West Los Angeles apartment.

SK *30 Miles from J-Town* opens with a section of poems called "Sansei Line Dance" that recall childhood experiences and the Japanese American youth culture of your day. In what ways has your family background and your upbringing influenced your poems?

AU My family on both sides has been in southern California for a long time. My dad's side was based in Montebello and my mother's side in Pasadena. I was born in Pasadena; I'm a Sansei, a third-generation Japanese American. My experience was different from many Sansei when we moved to Sierra Madre from Montebello in the mid-fifties. The Japanese American community within central Los Angeles was still very strong. There were big concentrations—in the Crenshaw area around LA and Dorsey Highs, in Boyle Heights, in Gardena. We moved out to the suburbs way before the other Japanese American families that later took the same route. So I was

Amy Uyematsu

raised in an almost all-white environment. That definitely impacted and distorted my identity.

sk In what ways does your poetry draw on that experience of growing up in an all-white environment?

au What spurred a lot of the poems in *30 Miles from J-Town* was racism, years of built-up anger, and wanting to tell the story of my experiences as a Japanese American. The environment I grew up in was blatantly racist. One of my poems has a reference to a cross being burned on the lawn of our Jewish neighbors. This was in the fifties. Mom has said that, when Dad was going to build our house on the Uyematsu nursery, property the family owned—this is in the sixties—the neighbors circulated a petition and sent it to the City Council saying they didn't want us to move in.

When I started junior high, I had a number of close white girlfriends from grammar school and Girl Scouts. Most of them dropped me. Maybe other Asian Americans wouldn't have reacted the way I did, but there was something in me that eventually led to expressing my anger and protest in the form of writing.

sk You talk about built-up anger that you've developed over the years. Asian American families, Japanese American in particular, are often portrayed as silent. In other words, family members repress all their anger until it ends up exploding. Was that part of your family experience, or was your family more open in talking about these problems?

au I think it was more open because I can remember both my mom and my dad talking about camp. The thing is they didn't talk so much about the bad side of it. They were teenagers during the war, and both of them had some good times in camp. My dad stayed in Manzanar only a year. My mom is a very pretty woman and had an active social life as a high school student in Gila. But I do remember my mother telling me how humiliating it was being put on the train to be sent to the assembly centers from Pasadena. So they were a little more talkative about the camp experience than other Nisei I've heard about.

There's my own silence. When I was the only Asian face within the whole fifth and sixth grades, people would talk about the "Japs" bombing Pearl Harbor. I didn't speak up. I would cry. My problem was being so sensitive to these things but not being able to articulate anything to the bigots who were saying them. And then feeling bad that they could see me in tears. On top of being mad about what was being said, I'd feel terrible because I was showing more weakness by crying in front of them. For me, writing became a way to take some control and express what I'm feeling about those devastating experiences.

SK So, in a sense, you end up internalizing it. Your poems about identity, self-hatred, and denial were some of the ones with which I could really identify. Do you think this is a shared experience among Japanese Americans?

AU It's hard for me to say because I don't know if my self-hatred was much more pronounced because I grew up in an environment where I was so isolated. There's a huge range and degree of self-hatred in victimized people and each person's ability to acknowledge it. For example, my ex-husband grew up in West Los Angeles, where there was a pretty big Japanese community. When he went to high school, he always had plenty of other Sansei classmates. One of the reasons we used to argue a lot in the early years of our marriage was that I couldn't understand: "Why aren't you madder at the white racist world? Why aren't you angry like me?" His experiences had been different from mine. He didn't get the kind of overtly racist treatment that I did, so his ego and his self-concept were a lot more intact than mine.

That's why I wonder about the Asian Americans growing

Amy Uyematsu

up in LA today. There are so many other Asian Americans to identify with. Are they coming up with a healthier self-concept? I hope so because, for me, it was extremely damaging having to constantly feel self-conscious about the way I look. I would hear through neighbors that boys wouldn't ask me out on dates because I'm Japanese. Classmates would be friendly at school but not invite me to social outings. My anger became so overwhelming that, when I went to UCLA, I cut myself off from anybody but Asian students. I joined Thetas, a predominantly Japanese American sorority at the time, and did everything with Asians. Everything.

SK In your poems, you differentiate in your youth between different types of Japanese Americans, between Westside and Pasadena, or between the cool and the uncool. Where does that come from?

AU Being from Sierra Madre, which a lot of people had never heard of, I would say we're from Pasadena. In high school, Mary, my younger sister, and I would go to downtown Los Angeles to big Japanese American dances. We would meet these rowdy boys from the city. I was really attracted to them because they looked good and their background was more dangerous, more glamorous than ours. In Pasadena, kids were so straight, so clean-cut. We'd drive into LA just to see these guys who dressed like inner-city blacks. They just seemed cool and hip, strong, proud of themselves. Sometimes they would ask me to dance, and, if I said I was from Pasadena, they'd make a face because Pasadena was considered real square. We were from the sticks.

So we began to notice right away the groupings of Japanese. The ones from the city and from Gardena were definitely the most popular. It's funny because Mary and I made friends with some boys from Long Beach who would drive up to Sierra Madre and take us to parties in the San Fernando Valley, to Japanese Americans out there. All these JAs from the suburbs got to know each other. We were stuck with each other.

SK The section of poems under "War Stories" tends to draw more on your understanding of your ancestors' experiences. In what ways does history or the construction of history influence your poetry? For instance, on the issue of Japanese American internment, what does it mean to you? And does it mean something different to you or your generation than it did to your parents or your parents' parents?

AU I certainly think it meant something different. I don't pretend to speak for the Issei and Nisei because I was born after the camps. I'm presenting a Sansei point of view about the camp years. I remember my mother was once a little critical of Sansei movement people for talking so much about the camps and most of these people were never there. "What makes them authorities on the camps?" Also, I couldn't communicate with three of my grandparents, who spoke only Japanese. If my grandpa who spoke English were alive now, I'd be asking him so many questions about the camps.

My impressions of camp are just based on fragments, little things I'd hear from my mom or my dad, and what I've read. When I took U.S. history in the sixties, there would never be anything on the camps in our textbooks. In my twelfth-grade civics class, I felt compelled to say something, but then I ended up crying.

In my writing and my attempt to understand myself as a Sansei, I have tried to dig up some family history. What was it like for both of my grandmothers? What are the stories behind each grandparent's leaving Japan for America?

SK In that sense, in what ways does Asia enter your poetry? Is this just your construction of what Asia (or Japan) means to you as a Sansei?

AU I wish I knew more about Asia. Our folks didn't have us

Amy Uyematsu

do any of the cultural stuff: no Japanese-language school, no dance classes. We didn't learn origami, judo, all those things that many JAs do with their kids. I was ignorant of Japanese culture. I've tried to learn Japanese and read about things in the culture that interest me, but not nearly enough.

What surprises me is that I think something Japanese innately comes through my poems. Maybe this is something a psychologist or anthropologist knows more about. I've heard of concepts like collective consciousness or racial memory. Some of the poems I've written are from a Japanese sensibility and groundedness. I don't know if I'm just kidding myself—but sometimes I feel like I'm writing with an older knowledge, going back many generations, a knowledge that was somehow passed on despite my not speaking Japanese.

SK But, at the same time, being identified with Japan or Asia has also been a burden on Asian Americans in some ways. If you take the internment, that was based on the supposed link between Japanese Americans and the Japanese military. So why should addressing the question of our relationship to Asia be a starting point for us as Asian Americans?

AU I don't know if it's a starting point, but it is a point we continually have to address because you can't look at our experiences here without seeing how it hooks up with what's been happening in Japan, China, or wherever else in Asia. I was thinking about why there isn't a Japanese American literature or a Chinese American literature, why they aren't treated separately. America has always treated us by the way we look because, to whites, we're all one big hodgepodge of Asians. We get mixed up because of the racism toward yellow people, and, as a result, we have to continually respond on that basis. There's a continual interaction with Asia that affects people's attitudes here. For instance, it's really important for Asian American women to be aware of historical facts like the military presence in Asia, the major wars in Vietnam,

Korea, the Pacific front during World War II. Many American men have been stationed in Asia, where they developed views of Asian women as prostitutes, bar girls, waitresses, and maids. For me and most of the Sansei women I know, that has had an impact on the way American men treat us and often think of us, as servile sex objects.

SK A later section of your book titled "More War Stories" deals more with the wars and struggles of your lifetime. Obviously, for the Nisei, World War II was a huge watershed in their life, as was the Vietnam War for the Sansei. What were some of the images that you were digesting at that time? What were the thoughts going through your mind?

AU A lot of us, because we were trying to deal with domestic racism toward Asian Americans, could see the racism that the military was promoting in our American GIs toward the Vietnamese people as "gooks." And of course all those movements were occurring at the same time—the black power, brown, red, and yellow—simultaneously with the huge antiwar movement, so it's natural that a connection would be made. Then there were the experiences of Asian American GIs who fought in Vietnam and were afraid of being shot at from both sides. When they came back, some of them gravitated right away to the emerging Asian American movement to share their stories. Other experiences included joining big coalitions against the war, and often the white leadership in those coalitions didn't want to hear us as Asian Americans. It was very ironic because they would be protesting the war and its racism toward Vietnamese and yet here we were, Asian Americans right among them, and they would be very patronizing to us.

SK "The Emergence of Yellow Power in America" [1969] originally appeared in the activist newspaper *Gidra* and was later reprinted in *Roots,* one of the first movement publications, of which you were a coeditor. Recent authors have cited this essay to exemplify the spirit of the Asian American movement that formed in the late sixties and early seventies.

AU It's funny for me to hear this because that paper was the term paper assignment for my "Orientals in America" class, the first Asian American studies class I took. Yuji Ichioka taught it. I actually fulfilled two course requirements with that paper because I was also taking a sociology class on different ethnic groups. We were reading *Black Power in America* by Stokely Carmichael for that other class,[1] and I really got into that book. So I linked the two. I was inspired by what I was reading by these black power advocates, and that was the framework I used, trying to relate it to what I was just learning about Asian Americans. Maybe what was a little different about the paper was how I tried to use existing population data. Interesting things occurred because of that paper: I got hired by the Asian American Studies Center later that year.

I've never met Frank Chin personally, but he hated this little student paper. In 1970, he criticized it and talked about its "chick authoress." Basically, he was saying, "She's gotta become more Asian. She's just aping or imitating black power stuff, and she needs to be saying something more original." I can hear what he's saying to me. It was just a phase. I was just getting into all of this. Some kind of consciousness was awakening in me, and black power was the model I used to see how it related to our own movement. But I can see where he thought I was parroting black power. There was some evidence of that in the early Asian movement as well as in the Chicano and women's movements.

SK Was this around the time you first started writing poetry?

AU At the end of that term paper I appended three poems. I'm not sure what induced me to write them. I wasn't reading poetry, but the feelings were so strong. What's interesting to me is that the best poem here [pointing to the original copies] is the one I didn't want my name on because it said *fuck*. This poem was a protest against Asian men who go for white women and my trying to speak for "yellow womanhood." These got printed because Mike Murase, who was then on the *Gidra* staff, was one of the TAs for the class.

SK But what really caught on was "Yellow Power." . . .

AU After a while it just became kind of embarrassing for me. There was nothing else around, so people kept using my term paper. It got much bigger than it was ever intended. There was a newspaper called the *LA Free Press* that was well known in the late sixties—kind of an underground paper—that even printed the first part of "Yellow Power." That got me correspondence from black inmates in prison saying, "We're so happy to hear a Japanese who's talking about how racism is affecting her people." I also got a letter from [the actor] James Hong, saying he was glad to see something in the media about racism toward Asian Americans.

SK Were the emotions and views that went into the writing of the student paper similar to what emerged in these poems? Or was there a difference between the way you articulated through poems and through the essay form?

AU The paper was not enough to effectively convey what I was feeling. That's why I had to write these poems. I didn't consciously decide, "I want to write a poem," but there was so much internal turmoil and self-revelation that the poems just came.

SK So was poetry more expressive?

AU I think it was; at least it was more satisfying for me.

SK Did you continue to work on poetry from that time on?

Amy Uyematsu

AU I did, without telling anyone. I was writing off and on during the years I was active in different groups. The Asian American Student Alliance at UCLA. I was in the Storefront, which was interesting because we tried to be a multinational group in the Crenshaw area. We were trying to ally Asian Americans (mostly Japanese) with the blacks in that community. During that period, I was writing poems. I even remember submitting something anonymously to *Gidra* once and having it rejected.

Some of the poems I was writing at that time were very critical of what I thought was a negative climate in those early movement groups, a pressure for everybody to be correct. "You should say only certain things if you write a poem. It should serve the movement." Whatever that means. "The personal stuff, that's all bullshit." I was reading Marxist-Leninist works and Mao Tse-tung on the purpose of art. It was difficult trying to be creative and be spontaneous because of all this pressure and narrow thinking on what it meant to be revolutionary. I was writing but didn't show it to anybody.

SK So the era was in some ways liberating and in some ways limiting.

AU Yes, but, overall, it was liberating. I did a lot of my work with women's groups—study groups and Asian American women's classes—where we'd talk about the whole notion of the triple jeopardy for Third World women—the triple oppressions from race, sex, and class.

SK The poems in the middle section of your book, "Even the Dying Women," revolve around female subjects. How do issues of gender work their way into your poetry? In what ways has feminism influenced your consciousness?

AU The first book is very much on JA identity, but I have at least one and a half manuscripts worth of poems right now that are more gender related. Women's themes keep coming up, whereas the racially motivated work isn't occurring as much as before. Even in *30 Miles from J-Town* there are many pieces from a woman's point of view: that of an Issei grandmother, a Nisei mother, or mine—a Sansei mother.

I relate strongly to women in Third World countries, a theme that comes up in some of my poems as I connect back to my own sexuality, aging, raising a son. I've done a number of poems about old women. They play an important part in my poetry. Something keeps drawing me to old women, and I don't know if it's just a real love I have for my grandparents and the Issei pioneers or a deepening understanding of my own womanhood. In the mid-eighties, when I wrote these old woman poems, Chris, my son, and I went south to the Yucatan and visited the Chichén Itzá pyramids. Seeing Mayan women all along this remote highway to Chichén Itzá greatly affected me.

At that time in my life, I was separated. My marriage had failed. I was having trouble forming relationships with men and was celibate for around three years. I found myself drawn to tribal women who hadn't been affected that much by Western, modern culture, and it definitely got into the poems. I began to have this old woman visit in some of my dreams. I would write the dreams down and bring them back to the poetry group I worked with. Some of the people there suggested that she was a spiritual guide, an embodiment of my own changing consciousness. And, in the same period, I started writing father-daughter poems because I never had a close relationship with my father. I began to see how some of my difficulties at the time were linked to that.

SK Can you discuss some of your artistic influences?

AU I mainly like to read ethnic writers and poets. I don't have the time to read as many books as I'm interested in, but I'm able to handle poetry books because they're shorter, smaller. My favorites are poets of color or poets from Third

World countries. Among my favorites are Pablo Neruda from Chile, Rumi, also Li-Young Lee. Cathy Song, Lawson Inada, and many other Asian American poets. I also read Native American poets; one of my favorites right now is Linda Hogan. Among the African American women writers, there's Thylias Moss and Lucille Clifton. Chicano poets—Juan Felipe Herrera. So these are all very ethnic. If I had lots of time, if I could quit my job and go back to school, I would like to learn Japanese kanji just so I could read Chinese and Japanese poems, especially the early ones, because I'm really drawn to the picture symbols and their multiple meanings.

Other influences would be art. I've written a few poems based on Japanese woodblock prints. I love Japanese woodblock. And some of the Japanese artists who do calligraphy. Also the Mexican painters Diego Rivera and Frida Kahlo. Sometimes a painting will inspire a poem. And music—especially jazz, R&B [rhythm and blues], Motown.

SK So classical form and structure do not enter into your poetry?

AU That's not part of my formal background, though I think basic poetic elements are still present in my work. On the other hand, I have worked closely with writers like Momoko Iko and Zen poet Peter Levitt, who has taught me so much.

SK Would you like your work to be considered a part of "Asian American literature"? Do you ever feel confined by that label *Asian American poet* or *Asian American writer*?

AU I definitely would like to be included as an *Asian American writer,* but I would also like to be in the body of *contemporary American women poets* or just *contemporary U.S. poets.* But *Asian American writers* is my priority. As far as how it helps or hinders, I think the literary establishment is open to minority writers right now. I hope this is going to be a lasting thing and not just a trend. There have been times when

I've felt some publications included me just because they wanted a few people of color.

The reality is we're still dealing with a literary establishment that's run by affluent white males. Who are they to decide what is good Asian American literature? What's genuine? Even among Asian American writers and editors there are debates on who's authentic and who's not. There are a few places where I've submitted—Asian American journals or ethnic journals—where, if I didn't do something that was specifically on a racial theme, my work wouldn't get considered. And that doesn't feel right to me because those aren't the only things I write about. As a poet, I'm going to write about everything, and, to me, my being Japanese American is going to come through somehow in all the poems even though it may not hit you over the head. Why do only certain themes qualify as *Asian American literature?*

Another thing that came up in the publication of *30 Miles from J-Town:* I had included some poems in the manuscript about Native Americans, whom I have always felt strongly about. My own understanding of American racism goes back to the initial mistreatment and genocide of American Indians. I'm also drawn to their cultural beliefs and values. In my limited knowledge of Asian culture, I see many links. But the editors recommended omitting those poems about Native Americans, telling me, "Those poems aren't as strong." I wondered whether it was because they weren't just about Japanese Americans and whether the editors thought I was venturing into territory where I shouldn't be.

SK Do you have a favorite poem from *30 Miles from J-Town?*

AU There is one poem—it's not my favorite, but it's one I regard as very significant—called "Three Pulls of the Loom." Some poems write themselves, but this poem took a lot of hard work. Each of the three sections shows different aspects of being a Japanese American woman. The first section,

Amy Uyematsu

"Immigrant," is about both of my grandmothers and the conditions that brought them to this country. The second section, "Sisters," is about what it was like for Mary and me as young women of color in a country that promotes white women as the ideal. How do young girls deal with that? Do you take it out on each other sometimes? Do you take it out on Asian men and on yourself? The third section, "Maya," came out of the period when I saw the native women in Mexico and saw how much they'd survived and retained a strong sense of self; this has meant so much in my awareness of what Asian American women are.

sk The poems in "Sansei Line Dance" that open the book are about a lack of identity or wanting to be something else, feeling lost. Then the "War Stories" are about turmoil, racism, and discrimination. Does "Harvest" [the poem in the final section of the same name] represent a coming to terms with the discordance in your life?

au The poem "Harvest" is about my girlfriend's father Mr. Ikeda. He's a gardener, and I've always felt an affection toward nurserymen and gardeners because that's so much a part of Japanese American history in California, so much a part of who we are. There were many men (like my maternal grandfather) who didn't become gardeners until after the war, when they couldn't find other kinds of jobs. Mr. Ikeda could retire, but he doesn't. His refuge within downtown LA is this lush orchid garden in the back of his house. "Harvest" was written after I'd seen the orchid garden and was really moved by it. He explained how he names some of the loveliest flowers after his daughters.

In talking about this gardener, I also tried to create the sensual world to be found working with flowers and plants. This was written after we left North Hollywood. We had a big plum tree and Japanese garden in North Hollywood, but no yard or trees here in West LA. I needed to talk about plants and flowers in this poem. Now that's kind of Japanesey, isn't it? Maybe it's in my background more than I realize because my other grandfather was a nurseryman, my dad, too. To me, one of the strong points about the Japanese experience here is this love of plants and flowers that we've retained. We make good gardeners and farmers. We make good landscape artists. When my father's family was interned at Manzanar—I don't even know if experts on Manzanar will tell you about this— there was apparently a whole cherry blossom garden that grandpa had trucked in from his nursery and planted in camp soil. I've always been glad that we brought that love of nature and love of that kind of beauty from Japan.

SK What does it mean to you to be successful as a poet?

AU Different things come to mind. One, if I'm writing poems that strike a chord in some Asian Americans—"Yes, this happened to us, too"—that's one element of success because I want more of us writers to be able to do that for Asian Americans as a testimony to the fact that we were here, this is what we experience, this is the truth as we see it. It's gratifying when Nisei or Sansei come up to me at readings and tell me, "You put into words what I feel." Another element of success would be if I'm exposing people to Japanese American issues, or women's issues, or something that they haven't thought about before, and they're changed by it. Their consciousness is changed. Another area for me personally is getting validation from writers whose work I like. Or when a poem takes me on a journey that really surprises me or helps me become more aware. Lately, I'm experimenting much more with form and sound and feel good when that works. If I can write a poem that moves the reader or listener, changes them somehow or makes them feel something strongly at that moment and even later, that's part of being successful as a poet—an added bonus to the deep satisfaction I already get from creating the poem.

Amy Uyematsu

Note

1. Stokely Carmichael and Charles V. Hamilton, *Black Power: The Politics of Liberation in America*. New York: Random House, 1967.

Selected Works by Amy Uyematsu

"The Emergence of Yellow Power in America" (1969). In *Roots: An Asian American Reader,* ed. Amy Tachiki et al. Los Angeles: University of California, Los Angeles, Asian American Studies Center, 1971.

"Near Roscoe and Coldwater." In *The Open Boat: Poems from Asian America,* ed. Garrett Hongo. New York: Anchor/Doubleday, 1993.

30 Miles from J-Town. Brownsville, Oreg.: Story Line, 1992.

"Mother's Day Poem to Myself." *Bamboo Ridge* 63–64 (Summer–Fall 1994): 46.

"Did You Hear What Happened to Mo?" In *Grand Passion: Poets of Los Angeles and Beyond,* ed. Suzanne Lummis and Charles Webb. Los Angeles: Red Wind, 1995.

"Dreaming of Fire on the Night It Rained." *Blue Mesa Review* (1995): 75. This poem appears in an issue of *Blue Mesa* entitled "Approaching the Millenium."

"Fortune Cookie Blues." In *Letter to America: Contemporary American Poetry on Race,* ed. Jim Daniels. Detroit: Wayne State University Press, 1995.

"The Ten Million Flames of Los Angeles." *Flash-Bopp Magazine,* 1995, 4–5.

"To Women Who Sleep Alone." In *On a Bed of Rice: An Asian American Erotic Feast,* ed. Geraldine Kudaka. New York: Anchor/ Doubleday, 1995.

"The Crossing." In *Charming the Spirit Within,* ed. Marilyn Sewell. Boston: Beacon, 1996.

"The Small Particles Which Lodge in the Eye." *Solo* 1 (Spring 1996): 93–94.

"Because the Rhythm of the Ballad Depends on the Bass: Acoustics of a Too Rapid Heart." *Asian Pacific American Journal* 6, no. 1 (Spring–Summer 1997): 111–113.

Words Matter

"The Fold." *Zyzzyva* 13, no. 1 (Spring 1997): 122–123.

"An Interview with Sesshu Foster, Author of *City Terrace Field Manual.*" *DisOrient* (Los Angeles) 5 (1997): 70–77.

Nights of Fire, Nights of Rain. Ashland, Oreg.: Story Line, 1998.

"With a Calligrapher." *Crab Orchard Review* 3, no. 2 (Spring 1998): 206.

Amy Uyematsu

15

Li-Young Lee

Interview by

JAMES KYUNG-JIN LEE

Li-Young Lee grasps for what is seemingly palpable yet ultimately elusive—to "speak" to another. This struggle to communicate first begins with a conscious effort to listen. Lee
hears the voice of memory, a past that fuses the familial with
the political. His biography has become almost folkloric: son
of Chinese parents who lived through the political turmoil of
Sukarno's Indonesia, exiled to several other Asian countries
before arriving in the United States, where his father became
an evangelical minister for a small community in western
Pennsylvania. We see moments of this rich narrative of history
in both his books of poetry, *Rose* (1986) and *The City in Which
I Love You* (1990), and in his latest memoir, *The Winged Seed:
A Remembrance* (1995).

Yet, if Lee is trying to excavate the regions of memory, he
is also pushing the language of remembrance to its circum-
ference, its limit. In his memoir, he asks, "Love, what is
night?"—and we realize that all four words in that sentence
are incalculable, indeterminate, profoundly metaphysical, yet
resolutely material. It is this movement of language that gives

his writing both intensity and humility. In this sense, Lee is a theological writer, one who allows the stones of words to reverberate, in a lyrical, groping "narrative."

JKJL You're known as a poet; how did you feel writing this memoir in prose?

LYL It was hard for me because I wanted the book to be one person's thoughts during a single night, and the way I tried to reproduce that was by seeing if I could actually write the book and plumb the depths of consciousness in one night. It sounded so easy; it was foolishness or even stupidity on my part. It was impossible, actually. It took me three nights, and it had taken me five years of processing to be able to write it in that time. I wanted the book to have the feeling of a single movement, a single gesture, and within that single gesture to contain many smaller, nuanced, subtle ones. It was like taking a ball or a stone and throwing it—that single arch. And I didn't want to fabricate it, so I planned to write it in one night. My other difficulty was not believing in narrative. I'm suspicious of the ulterior manipulation that goes on in narrative. Prose writers, of course, would differ with me. I thought of the book as a lyric moment and didn't know how to sustain that for two hundred pages.

JKJL Your book engages in several extremely lyrical moments. Was it more difficult to reach that state of consciousness crafting in prose than it would have been in poetry?

LYL I wanted to transcend craft. I was interested in the possibility of actual human utterance without revision—that seemed like life to me. We can't revise anything we do in life; I wanted the book to have that kind of trajectory. I would revise by writing the whole book over again. I had to make it up as I went along. As I was writing the book, I was pitching into greater and greater commitment. I wasn't allowing

Li-Young Lee

myself to look back or look to plot. If there is a plot, it's accidental or coincidental. It's a bonus.

JKJL There's a connection between your search for the momentary human connection and the search for that voice that you discussed in your interview with Bill Moyers.[1]

LYL That voice isn't a fabricated, premade voice. I sometimes hear it if I'm in the right state of tension. But sometimes, if you listen too directly, that voice disappears. So it's a peripheral voice that you yield to. Poetry for me is that other voice. I wanted to write a long prose poem.

JKJL How do you feel about the book now that you've completed it?

LYL I'm unhappy that it's finished, and I'm a little exhausted from writing it over, and over, and over again. I look at my work—all the poems that I write, everything—as a failure of a kind of perfection that I was trying to reach.

JKJL Does this sense of trying to seek perfection have anything to do with the constant metaphors of flight that reverberate in your book? The bird, the winged seed, emerges several times in the narrative. Even the letter *r*, which you examine in a significant portion of the book, becomes something fleeting. Were you trying to work with language fleeing us?

LYL Yes, exactly. Not only language, but experience itself. It seems to me that all the metaphors—sowing, walking, flying—express my inability to touch a human being, really touch another human being, in this case, my wife lying there. If everything is constantly elusive—experience itself, consciousness, language, poetry—then I never know what the work is. In a way, the book keeps exceeding me, language keeps exceeding me, and I keep trying to catch up with it. A lot of times there is slippage in the language. I'm real excited when that happens.

JKJL Some of the passages in the book became very difficult and challenging. I realized I'm not to let the narrative work as it goes. At certain moments I felt that you were trying to let the meaning escape. And chasing it.

LYL As I was wording a record of actual thinking, the meaning actually would escape. Thinking and thought are two different things. A thought is encapsulated and already dead. It's a noun. Thinking is a verb that means that it's in action, and I wanted to capture the action of thinking. That's why sometimes it defies the way we understand meaning in conventional terms. I'm hoping, too, that, if the book is read out loud, it speaks to the nonrational part of our consciousness. I'm interested in other forms of intelligence that inhabit us or that we're ruled by. Conscious thinking is maybe 10 percent of the way we actually exist in the world. I wanted to get into that darker 90 percent, the way the mind actually works, the way it doubles back on itself, the way it eludes itself.

JKJL Psychoanalysis talks about this kind of unconscious that we're unable to reach but that momentarily emerges. It's something that we forget but that comes back to us in our dreams. In these moments, this other voice speaks to us.

LYL It occurred to me as I was writing the book that it's possible for a sentence to exist without words, that a sentence is a rhythmic frequency and words are like birds that come to perch along that sentence. We see the birds. I wanted to strip the sentences just to hear the rhythmic frequency.

JKJL Grammar and syntax.

LYL Yeah, if we read it out loud, we can hear the beauty and rhythm of the sentence. That's a very old idea. Robert Frost talked about that. Sound is a lot more important to me than sense.

JKJL You're focusing on the action of thinking rather than

Li-Young Lee

the state of thought. Near the end of the book, you mention the importance of dying not as death. It seemed that, as the narrative was coming to a close, it was important to look at the movement of dying.

LYL It was important to capture flux. I can't stop thinking about love and death; no other issues interest me. Political issues don't interest me. Romantic love interests me only slightly. More than anything, a kind of universal love—divine love—and death and dying are what interest me. The momentum of dying and the act of making art are opposing forces. Making art opposes dying, but at the same time it gets all its energy from this downward momentum, this art into the abyss that all of us are a part of, that's the tension we feel in art that we enjoy.

JKJL You subtitled your book as a remembrance, and I'm wondering, What are you trying to remember? There is a constant indication of your wife in the book. Was it a personal remembrance for her?

LYL It was a personal thing to me. It seemed I was unable to communicate to any human being at all. All my life, I used to attribute it to being an immigrant. The things that are closest to me and dearest to me defy language. It seems to be some sort of ghastly joke. And while writing the book I thought, Well, let me address that directly—that inability to communicate with somebody I love very much, somebody very close to me, physically and emotionally. Why can't I communicate? Part of it is because language itself is both a vehicle of communication and yet an obstacle to communication. And the other thing is my feelings are somehow outsized. They seem to me frequently larger than myself, overwhelming. In that way, they seem to defy language.

JKJL There were moments in the narrative when the language became so unconventional that it forced me as a reader to move to a different realm. Could you discuss the way in which you negotiated the historical past, your past, with passages that move into moments outside those narratives of history?

LYL I'm a historical being and yet an entirely nonhistorical being. I'm both a person who was born and will die and **275** someone who was never born and will never die. I wanted the book to have that simultaneity of both the historical and the nonhistorical, the personal and the impersonal, the spiritual and the very human narrative. The lyric moment for me is exactly that, a moment in which all of who we are is simultaneously true—the contradictions, the paradoxes, the opposites are simultaneously negotiated. In other words, the book was impossible for me to write. And I liked the task because it was impossible. I might add, too, that the reason I'm suspicious of narratives is I've noticed that we can't be free of stereotypes as long as we're thinking with our rational mind. So it was important for me to take a breath and then go under, the way one goes under water, to try to escape all stereotypical views of what an Asian is in America, what an immigrant is, what a man is, what a human being is. The only way I could escape those stereotypes was to defy my own rational thinking.

JKJL Do you think it's possible to escape these narratives that are imposed on us?

LYL I don't know if it's possible or not, but it's important for me to live in a state of "nobodyhood." The culture we live in offers or imposes versions of "somebodyhoods" that are really shallow and false. The car we drive—that's a version of "somebodyhood." The woman or man we take to a party, who we marry, what shoes we have on—those are all really cheap, shabby, insufficient versions of "somebodyhood." The titles we earn, the awards we win. Those are all obstacles to the real gift of living—this consciousness that we have been gifted with momentarily. If I can attain a state of "nobody-hood," which is the same thing as the state of "everybody-hood," that's much richer and more full of potential than some false, made-up, Hollywood magazine, university, or cultural version of "somebodyhood." I don't know if that's possible, but that's where I'm headed. And so it was important in writing this book to remember that I was writing a personal history, but I also wanted to reach a detached voice. In a way, I was cutting my right hand off and letting it write by itself. Almost like automatic writing, but not quite.

JKJL Your story is grounded in your family. Your father looms over your poetry as well as over *The Winged Seed*. How do you negotiate this quest for "nobodyhood" with your familial history?

LYL Words have personal and impersonal connotations, and sometimes, if we don't hear the impersonal connotations, then a word loses its reverberation. The word *father* itself has personal connotations, yet, when I say the word, I can't help but hear impersonal connotations. All my work has been a struggle with the personal and the impersonal.

JKJL You mentioned before that you were trying to get beyond this father figure.

LYL It was a conscious effort, but, since that time, I've been a little more humble about it. I believe that each of us is given one sentence at birth and that we spend the rest of our life trying to read that sentence and make sense of it. We write hundreds of poems, and many books and paragraphs and lines, in order to understand that one sentence. It isn't a matter of switching subjects; it's yielding to whatever forces, whatever furies, sadnesses, whatever darknesses inhabit us.

JKJL There's a passage in the Book of Revelation in which everyone is given a stone that constitutes who they are. It's something that's given to you in a certain sense by God.

Words Matter

LYL Martin Buber called it *the stone of witness.* Yeah, it's that one stone. It was a useful arrogance to think I could switch stones or get beyond that stone. I've gotten humbler—trafficking with the muse really teaches you humility.

JKJL Your father was a minister. Do you still cherish the religion that your father taught you?

LYL Very much so. The whole enterprise of writing for me is spiritual. I'm at a point in my life where what's important is to discover a naked relationship between me and the greater self or the true self. In the Bhagavad Gita, they call it *the self.* They mean, of course, the godhead. The entrapments of Christianity or Buddhism or Hinduism—those are just entrapments—they're like crusts that I need to shed to get to the real kernel of truth. I think Christ was doing that in the New Testament. It's this naked relationship between me and the godhead, to become somehow united with the godhead. That has become absolutely necessary. I'm on the path, I hope, through meditation and prayer, practicing a certain way of life, a certain way of writing. The whole enterprise of writing for me is spiritual. My soul is at stake. I have this secret wish: I write to be a perfect conduit for a greater voice, and it means, of course, that I have to quit my own rational thought because real contact with the godhead defies rational thinking. It doesn't make sense in the world we live in, and yet it is the only refuge for me, not only because of my background, because my father believed it, but because it seems that any other refuge is willful foolishness. That's why this idea of "nobodyhood" is so important for me—if I can empty myself of my own willfulness, my own ideas, I'll make room for a greater selfhood to abide in me.

JKJL Are you still drawn to your father's evangelicalism?

LYL Every time I think I'm free of paradigms, I discover another one that was already installed. I'm trying to live a life

Li-Young Lee

without paradigms. And it seems to me that life moves at such a pace that, before we know it, we've already done something to jeopardize the well-being of ourselves and of the people around us. So, by the time I'm thinking, "Thou shalt not," the situation is over, and I'm sitting there thinking I should not have. It's important to be more fluid and more immediate. I'm trying to get beyond analytic thought. I'm trying to have my head right up against the nub of living. Life is happening to us so fast that I have to find a way in which I'm not submitting to it but yielding. I'm not even reacting, but I'm involved in a perfect, if possible, dance with it.

JKJL But people do respond to your work and categorize you, put you in a paradigm. Your name comes up frequently as representative of Asian diasporic literature. I was wondering, to what extent would you allow yourself to be classified as such?

LYL I never thought of myself that way. I've always stupidly thought that I was just writing poems, saying things that were closest to my heart, cocking my ear to hear what it was that I needed to say. That classification can bring attention to Asian American writers who are overlooked because they're Asian American. But, ultimately, if we're not careful, it can be a prison because, in America, we have poets and then we have Asian American poets. That's such bullshit. When I'm writing, I'm trying to stand neck and neck with Whitman and Melville, or, for that matter, the utterances of Christ in the New Testament, or the Epistles of Paul. Those are as important to me as and perhaps even more influential than Asian American writers. It's lucky that we live in a time where Asian writers are getting that kind of attention, but, in the end, it's not about that. It's something much more immediate, something much more close and necessary.

JKJL Would this search for immediacy even go beyond family?

LYL Oh, yes, yes. Sometimes I'm not even talking to a human being. I feel as if my ambition is to speak to God, to find a human utterance that makes sense to my God. Half the things I'm saying tonight I realize will sound lunatic to most people. And yet, when I write, I am speaking to a human "other" that is in everybody, not a specific somebody—a kind of greater everybody.

JKJL At the same time, you talk in your work about your family and their history of constant movement and exile. That's significant in thinking about what constitutes the writing of Asian Americans.

LYL Yeah, but that applies to the children of Israel, too. I always thought that trying to find an earthly home was a human condition. It is arrogant of the dominant culture to think it's not part of a diaspora. My hope is that somebody who isn't Asian American can read it and say, Well, I feel that homeless, too. The difficulty is that the earth is not my home, and that's why I feel this schism. It's so important for an artist of any kind *not* to identify with a group. You know what I mean?

JKJL And transgress those borders. . . .

LYL It's about transgression. So if the term *Asian American* empowers us, fine. But the minute it starts making us smaller than we are. . . . They're going to have to deal with Maxine Hong Kingston the way they deal with Virginia Woolf or any other major writer. They're not going to be able to sweep her into a little ghetto. She has already exceeded those boundaries. They're going to have to deal with her as an equal. In this way, I'm speaking to the Anglo community. To the Asian American community, I would say, "Yes, she's one of us!" But, to the Anglo community, I would say, "Don't try to ghettoize us," because the writers who are among us have already equaled and surpassed many of the Anglo writers they send up the slag.

Li-Young Lee

JKJL What is driving you now?

LYL My first love is poetry, and I'm trying to find a way to write sacred poetry, poetry that sends the reader to a sacred place or calls to a sacred place inside the reader. I don't know how to do that. That's my wish. That's what I meditate on and hope for.

Note

1. Bill Moyers, *The Language of Life: A Festival of Poets,* ed. James Haba (New York: Doubleday, 1995), 257–269.

Selected Works by Li-Young Lee

Rose. Brockport, N.Y.: BOA, 1986.

"The City in Which I Love You." *Grand Street* 9, no. 4 (Summer 1990): 103–109. Reprinted as *The City in Which I Love You* (Brockport, N.Y.: BOA, 1990).

"The Cleaving" and "The Waiting." *TriQuarterly* 77 (Winter 1990): 254–266.

"This Hour and What Is Dead" and "The Sacrifice." *Ploughshares* 16, no. 4 (Winter 1990): 60–63.

"This Room and Everything in It." *American Poetry Review* 19, no. 3 (May–June 1990): 38.

"The Cleaving," "The Gift," "I Ask My Mother to Sing," and "This Room and Everything in It." In *The Open Boat: Poems from Asian America,* ed. Garrett Hongo. New York: Anchor/Doubleday, 1993.

"Eating Alone," "Eating Together," "The Gift," "Mnemonic," "Persimmons," and "This Room and Everything in It." In *The Norton Anthology of American Literature,* 4th ed., vol. 2, ed. Nina Baym et al. New York: Norton, 1994.

The Winged Seed: A Remembrance. New York: Simon & Schuster, 1995.

"I'm on the side of literature"

16

Wendy Law-Yone

Interview by

NANCY YOO AND TAMARA HO

Born in Burma (now called Myanmar) at the end of almost a century of British colonialism, Wendy Law-Yone is an American author of Asian descent who conveys a particularly postcolonial and polyglot sensibility in her writing. Her father, Edward M. Law-Yone, was a notable figure of Burmese politics and letters who founded and published *The Nation,* the premier English-language newspaper of fifties Burma. He was later imprisoned by the government and eventually exiled for his political views and affiliations. His passions for writing, political critique, and resistance to the repressive, postcolonial Burmese regime find new form in Law-Yone's writing. At age twenty, when she tried to leave the country herself, Law-Yone was arrested and detained by the government, an experience she details in her short story "The Year of the Pigeon" (1994). After living in various parts of Southeast Asia for a number of years, she came to the United States in 1973, obtaining her B.A. in Florida and then moving to Washington, D.C., where she currently lives.

Law-Yone's memories of Burma, her experiences of growing up under a totalitarian government and emigrating to the States, surface as thematic concerns in her work. Her writing, however, is distinctive for its focus on what Law-Yone calls "stories of failure." Her novels contest the usual "success story" trajectory of American literature, just as her protagonists stubbornly contest traditional Western and Asian cultural expectations both at "home" and in their travels. Written from the perspective of a Burmese girl emigrating to the United States, Law-Yone's first novel, *The Coffin Tree* (1983), received considerable critical acclaim for its eloquent representation of exile, alienation, and madness. Her second novel, *Irrawaddy Tango* (1993), which was nominated for the Irish Times Literary Prize in 1995, deals with similar themes, although the plot and protagonist differ radically from those of her first book.

Like many other Asian American and postcolonial writings, Law-Yone's works critique official versions of history from the perspective of the forgotten and the oppressed. The postcolonial/emigrant storyteller claims cultural memory as her own property and path to power and resolution. Often narrated through the position of a marginalized Asian woman emigrant/exile, Law-Yone's works attempt to undermine the social hierarchies enforced by dominant, male-centered versions of history. Ultimately, Law-Yone's protagonists, like she herself, are survivors, not only of a troubled history in Asia, but also of an American system that attempts to confine, define, or limit their individuality and agency.

NY Tell us something about your genesis as a writer.

WLY My career in letters began early, in Rangoon, Burma, where I grew up. It was launched by an illiterate maid. She was a great flirt who attracted suitors, some of whom declared themselves in letters. Since she couldn't read, I became her personal reader; later, I became her personal writer. I can't remember how old I was when this began, but answering her letters was the first memory I have of writing something important. I mean, not just writing words, but shaping thoughts, making statements. The sense of importance came from feeling needed, useful, powerful, but also from seeing that writing had real consequences, actually made things happen.

NY Was there ever a time when you actually sat down and thought, "I'm going to be a writer?"

WLY I do that every morning. And every night. But to answer your question another way: No, there wasn't that single illuminating moment when I decided to become a writer. I never thought it would be the one thing I'd focus on in my adult life. There were many other things I wanted to do. I wanted to be a concert pianist for a time. Had my father not been arrested, I would have gone abroad to study music. I once won a scholarship to the State Conservatory in what was then Leningrad. If I'd taken that road, who knows? I might still be in Russia now, writing Russian novels instead of just reading them.

NY Did your family play any particular role in your writing?

WLY Families play a role in everything, don't they? Blindfolded, they can put a finger on your most sensitive nerve. There's a medical term: *insulted nerve.* They go on insulting that nerve in you. It's also known as *family love.* It can drive a person to write.

~ My family saw me as secretive. Given all that sub-rosa letter writing, I guess I had an early start. But secrecy was important for me on other fronts, too. Ours was a large family— three boys, three girls, assorted relatives. In a big household, one has to fight for privacy, and privacy rights require secrecy. It became a family sport to uncover my secrets. I remember an uproarious game of tag enjoyed at my expense. One of my relatives had found an essay I'd written. It was my reaction to being found out that set off the fun. I should have pretended indifference—instead I panicked. My tormentors ran around the house, reading out loud, in relays, from that incriminating page. I managed to snatch it out of their hands, to run and hide it once or twice, but somehow it was always found and redisplayed. It was a vapid little essay called "A Rainy Day," a school assignment I'd dashed off expecting no one to see it but the dullard of a teacher who'd assigned it.

This incident impressed on me the importance of never assuming that what you write will go unread. It gave me a taste of accountability vis-à-vis the written word. I owe that to my family—that and my lingering inability to describe a rainy day.

NY Your father was a newspaper publisher while you were growing up. What influence did he have on your development as a writer?

WLY The greatest debt probably is due to my father. The newspaper he founded and published, *The Nation*, was the leading English-language daily in Rangoon. Aside from the pervasive influence of the newspaper business on the everyday life of our family, he imparted to us—to me anyway—a sense of constant and utter involvement with language. As a child, it seemed to me that, if he wasn't talking, he was writing. Even when not actually *at* his old Smith Corona, hammering out his copy at breakneck, two-fingered speed, he was writing all the time. It was literally scribble, scribble, scribble. He had a habit of writing with his forefinger on any surface close to hand: on his lap, a table top, the arm of a chair, the arm of a child. Sometimes, he'd be smiling to himself, quite pleased with a thought, a turn of phrase he'd just scribbled.

My father's love of the written word was surpassed only by his love of the spoken. When not writing, he was talking. Or thinking about talking, preparing his next story, gearing up for an argument, waiting to deliver his next opinion. He was always playing to an audience. He did pause to give others the chance to talk, but then he was not so much listening as regrouping, rehearsing his next story or pronouncement. He had the storyteller's gifts: the sense of drama, the absolute confidence in the importance of his story. He made language seem delectable. He would introduce, in the course of conversation, a word or phrase he was taken by—introduce it in a proud, almost proprietary way, as if he had personally discovered it. Sometimes he rolled the word around in his mouth, tasting it, savoring it. I don't know why such unkind things are said about people who move their lips while reading. My father did it all the time, even making sibilant sounds now and then, the better to digest certain words. I mouth my words when I read, too, although I try to keep it silent, at least in public places.

I've often wondered whether my father's sense of discovery and pride of language didn't come from growing up in a remote region of northern Burma, where reading and writing were still something of a luxury, a privilege earned only by effort and dedication. His own father, a native of Yunnan Province in neighboring China, was determined that his son be educated at the best school—which, at that time, in that part of the world, was a Christian Brothers school in Mandalay. The remarkable thing was that my father began learning English only then, at age fourteen or so. By the time he graduated, he had won the governor's gold medal in English— quite a feat, considering the high standard of English in those days, when Burma was still a British colony. But coming to the language late gave him a special appreciation of it, I think—an appreciation I share since I, too, came to the English language late, in a way.

I was born in 1947, one year before Burma won independence from almost a century of British rule, so, although my father's generation was well schooled in English, I grew up in the period of nationalism when English was no longer the official language. In schools, it was devalued, taught more as a second language or by default, that is, restricted to subjects where translations of standard texts into Burmese did not yet exist—or were inadequate. So, while I grew up speaking English, I was not *schooled* in it, did not feel confident about my grounding; and, even now, after some twenty-five years in an English-speaking country, the sense of foreignness, of not being completely at home in the language, is still with me. Looking back, I see that, as a young adult in Burma, learning more and more about the use of English, trying to express myself in it, I was learning only to imitate it. I had to wait a long time, until I was actually living—and writing for a living—in America, before I could learn to use it *inventively*.

NY Were your parents always concerned about your education?

WLY My parents were not overinvolved in my education; in fact, they were hardly involved at all. My father was seldom at home because he was caught up in his work; my mother wasn't really that concerned with my day-to-day progress at school. But the importance of doing well was clear to all of us. It was understood. My father in particular minced no words when it came to mediocre marks. I remember one of his pronouncements on seeing in my report card one or two Bs among mostly As: "Only fools get Bs." He talked like that—brutal talk by today's standards, but all of us learned to laugh at his excesses. We had to. On hearing that one of my brothers had flunked a difficult exam in med school twice in a row, he sniffed in contempt and said, "Damned fool's failed again." It became a family joke to say, "Damned fool's failed again," whenever anyone screwed up. My mother was less judgmental in matters academic, but in her own way she was as exacting—and as disapproving of underachievement.

NY Tell us something about the writers who have impressed or influenced you.

WLY Naturally I was drawn to writers for whom English was not their native tongue. Joseph Conrad was a great model. I wanted to use large words just so. I was fascinated by multisyllabic words, the way they looked on the page, how they sounded, where you put the accent. In my early stages of literacy, words were like a puzzle, a game. I had a good memory and flaunted the knack of remembering spellings and pronunciations others couldn't remember. I was proud of this talent and never lost an opportunity to show it off.

As a child I read very little—little that stands out anyway. What I did read I had a way of taking out of context, remembering for the wrong reasons. I happened to read *Catcher in the Rye* when I was quite young, and the thing that struck me was the writer's bluntness in talking about someone with his thumb up his nose—the kind of detail I had not previously encountered in my usual reading fare, which consisted mostly of English schoolgirl adventures, Nancy Drew mysteries, and the bland poetry of textbook anthologies that came our way.

I seemed to "get" only bits and pieces of things I read until I was sixteen. Then suddenly I read books in a different way, not just for words and isolated thoughts, but for interconnected ideas and feelings. At one stage of my haphazard sampling of English literature I read a few issues of *Encounter*, the British literary journal. Here I came across short stories, essays, and analyses of literary issues the sources of which were unfamiliar to me. There was no earthly reason for me to be interested in such arcane intellectual subjects and debates—often involving Russian writers like Sinyavsky and Daniel, if I remember correctly. But, for reasons I cannot now explain, I felt drawn into the world of ideas, as if I had a stake in the outcome of those elegantly reasoned arguments. All this without a clue to the backdrop of the subjects in questions. I just liked participating in complicated ideas and their expression.

From there I went on to read Sartre, Camus, Simone de Beauvoir—more head-scratching stuff I somehow enjoyed

Wendy Law-Yone

without understanding. Then I studied German; and, myste-
riously, almost instantly, I felt an affinity with the language, a
language in which the poetic and the concrete came together
in ways that made perfect sense to me. Since German, then,
was my first *literary* language—the language in which I first
began to read seriously and then to write—it affected the way
I expressed myself in English for some time to come. My first
grown-up poems were written in German. One of the large
German publishing houses wanted to publish them, but they
never did see print because I failed to produce the additional
poems necessary to complete the volume. You have to be seventeen, I guess, to possess the gall to write poetry in a foreign
language. But this was an extraordinary moment in my mental and creative life; it was like speaking in tongues all of a sudden. I'll never understand how it happened, exactly.

NY So English is actually the third language in which you
became literate. How did you come to your passion for
German in Rangoon of all places?

WLY It was pure accident, a happy outcome to a most
unhappy time in my life. I had just finished high school and
was on my way to study music at Mills College in Oakland
when my father was jailed as a political prisoner. This was
1963, a year after the coup that brought the new military junta
into power. The junta was still conducting mass arrests, and
my father was among those thrown into prison without
charges or trial. He was in jail for five years. During that time,
we never saw him once. As members of his family—as relatives of a political suspect in a police state—we were given the
usual treatment. We were watched, our telephones were
tapped, and I for one was denied entry to the university simply because I was my father's daughter. Trapped in Rangoon
with no opportunities for study and no prospects for the kind
of education I craved, I was bored and desperate. Then I discovered the Foreign Language Institute, where someone I

knew was taking an intensive course. The German professors allowed me to attend classes unofficially, so every weekday for the next academic year I ended up studying German for six hours a day.

NY Are there any particular German writers whom you admire?

WLY Reading Kafka for the first time was unforgettable because the world he described was so similar to the one I was experiencing in Rangoon—the dark, somber world of the police state with its backdrop of farce. A world at once ridiculous and awful. And everything so arbitrary, so without rhyme or reason, it didn't matter what you did. The guilt of it! The nightmarish sense that you, the persecuted, are somehow to blame for the otherwise inexplicable conditions—along with the helplessness in the face of arbitrary rule (of government or fate)—really spoke to me.

In addition, I loved Kafka's style. The irony and slyness in every sentence was sheer delight. I was affected on so many levels that for a long time I thought I could claim a special insight into his work. Then I read a critic who pointed out that it was a common experience for readers of Kafka to feel uniquely qualified to enter his world.

NY How did your family cope during your father's time in jail? Did your mother have a source of income to support such a large family as yours?

WLY She had no income other than the proceeds from what my father had made from his newspaper, which must have been substantial since there was no change in our standard of living—at least as far as I could tell—all the time he was in jail. But bear in mind that a high standard of living in a country like Burma is different from what you might imagine among the wealthy in, say, other developing countries—like parts of Latin America—where the disparities between the rich and

Wendy Law-Yone

the poor are greater. We were well-off before my father was arrested and remained well-off during his imprisonment—we had the same number of servants, the same number of cars. The deprivation was more psychological than material.

NY Your father's newspaper was shut down, too?

WLY Yes. It was allowed to run for maybe close to a year, and then it was shut down.

NY Can you tell me about your experience of coming to America? You have such a dark vision of America in your novels, and, as you say in *The Coffin Tree,* there is a sudden draining of color when the character arrives in America. Is this related to your own experiences?

WLY I had a fairly easy time, compared to what a great many immigrants have to suffer. I had the language; and some of my family were already here. But the shock we've all felt—the jolt we've had in common—is that clash between the expected and the actual. In the imagination of most would-be immigrants, America occupies a very special dimension. The expectations are enormous—and full of distortions. Going to America is not just going to another country but the end of one existence and the beginning of another. America has something of an aura of the hereafter. I've always liked that line in Dostoyevsky's *Crime and Punishment* where, before killing himself, a character says, "I'm going to America."

What I have discovered, though, from the many stories I've collected about immigrants is a stubborn unwillingness to express disappointments in this great idyll, this fantasy land. No matter what disasters befall them, what hardships they meet, they're reluctant—or maybe just scared—to admit disillusionment. Most immigrants I've met put a touchingly good front on things. "Well, yes," they'll say about their troubles in America, "my nose has fallen off, my arms have been cut off, but I'm glad I came here." It never fails to amaze me how much people are willing to bear just to be in America.

NY   Certainly, you can see the negative representation of America in your novels. Why this total debunking of the American dream?

WLY   I like to focus on stories about failure. Success isn't nearly as interesting to me. But the particular ways in which people—especially newcomers—fail in America is something I find worthwhile exploring. In my second novel, for example, Tango, the heroine, starts out with a lot of promise—a lot of spunk and verve—and ends up as a nobody in America. Readers have asked me how this is possible—how someone like her can become such a nonentity. My answer is to point out how Tango realizes that, in order to become American in a "successful" way, she is expected to open herself up to the process of healing that people in this country are so obsessed with. The obsession with sharing pain is widespread in America in every sense of the word: If pain is spread around and shared, then everyone is magically healed. This is a quintessentially American belief.

Tango realizes in some way that, in order to hold on to what is truest and most authentic about her, she must not go that route. She has to remain true to her past by hanging on to it in all its shameful, awful aspects. She fears in some indefinable way that healing will mean becoming something else. So she remains quite perverse and bloody minded in her approach to Americanization. She is not a successful immigrant in the generally understood sense. She does not become a CEO. But holding on to the painful past allows her, some twenty-five years later, to return to her homeland and seek—let's call it *major restitution*.

NY   Which brings me to the whole business of insanity in your novels and how it's related, particularly in *The Coffin Tree*, to displacement.

Wendy Law-Yone

WLY A natural outcome of displacement is that one's reality changes. In *The Coffin Tree*, the characters' lives in the old country had run along a groove cut by habit and tradition. Suddenly to be thrown out of this groove, to be cast into a world without the old markers, the old protections, can alter one's reality in the most profound way. Everything is ambiguous, everything is open to misinterpretation—as in a state of insanity.

NY Tell me more about your fascination with madness. In your books you're concerned with characters who are either schizophrenic [*The Coffin Tree*] or megalomaniac [*Irrawaddy Tango*].

WLY One of my brothers is a psychiatrist. At one point during his medical residency in Rangoon he worked at what we then called the lunatic asylum. The stories he brought home were staggering. The appalling conditions aside, the characters he described—their bizarre behaviors—were at a certain level enviable to me. Maybe this sense came from living in a culture that was otherwise so sensible, so polite, so restrained. Outrageous behavior seemed possible only if one was crazy—or in some unassailable position of power. Tyrants and lunatics alone, it seemed, had the license to vent themselves so flamboyantly. I came to associate madness with power. The irrationality of power, the power of irrationality.

NY How do you begin shaping your books?

WLY I can't remember so clearly any more about the genesis of *The Coffin Tree*. What I do remember with both *The Coffin Tree* and *Irrawaddy Tango* is that in the germ of each novel was a *feeling* that strained for expression. The challenge in the early stages was to find a story to fit the feeling. The feeling with *The Coffin Tree* was one of sadness and loss. With *Irrawaddy Tango* it was rage.

NY When did you start writing your first novel? Was it after you came to America?

WLY Actually, before. And after. I remember starting something in Kuala Lumpur, where I was living between 1970 and 1972. I wrote a little story about the brutal treatment of a madman, a basically harmless character. It was a bit of nothing as it stood then, but it got enclosed in another, bigger story that grew over time. I guess I knew I was writing a book, but the story kept changing in so many ways. Every passing year brought new opinions, new influences that clamored for inclusion. Finally, I had to put an end arbitrarily to this never-ending effort and say, "That's it. I'm not doing anymore." The result was my first novel, *The Coffin Tree*.

Books suffer from being dragged out over too long a time. You'd think I had learned my lesson. But along comes my second novel—and what do I do but the same old thing.

NY How long did it take to write?

WLY Ten years from start to finish for each book.

NY How comfortable are you with the label *Asian American writer*?

WLY There's no getting away from it, is there? I'm Asian, I'm American, and I'm a writer. You can't fight labels, anyway. They're part of the convenience culture. People want quick ways to classify and identify; it makes the sorting of information and opinion easier. Labels help them accept or reject things, persons, ideas, with a minimum of thought. The convenience is not for the labeled, obviously. No one appreciates being arbitrarily, unfairly, or inaccurately named. Everyone prefers to be unique.

NY Do you feel limited or empowered by such a moniker?

WLY I wish I were indifferent to labels, but genuine indiffer-

Wendy Law-Yone

ence is difficult to achieve. After all, the person who refuses to wear a shirt with a little polo player or an alligator on it cares as much about the label as someone who buys the shirt for that emblem. If I were truly emancipated, I wouldn't care one way or another about having a little Asian American polo player on my shirt—or next to the ISBN numbers on my books. I care enough not to want it.

NY But would you say that there are any particular obstacles or opportunities for an Asian American writer?

WLY I'm not sure what you mean by *obstacles or opportunities*. Obstacles to what? Self-expression? Getting published? Opportunities for what? Fame and fortune? Critical success? The life of a writer is one unending obstacle course; I don't know if being an Asian American writer substantially changes that course. When younger writers ask me about the prospects or profitability in writing, my heart sinks. Writing is not a career choice. You write because you have no choice.

NY What kind of audiences do you have in mind when you write?

WLY The audience I have uppermost in mind while writing is the page. I mean this literally and sincerely. Nothing matters to me in the act of writing save the preoccupation over the best word I can put on the page. It's the only way I know how to write: word by word, then phrase by phrase, till it looks right, sounds right—not to any phantom audience, but right there in front of me, on the page, where the real stage is.

NY Do you feel split between the so-called mainstream and ethnic audiences? What kind of response have you got from either community?

WLY I can't imagine how one writes with concepts like *mainstream* or *ethnic*. Nor would I know how to codify the responses to my writing—to keep track of which reactions came out of which community. The reactions to my books have been as varied as the people who read them. I can't even speak for one specific community—my compatriots, the Burmese. I honestly don't know whether a Burmese reader gets more out of my novels than a native-born American. Obviously, the former will have a keener appreciation of certain aspects than someone who has never been to Burma. Nonetheless, I hope the average American (whatever that means) will find other aspects to enjoy or recognize. That's the beauty of literature. It isn't beholden to any special interest group.

Are the responses encouraging or disappointing? I suppose they must be encouraging. I don't believe I'd be dedicated enough to keep on working in the face of sustained disappointment.

NY Do you feel you have a fairly tough ego?

WLY The strength of the ego in relation to the work I do is critical in more ways than one. If we are talking about the ego in its popular meaning, as a self-confidence, a certain invulnerability to the slings and arrows of criticism, I'd have to rate my ego as average: I love approval and feel prickly about criticism, no matter how "helpful." But one's ego gets tougher with time and maturity. When you begin to see success and failure for what they are—just other people's opinion in both cases—that's when you start to rely on your own opinion as the standard, not on the dictates of others.

There's another sense in which the ego, I think, serves an important function in my work—that is the psychospiritual sense of the ego as an individual, a self that believes in its uniqueness, in the importance of its own judgments and assessments, hopes and fears, likes and dislikes, rights and freedoms. The ego in the Western sense, in other words. In much of the East, by contrast, the ideal is to be *rid* of the ego, of this individuation that demands a finding of one's center in the pursuit of authenticity. As Joseph Campbell has pointed out, the freedom we think of in the West, the freedom of an individual to be what he wants to be, do what he wants to do, means in the East the freedom *from* impulse. This fundamental difference is reflected in the way artists fulfill their roles in Western and Eastern countries. The role of the artist in the East is not to question and challenge the nature of reality but to *reconcile* society with reality. Self-expression in the Western sense is not the task of the artist in the East. Rather it is affirmation, repetition, the subjugation of the ego's very desires and ambitions that preoccupy those in the West.

This is a labored way of saying that I hope my ego is tough in both senses of the word—that I am not only confident about my task as a writer but committed, despite my roots in the East, to the task of the ego in the Western sense.

NY Are there invisible censors that interfere with your work?

WLY The censors—both invisible and apparent—are all too present in any writer's life. The apparent ones are sometimes easier to take on. In totalitarian regimes, for example, state censorship is a moral challenge that any self-respecting artist expects to undertake. It may even be the charge, the catalyst, that produces the kind of ambiguity and complexity we admire in the works of Russians and Eastern Europeans writing under communism, say. Institutional censorship—whether imposed by church or by state—is harrowing but not without its dividends in artistic ingenuity.

The invisible censors are sometimes more demoralizing. I'm talking now not about the so-called internal critics that writers like to blame for their lack of productivity, or creativity, or whatever inhibits their imagined optimum performance. I mean by *invisible censors* the kind of economic pressure and public opinion that forces us to compromise ourselves. So much in this cultural climate conspires to browbeat writers and all other artists into producing for maximum profit and exposure. Nothing seems to have changed since George Orwell observed that "any writer or journalist who wants to retain his integrity finds himself thwarted by the general drift of society rather than by active persecution."[1]

Isn't this the real enemy of free speech in the so-called free world? Censorship of a less identifiable kind: more sophisticated, more insidious, more corrupting than the big book-burning brutes we can easily recognize.

NY Do you believe that there is such a thing as Asian American aesthetics? An Asian American literary tradition? Do you see your work as growing out of it?

WLY Trying to define concepts like *Asian American aesthetics* or an Asian American literary tradition is too slippery a task for me. Being Asian, like being European, carries some well-known implications that suggest a certain cultural homogeneity. But, when you think of the differences that separate the Chinese from the Japanese, the Japanese from the Indians, and so on—each of these cultures so essentially Asian in its own way—you have to wonder about the usefulness of concepts like *Asian American aesthetics.* Surely the complexity of Asiatic cultures isn't reducible to the uniformity implied by a term like Asian—let alone *Asian American?*

Of course Asia will always figure in my work, whatever I end up writing. I could write a musical set in Scandinavia, and even then I have no doubt that Asia would sneak its way in. The perspective and sensibility that come from being raised in Asia will continue to permeate my every effort, I suppose.

NY What about your background in Burma? Are you drawing on Burmese literary tradition in your novels?

WLY I'm not drawing on any Burmese tradition I'm aware of. In fact, the kind of novel I'm trying to write would be impossible in Burmese, not only because of the inadequacy of

Wendy Law-Yone

my language after so many years abroad, but because the language necessary for the books I attempt—the language of psychological scrutiny and insight—simply doesn't exist in Burmese. That's why I could never write my novels in Burmese.

NY Were you trying to create a recognizably Burmese heroine when you wrote *Irrawaddy Tango*?

WLY No. I was trying to create a memorable heroine who happened to be Asian. So many of the novels set in Southeast Asia—some of them acknowledged masterpieces I admire for other reasons—seem to portray Asian protagonists in such unsatisfying or ludicrous ways. An example that comes to mind is [Graham Greene's] *The Quiet American* [1956], one of the best novels ever written about Southeast Asia. There you have this central character, a Vietnamese woman. It is her effect on the two men competing for her that gives rise to most of the interesting issues in the book—yet she is not only monosyllabic but almost ghostly by definition. Graham Greene would disagree, but there was one heroine I found lacking in quite essential ways.

I wanted to create a woman different from the types usually portrayed by Westerners—or by Asians, for that matter. As a result, I may have created a character who isn't so likable—as I've been told by some readers. Oh, well. I didn't create a likable character, then.

NY Your novels are often read as autobiographical. How do you feel about that?

WLY Oh, I'm very pleased. It means I've told a plausible lie, a believable yarn.

NY In what ways does gender shape your writing? How easy or difficult is it to empathize with the other sex?

WLY Trying to figure out how gender shapes my writing is like trying to figure out how being Wendy Law-Yone shapes my writing. I don't know—nor do I particularly care—what it would be like to write as a male. But I don't think empathizing with males is difficult for women—or vice versa—unless you think of the other sex as the enemy. The enemy for writers is not the other sex. The enemy, to paraphrase Emily Dickinson, is what distracts.

NY Do you feel a sense of social purpose in your work?

WLY If there is a sense of social purpose, it isn't premeditated. I have no aspirations to change the world through my books—only to show the way it is and, simultaneously, the way it could be.

NY Do you feel that art should be for art's sake?

WLY Only if we are talking about Mr. Buchwald.

NY What is the role of memory or history in your writing?

WLY Memory is everything for writers like me, who are not free to return home at will. For a long time, the political situation in Burma was such that I couldn't go back. Now, even as the country reopens its doors to tourism and foreign investment, I'm still in doubt about whether I can—or should—return. After all, the regime in power now is the same regime that jailed my father and me along with thousands of others, the same regime that has caused a generation of Burmese untold misery, the same regime that continues to persecute, imprison, brutalize, and kill people with impunity. Just because the barbed wire has come down in recent days doesn't necessarily mean one can go back in unscathed.

No. Other immigrants can rely on periodic refreshers; we exiles have only our memories as witnesses. But only our memories will finally set us free. History, after all, is the version of the victors. The history books are slanted in favor of the successful conquerors. Literature, on the other hand, documents the version of the conquered. I'm on the side of literature.

Note

1. George Orwell, "The Prevention of Literature," *Polemic,* no. 2 (January 1946): 4–14.

Selected Works by Wendy Law-Yone

The Coffin Tree. New York: Knopf, 1983. Paperback, Boston: Beacon, 1987.

"The Year of the Pigeon." In *Without a Guide: Contemporary Women's Travel Adventures,* ed. Katherine Govier. Toronto: Macfarlane Walter & Ross, 1984. Reprint, St. Paul, Minn.: Hungry Mind, 1996.

"Ankle." *Grand Street* 7, no. 3 (Spring 1988): 7–24.

"Life in the Hills: Students Who Fled the Brutal Crackdown on Pro-Democracy Demonstrations Last Year Have Found Refuge of Sorts among Burma's Ethnic Insurgents." *Atlantic,* (December 1989): 24–28.

"Drought." In *Slow Hand: Women Writing Erotica,* ed. Michelle Slung. New York: HarperCollins, 1992. Reprinted in *The Gates of Paradise: The Anthology of Erotic Short Fiction,* ed. Alberto Manguel. New York: Potter, 1993.

Irrawaddy Tango. New York: Knopf, 1993.

"The Burma Road." *Asian Art and Culture* 9, no. 1 (Winter 1996): 4–11.

17

Gary Pak

Interview by
BRENDA KWON

Growing up in Hawai'i is an experience that is often difficult to explain, although Gary Pak does a pretty good job. The way he sees it, there are racial divisions there like anywhere else, but you don't have to go around with your ethnicity "on a picket sign." In *The Watcher of Waipuna*, you see Rosita, a Hawaiian *mahu* (homosexual) descended from *ali'is* (Hawaiian royalty); Tats Sugimura, a Japanese potato farmer; and Marianne DeSilva, a Portuguese teenager who gives birth to a child surrounded by suspicions of God and the devil. But Pak's stories aren't about *pākēs* (Chinese), *yobos* (Korean), *pilipinos, japanee, portugee,* Hawaiians, or *haoles* (white person; lit., "foreigner"). They're about the ways people in Hawai'i relate to one another amid a landscape of colonialism, war, the struggle for land rights, and the struggle for Hawaiian sovereignty. They observe how communities form in Hawai'i and the way locals interact with one other, whether it be over the building of a freeway or the rumblings of a volcano. Above all, you get the sense that, in trying to understand it all, Gary Pak's just trying to tell a good story. And he does.

Besides *The Watcher of Waipuna,* Gary Pak has published several short pieces, including "Catching a Big Ulua" and an excerpt from *Children of a Fire Land.* At the time of this interview, his novel *A Ricepaper Airplane* was still in progress, but the novel has since been published (1998). He teaches at the Kapiʻolani Community College and lives with his wife and three children in Kāneʻohe.

BK When did you begin to write, and how did you decide to become a writer?

GP Seriously, it was 1980, when my first son was born. Before that, I used to write poetry and stories, but it was more like a hobby or something to get off my chest. But to commit it to paper, to revise it and get things published, that wasn't until 1980. There were many stories to be told in Hawaiʻi, in my family, in the community, and they were important stories. Looking at my son who was just born, I felt that maybe we should write these stories down, commit them to paper, so that my son and others would be able to read them and have that as part of their cultural experience.

BK Have your children read *The Watcher of Waipuna?* What do they think about it?

GP My oldest son has read it cover to cover. He likes it. In fact, one of his projects in school for English was to write a short story, and he used my first story, "The Gift," as his model. He changed it around, of course. My other son has read parts of the collection. My younger daughter is too young, I think. She can read, but mostly Dr. Seuss books.

BK Do you feel you're writing mostly for them? Who do you see as your audience?

GP As a writer I'm coming from a certain community that speaks and thinks a certain way, but I'm writing for a broad audience, for whoever wants to read it. I'm not necessarily writing for the person who lives down the street from me, although, if that person reads my stories, he or she might come to me and say, "Hey, I understand what you're saying." The identification, the unity, is very strong in Hawai'i. When I'm writing a story, I guess the audience must touch my mind, but it's not a conscious thing on my part. It sounds simplistic, but, when I'm sitting down with my computer, I'm just trying to tell a story: a beginning, a middle, an end. I think a lot of writers do that; they just try to write the best story that they can, and, whatever it takes to write the best story, they'll do it.

BK So you don't necessarily take into account a split between local and "mainland" audiences when you write?

GP Well, there is a difference because the local audience is going to pick things up right away. I was talking to a teacher at the University of Hawai'i who uses "The Gift" in her class, and she said that the kids there noticed the pidgin I used was from the sixties. The kind of pidgin we use now is a little different. So the students are very critical about it. This way of looking at the language you might not get on the mainland. You might have a hard time just trying to figure out what everything means, but then it's a process of just being aware or just keeping at it.

BK How did your family feel about your becoming a writer? Did you feel any resistance from them?

GP Not really. My parents were always supportive, but mainly it was my wife who supported me. She felt that, OK, if you want to write, write. And she actually was and is my editor. I have her read my things, and she's always been my critic, putting me on hold, like, "Hey, this doesn't sound right," or, "This is OK." She's been very supportive, and I really didn't feel resistance from anyone except for maybe one

Gary Pak

member of my family, who said, "Don't write about me!" Basically, "You better not write that!"

BK About that one member of your family who didn't want to be in your stories, is that because your writing is autobiographical? Do you ever feel concern over how your family and friends will react to your work?

GP All writers tap into their lives no matter what, and, as for my work being directly autobiographical, I don't think so. But I know that, for example, "The Gift" comes from my childhood, from growing up in a community in Kāne'ohe. Yes, it is autobiographical, but it's not intended to be. The setting, the characters, and the language are very much a part of me, and in that sense it's autobiographical. In terms of my family, most of them, I would say 99.9 percent, are tickled if I write about them. I was invited to be a participant at the Cornell symposium on Asian American identity, and I wrote an essay about a family gathering at my uncle's house, and they were all tickled because I mentioned their names. But, no, I don't worry. My family is pretty close, especially on my mom's side, and I'll never run them down anyway. Besides, my characters are not direct characterizations of people I know. I think other writers have said that their characters are composites of people, so you can't really say, OK, this is so and so. They're not. The characters are not specific people.

BK Who are some of the writers who inspire you in your writing, and what is it about them that moves you?

GP There's a lot of them, and they've helped me or given me inspiration in different ways. In terms of voice, I like Milton Murayama. He's given me the inspiration that, Hey, he was able to write that way, and we can take chances. When I first read John Okada's *No-No Boy*, I thought that technically he could have polished the book more, but the spirit and the passion in the book really hit me. And Latin American authors like Gabriel García Márquez, Mario Vargas Llosa, Alejo Carpentier, Manuel Puig just overwhelm me; for one period, I was reading nothing but those writers. Of course, I love American writers. I used to read a lot of Doctorow, and Faulkner, and Stephen King. I really liked Stephen King for a while. He has a way of developing the plot, the suspension. The local writers in Hawai'i have been a real home mood for me, like Darrell Lum and Wing Tek Lum. And John Dominis Holt always has a place in my heart because of the fire and passion, the things that he writes about—Hawai'i, being Hawaiian, like *Waimea Summer*. I also like James Joyce. Sometimes I'll read parts of *Ulysses* or *Finnegan's Wake,* and I just don't understand what's going on, but the language is so overpowering. Another writer that did that was Keri Hulme, the Maori writer. She's amazing. Powerful.

BK Do you identify as an Asian American writer?

GP Yeah, I do. I also identify myself as a local writer, and a writer from Hawai'i, and just a plain writer. The thing is, I accept all these names. I'm very proud to be an Asian American writer, and I'm proud to be a Korean, but I don't go around with it on a picket sign. I think what happens is that it comes out in my writing. My father has always been very nationalistic, always proud, and it kind of rubbed off on me in a sense, but, then again, it's not something that I have to prove. It's there. I'm proud of what I'm doing. In certain places, people tell me that I'm an Asian writer or an Asian American writer, and I say, "Yeah, you're right." In some places, I'm a local writer, and I say, "Yeah, you're right." I take it all. As long as it's not degrading or derogatory, as long as they're not putting it in that sense, I'm proud to be in those traditions.

BK During the strategizing cultures conference at UCLA, Ricardo Trimillo recounted a story about flying into Los

Gary Pak

Angeles from Hawaiʻi with a colleague, and the moment that the plane landed the colleague turned to him and said, "Well, we're Asian Americans now." Do you see any difference between being an Asian American writer and a local writer or even a Korean American writer?

GP In a sense, geography and culture make the definitions sharper. When I go to the mainland, all of a sudden I'm very aware of how people see me. They see me as Asian American or Korean American or whatever—a "minority." That does affect the way I see myself. In Hawaiʻi, the definitions are much looser. And the writing is very different. Asian American writers on the mainland and in Hawaiʻi write differently in the way they look at character, the world, and identity. In Hawaiʻi, the cultures are a bit more integrated, and I say *a bit more* because there still are divisions among races in Hawaiʻi. You can see it in the politics, in the kinds of voting that happen. Some people will trust a certain race more than another. But the division is not as sharp, and it's much more tolerable than on the mainland. Although I've been in situations on the mainland where things have been nice, I've also experienced harsh things. When I went to the mainland, I lived there for four years, and I realized that, Hey, this is something I've taken for granted—being local, being Asian. When I came back, it was something that was very sharp for me, and it took some time for those sharp edges to smooth out. But, then again, that awareness was still there. I've also faced harshness here, but here things are a little smoother. I'm able to do more things, take more freedoms, just feel comfortable. That's what it is, feeling more comfortable in my role, or just being a writer.

BK Do you feel it's a plus or a drawback to be called an *Asian American writer*?

GP There's a positive and a negative to that. Whenever you give any person a name, a category, it's already limiting. It's a plus, too, in the sense of identity, unity. It depends on the individual. If you're going to take it as a negative, then it's going to be a negative for you, and it might affect the way you write. You have to understand that there are barriers out there, no matter who you are or what you are, and it's a matter of overcoming them. In terms of the writing, all writing for me is universal, no matter what it is. If you write about an Asian American family growing up in LA, there are still a lot of universals in that. There are these critics who say, "It's Asian American," or, "It's about an urban Japanese family in LA." It gets categorized more and more, but I think that, in all good writing, there's the universal, which transcends all these things. It's also a matter of readers and critics being aware and being open-minded about what's on the paper.

BK There's been a lot of debate over universalism, over the fact that it's been used to erase distinct cultural differences in the name of larger *human*, meaning "white," commonalities. How do you feel about this?

GP That seems to be another thing because that's saying we're all the same. It's the flip side, not really understanding what the situation is and the fact that the world is very different. There are all kinds of textures and colors, not only in races, but in everything—ways of thinking, ways of looking at the world. There are so many different ways of seeing. I think the human project is to try as much as possible to understand all these ways of seeing and also to respect these ways.

BK The Hawaiian and pidgin words in *The Watcher of Waipuna* are not glossed or italicized. Was that your decision?

GP I know consciously I didn't want that because I felt that this is part of the language—no need to italicize it, no need to put a marker on it and say, "Hey, this is a different kind of word." I'm coming from this sort of culture, from this com-

Gary Pak

munity, and this is the language. It's nothing unique to me as a writer, and there's nothing unique about it to a lot of other readers. This message has to be brought out to other readers who maybe are not familiar with this, and I think it's healthy. I know at times in my copy I italicized words, and then I knocked it off, and I thought, This is part of our language, part of our culture, why should I make it look unique? Some people might have a hard time trying to figure out what the words mean, but it's a process of just being aware. People on the mainland, if they keep on reading, once they start getting the hang of it, they're going to get a much deeper understanding of our culture, the way *we* had to learn about other cultures in Hawai'i. I think we understand a large part of the culture of the mainland because of what we've gotten: movies, television, books we had to read. We had to learn how to read Hawthorne, Melville, Shakespeare. And even the modern writers—we have to learn how to read them. It's the same thing.

BK Did you ever feel like a minority as a Korean American in Hawai'i?

GP I didn't have very many Korean friends. My father was a member of a Korean organization here, and it was composed mainly of local Koreans or second-generation Koreans. That was my attachment to being Korean. Of course, my parents spoke Korean at home; they spoke Korean when they didn't want me to understand what was going on, and after a while I picked it up. My family is very Korean in terms of food and things, but it is also really intermarried. You go to my family gatherings, and you don't see "real" Koreans. I mean, my father and mother are Korean, so I'm Korean. But, growing up, there were no Koreans except for my cousins who lived right down the street from me. And, around here, we had all kinds of people. We had Japanese, Filipino, Chinese, Hawaiian, you name it. In my childhood, we didn't see each other as being Japanese or Korean or *haole* or Hawaiian—maybe *haole*. There were one or two local *haole* families living in our neighborhood, but the kids, we all integrated together. It was always, "Eh, that's my friend." Even today I see them and say, "Eh, howzit?" And that's the kind of community it was. It was a working-class neighborhood; we didn't have any rich kids around us. We just were all in the same boat. We had the fun of our lives then, when I was growing up.

BK You said earlier that, when you sit down to write a story, you're just concerned with a story: beginning, middle, and end. But your stories in *The Watcher of Waipuna* seem very consciously political, and they address a lot of issues. Do you try to instill a sense of social purpose in your work?

GP All art has some kind of political or social bearing. It has to. We all live in a society, and whatever we write has some autobiographical bearing. Whatever we think surfaces in our stories. When I write a story, I don't purposely say, OK, I have to write a political story or a socially responsible story. I want to write a story, but I guess through my understanding, or my way of seeing life in this society, this community, this world, politics do come out, and a lot of contemporary issues have come out in my stories, like land rights, for example. It's such an important issue in Hawai'i. For "The Trial of Goro Fukushima" for example, Marie Hara gave me this story about the Goto trial on the Big Island around the turn of the century, about a worker who got lynched by three *haole lunas* [boss, supervisor, overseer; plantation foreman] because he could speak English and he was helping out the other immigrants and Japanese workers. The *lunas* got off, one dollar apiece, and I just thought that was such an injustice. And that was the seed for "The Trial of Goro Fukushima." I didn't write it right away. I needed that image, that opening image,

Gary Pak

or that opening line—that's how I write. The language has to be clear to me, and, once I have that opening, I just go with it. Wherever the story goes, it goes.

BK   About "The Trial of Goro Fukushima," the priest is implicated in Goro's lynching as well. What are your feelings about the missionaries and the missionary legacy in Hawai'i?

GP   I try to play on the contradiction of religion. Religion played a strong unifying role in the community, and it still does. But religion has its contradictions and its internal conflicts. You're going to have people like that priest who say one thing and do another. And they're only human in that sense. I'm not religious, but I do see that religion has played a unifying role. And there's a negative side to all that, too, because it's also been a scapegoat. People point to the missionaries as one of the reasons why Hawai'i has become the way it is. The missionaries came in with the religion, and there's that saying: They put the Hawaiians to pray to the God above, and in the same breath they stole the land from below. That has a strong truth to it, and, historically, I don't think you can deny it. But they also came at an opportune time, when there was a void and the *ali'i*, the Kamehameha *ali'is*, realized that they could use the missionaries.

BK   As you mentioned, many of your stories in *The Watcher of Waipuna* bring up the issue of land rights, and some illustrate the ways in which colonialism is still visible in today's local life. What is the role of history in your writing? What is your position on Hawaiian activism in the islands?

GP   First of all, history creates a very important background to my writing, for example, in the first story in *The Watcher of Waipuna*, "The Valley of the Dead Air." With all the various land struggles that have been happening in the islands, the common people are saying, "Enough is enough." The land is really for the people who use the land, not for these landlords or absentee landlords who just collect money off them and sit pretty. The people who actually labor on the land are the ones who should reap whatever benefit comes from the land—the produce, the *mana* [supernatural or divine power], the life, or the spirit. Since the early seventies, there's always that realization that, when people start getting together, the feeling is there—their sense of *mana*, their sense of power, being linked together, being able to forge communities together to demand these things. Along with that, I've always been supportive of the land rights in Hawai'i, of the Hawaiian indigenous peoples getting what was stolen from them. That's being kind of blunt. You can say *legally stolen* or *illegally stolen*, but that verb is *stolen*. It was taken from people, but it's not a simple thing either. If you look at history, there's the *ali'i* along with the colonial forces. But the main thing is that these colonial forces have come to control the land, culture, language, and everything. I've always been supportive of people fighting for their rights.

BK Every time I come back, I notice that a little bit more of where we used to hang out is cemented over. A few years back, Point Panic was all cement walkways and park benches.

GP I used to body surf down there. I haven't done it for years.

BK Yeah, it's really different, and it seems like a lot of it was done for tourism. In "The Watcher of Waipuna," another story about land and land rights, Gilbert is very sympathetic in his desire to hold on to the land as opposed to selling it to the developers. Are your feelings about land development in the islands similar to his?

GP I think that, if it benefits the people, it's OK. Certain kinds of development are important. I don't say all development is bad. We need a sense of nostalgia, we need a place where we can go back and reflect, and it's not going to be

Gary Pak

that way all the time. But it is part of human nature that we want to have a certain attachment to a place, that sense of unity. We go back, and we don't want to be alienated. I remember that, when I came back after several years on the mainland, I just thought, Wow, they're building a freeway there at the back of my house where I used to go hiking. And I was thinking, This is not right because I remember the times when I was a kid. Perhaps that was one of the reasons why I did write a story like "The Gift." To recapture a really nice time. One thing about writing—we sometimes overlook it— is that, when you read something and you feel good about it, you want to have this optimistic vision of the world, of human beings. One thing I'd like to try is to get that kind of uplifting. Sometimes it doesn't work out; the story doesn't turn out that way. I think one sixties activist said that nostalgia is like a mild form of depression. Part of life.

BK How does gender shape your writing?

GP I think gender does affect my writing. I wrote a story about a cabdriver ["My Friend Kammy"] that was published in the *Hawai'i Review*, though it wasn't included in this collection. It was about a cabdriver driving down Hotel Street in Waikīkī and how he picks up hookers. Part of it is an internal monologue about hookers and what they do, and, after I wrote it, my wife said, "Hey, that's terrible! You're knocking women?" And so I had a debate with her. She was affected by the sixties, too. The "politically correct" thing has been exaggerated and distorted by both sides in certain ways, especially by the more conservative side. But there is the thing of being responsible. Whatever you write, you're responsible for it being there, and, once it gets published, it's not your baby anymore; it just takes off, and people are going to be critical. If I feel that, in the story itself, I need to portray a character in a certain way and it's going to border on stereotyping, I just have to let that go because I feel that that's part of the story. Sometimes you just have to say, OK, look, I know what this is about, what this word means or suggests, but I have to be true to the art form.

BK In "Watcher of Waipuna," Lucy ends up having a change of heart and decides not to take the land from her brother Gilbert, but what do you feel about Lola, who remains greedy up to the end?

GP Lola came off like a very stereotypical character. But then there are people like that. In the course of this story she's not going to change; maybe later she will. I think that, because Lucy has a change of heart, there's hope for Lola. The human character, the human condition is very complex. I guess I want to be optimistic and say that people can change for the better, no matter what. I wanted to give Lucy that dimension and hopefully maybe Lola in the next story.

BK You write from several different points of view, which are not necessarily from a Korean male perspective. Does that come from having grown up in Hawai'i? Do you feel that more Asian American writers should feel the freedom to do this—to write outside their ethnicities and genders?

GP It depends on the writer. If the writer's comfortable doing that, then I think, Yeah, why not? Because it's true to the writer's own sense of identity or sense of community. I have a very strong sense of community, of where I've been living for most of my life. I feel very comfortable. Maybe I do stereotype characters, but I feel like I have a sense of fair play. Going back to what I said earlier, it's whatever the writer feels comfortable with because, if the writer doesn't feel comfortable with bringing in many different voices, it's going to show. The writing is going to be very hard; the characterization's going to be forced. I've read that in the work of some local writers living here, writers who have been living in the islands for a while, who feel that they're comfortable, or they

Gary Pak

feel they want to write in this way, with this community of voices in their stories. But, while reading their work, I can see a real tension, a very tense kind of flow to the writing. Rather than going smoothly down a creek or down a stream, there's rocks. It may not be apparent to the writer, but maybe the pidgin or the characterization might be too forced. On the other hand, I feel that, if the writer wants to do whatever he or she wants to do, fine, do it. If you want to write about something and you have no knowledge of it, do it. But you have to remember your judge is going to be your audience. Your audience is going to read it and determine if they like it or not. That's the whole idea of writing, too. You can have your failures; you can have many failures.

BK So you don't necessarily worry about a mainland gay male saying, "Well, I thought your portrayal of Rosita was very demeaning."

GP It might have crossed my mind, but it really doesn't bother me. I felt that my characterization of Rosita is just how I felt about it. I thought it was true, that it wasn't demeaning. The demeaning part came from the other characters looking at Rosita. Rosita was strong. The story was told from the kids' point of view—how they saw Rosita, how their perspective was either challenged or directed by their parents and by other people. Yet they were able to see Rosita through a much fresher perspective, by seeing what he did, and the honesty and pureness in his heart, put above the fact that he had a certain sexual preference. He was concerned about his community, about the kids, and the kids in their very limited, very fresh, very open-minded perspective were able to see that. It's the grown-ups who have their minds made up about Rosita and his homosexuality. One thing about the story that I was hoping would come out is the fact that we need to trust children and their point of view. The way they look at the world is a fuller, much more honest, and much more pleasant and beautiful way. We sometimes tend to be very rigid in the way we see things, and we're not willing to change. We're right or wrong, whereas children have genuine feelings about things.

BK What other projects are you working on now?

GP Right now, I have a work in progress, and the title is *A Ricepaper Airplane.* I call it a *work in progress* because I'm afraid to say *novel,* which is a loaded word. People say, "It's a novel!" and all of a sudden they start fantasizing. The problem I had was with the unity of voice. It's a fractured kind of novel. It has different points of view; it jumps in time. But I'm finally getting some sense of unity of voice in it, and I feel good about that. It's been a long time coming. I worked on this thing for over ten years.

BK Can you say something about the plot?

GP The basic plot is about a Korean immigrant worker, Sung Wha—who is modeled after my grandfather's friend—on a plantation around the twenties, and he has this vision of building an airplane to fly back to Korea. He lives in Wahiawā, and so he has a dream, and the whole idea is about him trying to fulfill this dream, even though from the start you know he's not going to do that—he's not going to fly the airplane. He builds it on the bare skeleton of a bicycle, builds the wings with bamboo and ricepaper, and he wants to pump his way back to Korea. Technologically, it's not going to work. But the whole story is about his life, really, and how he's able to create these dreams.

The opening scene is in a hospital bed, on his deathbed—he has cancer of the lungs—and the first narrative is his nephew's. Sung Wha tells the nephew all these stories, and the nephew is fascinated by them. And the nephew already knows about some of these stories, like the ricepaper airplane, because he was there when his uncle was building it. But then Sung Wha starts talking about his life, and he has so many experiences. In one story, he and his cousin Eung Whan—who is the nephew's father—are back in the village, in a section of what's now North Korea, and they get into trouble with the Japanese. That was the time of the Japanese occupation. The Japanese come in and terrorize the village, and Sung Wha and Eung Whan get really pissed off, and they start attacking the Japanese soldiers with their hoes, so they become criminals and have to flee into the mountains.

To make a long story short, the uncle goes to China, becomes a revolutionary, and erroneously gets deported to Japan. Somehow, he escapes the prison in Japan, and he gets sent to Hawai'i and has all these visions and dreams of going back to Korea, back to Manchuria, where he got married and had children, but he never does. He remains in Hawai'i and becomes a trade union activist, leading some strikes on the plantation. He's a real rebel to his last breath. So the story charts his life, and the ricepaper airplane is more like a symbol, the whole idea that he's able to have these dreams. Some of them have been huge failures—he's never able to go back and be reunited with his family. Yet, with all these adverse forces going against him, he's still able to hold on to his dreams. That's the feeling, the underlying theme: we dream of things, and we have to keep on with those dreams.

Selected Works by Gary Pak

From *A Ricepaper Airplane*. *Chaminade Literary Review* 1, no. 2 (Spring 1988): 104–113.

"My Friend Kammy." *Hawai'i Review* 12, no. 2 (Fall 1988): 61–73.

From *A Ricepaper Airplane*. *Chaminade Literary Review* 5 (Fall 1989): 159–176.

"Catching a Big Ulua." *Bamboo Ridge* 47 (Summer 1990): 17–27.

From *Children of a Fire Land*. *Bamboo Ridge* 47 (Summer 1990): 28–41.

From *A Ricepaper Airplane. Amerasia Journal* 18, no. 3 (1992): 17–31.

The Watcher of Waipuna and Other Stories. Honolulu: *Bamboo Ridge*, 1992.

A Ricepaper Airplane. Honolulu: University of Hawai'i Press, 1998.

319

Gary Pak

18

Karen Tei Yamashita

Interview by
MICHAEL S. MURASHIGE

From the time I was young, Gardena, California, has been associated with Japanese Americans. I can recall weekend trips to my cousins' house, set midway down a cul-de-sac inhabited almost exclusively by JA folk. The markets in town actually had Japanese food—*ochazuke nori,* big white bags of Japanese rice, *kaki* in the right season—not just the "Oriental" section I was used to, stocked with bright orange cans of Chun King's "delicacies from the Far East." In the neighborhood, younger kids were playing pickup basketball or kick the can until dark, the older ones congregating around somebody's lowered Celica or Capri. And *all* the kids ate rice for dinner every night. No matter if dinner was steamed fish or spaghetti, *okazu* or burritos, there was always rice on the dinner table, sitting in a National rice cooker. In a way, it was a coming home for a JA kid growing up in the, then, almost Asianless wilds of San Gabriel.

On a summer day in 1993, driving south on the San Diego freeway toward Gardena and brunch and an interview with Karen Tei Yamashita, these are some of the things that I was thinking about. And, certainly, if things have changed since those days in the early seventies, then there's still a very JA feel about Gardena. At the time, I had not yet met Karen Yamashita and had had only a few short conversations on the phone with her to set up the interview. So, driving up to the house, a typically flat southern California suburban number, I expected to find confirmation of some of those childhood memories and associations I had held on to.

The two things that I noticed when I walked into the house were, first, that she didn't make me take off my shoes when I came in (though I did) and, second, that the music coming from another room was a slow samba—Alcione, Beth Carvalho, or something like that. In addition, the space in the main room of the house was almost entirely taken up by a number of large and colorful pillows in the shapes of various cars, two to three feet long each, and two fake sushi so big that they thoroughly put to shame their smaller cousins that dress the front windows of Japanese restaurants in Little Tokyo. After a number of apologies for the "mess," Yamashita explained that the cars and the sushi were props for her upcoming work, *Noh Bozos,* a multimedia performance about JAs living in southern California and, especially, Gardena.

What followed was a fun afternoon of food—mushroom omelets, not *musubi,* sushi, or little teriyaki chicken wings—and conversation. We (meaning Yamashita; her husband, Ronaldo; daughter, Jane; son, Jon; and me) talked about Ronaldo's work as an artist, Jon's recent soccer tournament, and the real artist of the family, Jane, and her various family portraits. And then, of course, we talked about Brazil and LA.

Yamashita went to Brazil in 1975 on a Thomas J. Watson Fellowship to study Japanese immigration to Brazil. But what started out as a one-year project turned into a nine-year stay during which she got married, raised a family, and began her career as a writer with the two books that grew, more or less,

Karen Tei Yamashita

out of her experiences during that period: *Through the Arc of the Rain Forest* and *Brazil-Maru*. After her return to southern California in 1984, she continued to work creatively, writing pieces on Brazil for the Los Angeles JA newspaper, the *Rafu Shimpo*, translating Brazilian literature, and, most notably, creating a number of multimedia/stage performances, including *Hannah Kusho: An American Butoh, Tokyo Carmen vs. L.A. Carmen*, and the musical *GiLAwrecks* (in collaboration with the composer Vicki Abe). In her most recent novel, *Tropic of Orange*, Yamashita writes about what it means to live in southern California: the daily labors of living in and through the contradictions that the contemporary global world has thrown up in Koreatown, in downtown LA, and also in Mazatlan and at the U.S./Mexico border.

MSM How did you actually find information to get into the market side of writing?

KTY Well, I had done some translations of Japanese Brazilian poetry. When I got back to the United States, the editor I'd worked with, Alan Lau, said, "If you've got some work that you're trying to show, here are some publishers that would be interested in Asian American work." I thought to myself, if they're interested in Asian American work, what are they going to think of *Through the Arc of the Rain Forest*? So I said, "Well, give it a try." All the houses were small. So I sent a sample over to Graywolf—a small house in Minneapolis. They looked at it and liked it enough to see the manuscript. Then, on their suggestion, I rewrote the book, but, when I rewrote it, they didn't like it.

At the same time, the publisher at Coffee House, Allan Kornblum, personally wrote me a note: "I know I asked you this six months ago, but where is your manuscript? I'm still very interested in it." And then, sometime in the next year, I was homesick, and I got this call from Allan Kornblum: "I want to publish your book." And he started to talk business. After I hung up I called Ronaldo and said, "I just hung up with someone who really wants to publish that book!" It was very lucky. I'd sent the manuscript out to fifty or a hundred different places, not knowing what I was doing, and, toward the end, I was starting to send it to science fiction publishers.

MSM Why?

KTY Because there was no clear niche for what I did. It wasn't Asian American feminist literature; it wasn't magic realism; it wasn't science fiction. It was very hard to write a query letter for something that the author herself had a very difficult time describing.

MSM If you were forced to classify *Through the Arc*, what kind of book would you say it was?

KTY That was and still is my problem. I think a lot of Asian American authors or authors of color find merchandising their work difficult because bookstores and publishers and publicists are looking for niches for these books. I would say, "Well, this is a story that has a Japanese man with a ball in front of his head. It has an American with three arms. It has a man and his wife raising pigeons. . . ."

MSM How conscious were you of the relative difficulty of marketing books as you were writing the second book?

KTY The second book is really the first. I went to Brazil in 1975 on a fellowship to study Japanese immigration to Brazil. I spent the first two, three years researching for that book, and the rest of the time—in between raising a family—I wrote the first draft of *Brazil-Maru*. In those days, it was a much longer, ponderous book. Back in this country in 1984 I rewrote it. By that time I was really tired of it, and so, following Ronaldo's suggestion and my own needs, I started to write *Through the Arc*.

Karen Tei Yamashita

Ronaldo has always had these oral tales he's told, which are conceptual. He's an architect and an artist, and so his ideas for stories are more conceptual. I had stored a lot of these stories in the back of my mind, and, when I decided to write *Through the Arc*, I pulled some of those stories together; in many ways we collaborated. I started to write the first six chapters, and every evening I would say, "Well, I got this far. What do you think happens next?" We would talk the ideas around, and that's how that book got written. It was a respite from Japanese immigration to Brazil and my inability to get anybody interested in the material. But everybody in this country was in the throes of redress then, so this whole idea that something might be happening with another immigrant community in South America wasn't of the greatest importance.

Then I got together with a friend named Ryan Shiotani, and we did a long article on the history, culture, economy, and politics of Brazil for the *Rafu Shimpo*. I had kept all my contacts in Brazil and continued to work, but not in any other way except to write feature articles. I translated some articles done by journalists in the Japanese Brazilian community. And a friend of mine, J. K. Yamamoto, published them in *Hokubei Mainichi* in San Francisco.

The year that I came back, I also did a work-in-progress play at East-West called *Hiroshima Tropical*. That play was about a family in São Paulo that goes through a great tragedy. After World War II had ended, Japanese Brazilians spread a rumor among themselves that Japan had won the war. Part of that tragedy is about the infighting that happened in that community because of that rumor. When I did that work in progress, there was some questioning—not by East-West, but outside—of the timing of the play in terms of redress, internment, and the politics—since a play like that can show that, indeed, there had been a strong nationalist sentiment among a portion of our community. So I sort of let it die, and I never went back to it. But those issues, which are real, are worked through in *Brazil-Maru*. If you look at [John Okada's] *No-No Boy*, you'll see that, in the very, very first pages, Ichiro talks about a letter his mother has received from Brazil.

MSM The ships are coming.

KTY The ships are coming. So the issues are there, but we haven't been very outspoken about them. In that sense, too, I needed to put *Brazil-Maru* away for a while. I'm glad I did. I had a great time writing *Through the Arc*. The collaborative process, too, was a pleasure. There was a point, though, when I didn't know how the book was supposed to end. And I remember saying to Ronaldo, "I need to know how this all ends. We have to think this through." He said, "Don't worry. I'll think about it." A week went by, and I said, "Well, what do you think the end is?" He said, "Give me some time, give me some time." And I said, "You know, I'm at the point where, if I don't know what direction this is pointing, I really can't carve this work." So at some point I made decisions about how the work ends and how I would bring all these disparate characters to bear on the story. When I finally knew that, I could structure the chapters and segments. I had a finished product in about a half year, and then I worked on it for another half year until I had all the pieces together.

MSM Do you feel you have more creative control than you might have had at a big publishing house?

KTY I don't know. I think it's different with every editor. Coffee House made suggestions, but it was up to me, ultimately, to make decisions on changes. One of the things they suggested was to remove the ball as the narrator [in *Through the Arc of the Rain Forest*].

MSM Then who would tell the story?

Karen Tei Yamashita

KTY It would be third person. While I went along with a lot of changes, I just couldn't make that one. I like the ball for a narrator, and I think it was wise to keep it.

MSM What are some of the advantages of having this ball?

KTY Well, the first versions of the story were told in third person. The advantage of having the ball as a narrator was that it gave me a lot of latitude in how I might tie segments and all the characters together. It was a way to have a singular vision running through the book. I was toying with the idea of having Kazumasa tell the story, but Kazumasa is too nice a guy, and I couldn't have him be all seeing. I couldn't have him see portions of Brazilian life because he's a recent immigrant. The ball was the next best thing.

MSM You talk about Kazumasa as a recent immigrant. Are the kinds of thing that he's experiencing the same as what you went through when you went over in 1975?

KTY I guess so. I spent so much time studying that immigrant community that I *had* to put a Japanese in. One of our mutual friends is a painter and actor in Brazil who emigrated to Brazil from Japan after the war. In many ways I based Kazumasa on him, although Kazumasa is probably a much later immigrant. There were things about this person that were open to the changes that he might encounter in Brazil, and I like that in him. I also enjoyed seeing how the Japanese culture could move into the Brazilian one, and absorb it, but continue to hold its own, and how the stodgy things about Japanese culture could be molded or torn away.

MSM Another thing that I was wondering about were the lists. I love those lists that you have: of products, of ideas for products, and for different kinds of people. Is that something that you consciously added to the book, or did the two of you come up with them together?

KTY I think that's just my style. If Ronaldo wrote this book, it would probably be fifty pages! He would have done it in a very precise and choppy manner.

MSM So what did you add to the book that wouldn't have been there in the fifty-page version?

KTY The story line, the literary fooling around and planting of metaphors throughout. I diagrammed the way the book would flow, what the subplots and big plots were, the division of chapters, the structure. The collaboration came with the conceptual work. If there were places that I got stuck, I would call Ronaldo at work and say, "What happens next?" Ronaldo would, out of the blue, start saying, "Well, you know, it might be that this happens, or maybe this. . . ." Then there was a choice of directions to take, and, after a while, I would say, "This is going to happen," and he would say, "Yeah, and then this happens." Some basic things that are Ronaldo's ideas are the man with three arms and the ball, but they were all hooked up to specifically Brazilian characters and situations, and I made them into international beings. So the original man with the ball was a Brazilian. In Ronaldo's original story he's riding on a bicycle with the ball. At some point he falls in a pool of mud, and the ball gets stuck in the mud and gets deeper and deeper. He starts to lose his relationship to this ball and so stuffs his head into the mud, trying to retrieve it, and dies.

The guy with three arms is a story about a Brazilian on the street who spends his time picking pockets. He goes from bus to bus, and he can always hold on to both straps because he has this other arm that can pick pockets. At the end of the story the police apprehend the guy, and they take two of his arms and hands, and he's handcuffed. Ronaldo always has this place where he says, "Well, he's handcuffed in the back. But he always has this other arm in the back to go, 'Fuck you! Fuck you!'"

Karen Tei Yamashita

MSM I can see a lot better now how the meeting of the two-hundred-page version and the fifty-page version produced this book.

KTY And, then, this book was written here, in this country, after we had been in Brazil for nine years. It was also my way of trying to pull that experience together in my own fashion. Every now and then I meet people who lived in Brazil who read my book and say, "There's something you *can't* describe that is *here*. And this is how it feels to be in Brazil." And that *is*. That's why the whole idea of the book being any sort of magic realism is on the edge of making no sense. Brazil has a very middle-class structure that involves international technology that comes from this country and from Japan, yet next door you have people who have no relationship to that technology or who use that technology in a manner that has nothing to do with it. As Ronaldo says, you may go to a small, rural place, and someone there has gone to a lot of trouble to buy a refrigerator, but he has no electricity to hook the damn thing up. So what does he use the refrigerator for? Well, when you open the refrigerator, you'll find it's cupboard space. All the sheets and the towels are neatly stacked up in this refrigerator. And that's the kind of thing *Through the Arc* is trying to convey about living in a country that's both developing and developed—and has an Indian and aboriginal culture that is undiscovered and dying. It has an urban culture that is highly cosmopolitan and also very imitative and a government that has pursued policies of bringing this technology into the country. All those things are in this rather strange mix. It's very real.

I wanted these strange features to be absolutely natural. Brazilians themselves are always talking about their "melting pot," about how their prejudices are based on class and not on race and how they're beginning to be so mixed that race doesn't matter. It's not entirely true. But, to the extent that there is a very generous and gracious acceptance of strangers and people who come to visit Brazil, many people feel that there's an endearing quality about the country. I wanted that to be there—the man with three arms or a man who had a ball in front of his head would be accepted. Without question.

MSM The way I always describe the book to other people is to say, "This is a book that you can read before you go to sleep" because you can do it in small chunks. The chapters are short, and they break off and go someplace else, so you don't need that continuity in the reading experience to get a sense of what's going on. Is that the way the book works?

KTY Yeah. One thing that becomes apparent in Brazil right away is people's attachment to the soap operas. When I was living in Brazil, there was one particular channel called Globo—and it was *global*. Everyone is tuned in to the soap opera. There are people you can't phone at that hour because they will not answer the phone because they're going to be missing the soap opera. The soap opera is sort of the common consciousness—part of the national identity—because the television has become so prevalent in that country. Even in rural areas poor people will have a television *somewhere*. So, for a period of three to four months, as you go through the story of the soap opera, many things—music, jokes, trends, political focus—seem to have at least something to do with the soap opera. As it gets toward the end of the soap opera, I'd say they have 80–90 percent viewership because people have to see the last episodes. I thought the soap opera would be a good way to talk about Brazil because it's so much a part of the psyche of the country. And soap operas have been a way for people to criticize society and the government in a hidden manner. For me, the ability to cut everything up into chapters that have their own endings made it possible to write the book over a period of time.

Karen Tei Yamashita

MSM You mentioned that, in the novelas in Brazil, they slip in this social commentary/critique. Is that what you're doing? There are references to environmental problems, especially with the multinationals, as well as a number of smaller references to class structure, how money is distributed, who has power, who controls what, and so on and so forth. Is that something that you were consciously working at?

KTY Oh yeah. In a country like Brazil, you can't *not* talk about politics. You can't talk about things that impinge on people's lives and not talk about class structure. The multinationals are very powerful in the country, and that becomes very obvious as soon as you begin to live there. Johnson and Johnson in our country is a company that provides nice products for babies—Q-tips, soft things. In Brazil, Johnson and Johnson is an all-pervasive company. Drug stores have nothing but Johnson and Johnson products. And all of a sudden you get more of a predatory vision of this company that you don't have here. The same thing would be true of chemical companies like Dow. All of a sudden these companies are bigger than life in Brazil. Car companies—Volkswagen, Fiat, Chevrolet, Ford. Big companies. Nestlé is another one.

MSM Infamous in Africa.

KTY Yes, it's infamous. But in Brazil you don't really have a choice. It's Nestlé. When I had my kids there, that's the formula milk they brought out. And it's not just Nestlé formula: it's Nestlé's chocolate, Nestlé's sweetened condensed milk, Nestlé's powdered milk.

MSM Where does the artist or writer fit into that system?

KTY That's a big question. In *Through the Arc*, where I fit in is to tell the story by the use of juxtaposition and satire. It's a very small part that I play. I can say only that I want to write about it with some honesty and integrity. I would find it hard to write a book without ideas, without political content, or without a vision. I would find it hard to simply write about some family saga. I guess the answer is more in creating the questions, creating an awareness.

MSM How does humor fit into that?

KTY Humor is a way to ease it into people's consciousness so that they can be more accepting of it. I don't think anybody appreciates being bashed over the head or being preached at. But it's also a way of looking at a world that's complex and contradictory. If you deal for an entire week with the bureaucracy, you begin to feel that you're not in the real world. It becomes a very strange world.

MSM But *Brazil-Maru* was a very different kind of story, right off the bat.

KTY Right. I'd been working on it, as I said, for all those years until I came back to this country and rewrote the whole thing again. At that point, Coffee House said, "What else have you got? We think we'd be really interested in anything you've got." And they were interested in *Brazil-Maru*. So I spent the next year rewriting it. I buckled down and started carving.

I wrote it five times from beginning to end. It was hard because I'd interviewed hundreds of people and I had bits and pieces of their lives all filtered through this book. There were just too many characters. Every time I rewrote it, I had to take one out. I'd take somebody out and then combine those experiences or find somewhere to put them or remove them to make the book readable. It all made sense to me because I knew all these people. But I honed the story to make it make sense to anybody else.

MSM You say that there were—and I think there still are—a ton of characters. But you also mentioned that you knew all

Karen Tei Yamashita

those people. Did you mean the real people behind those stories?

KTY Yeah, so the natural inclination, when you're telling this big epic tale, is to take those people, and tell the story, and then not understand that three people could be one person and you can combine characters. But the stories were still too close to me. So, in the beginning, this whole thing was very difficult, and I really learned how to write, having written that five times. I tell you, I cut my teeth on that.

MSM What did you learn through those five rewrites?

KTY I discovered that there was this process. I don't think it would ever take me so long to write a book now, but at that time I was doing many things at once. I was trying to figure out a history for an entire group of people. That meant I had to do many interviews to find out the entire story. And I was following one story in particular, but then I was also using that story to tell the larger story of an entire immigration. Where are these people coming from, and why? This is an immigration of a million and a half people, so it's really big. I was telling only this little story in this immense tale, trying to make this tale also reflect something larger.

What I came to Brazil with was a conversational ability in Japanese so that I could conduct interviews. But I couldn't read Japanese. I couldn't take the old newspapers and read this material. The Japanese Brazilians have their own little study center, and they've been continually doing research on their stories, in Japanese. I just didn't have access to it. So my manner of getting material was to listen to people tell stories and to pull all these stories together.

I wanted to find out about rural life because the majority of these people went to plantations and worked as contract labor on coffee farms. Or they went into these Japanese colonies, bought parcels of land, and pioneered virgin forest. I got their stories in incredible detail.

People tell you, "We pioneered a new life here. We are schooled in Rousseau and Tolstoy. Have you read them?" These are Issei. And I thought to myself, "My grandmother never read Tolstoy! My grandfather never read Rousseau! He never asked me these questions." It was a revelation to meet people who could say, "I was most influenced by a book I read in my early youth before I left Japan, a book by Jean-Jacques Rousseau called *Emile*. When I read that book, I wept." You know, this man is telling me this, and I'm thinking, "You *wept* reading *Emile*? I thought that book was so dry." But I was impressed. It was fascinating to hear an Issei telling you, "I came to this country because I wanted to come here. I wanted to start a new life. I believed that there are things about my Japanese culture, my past, that could flourish in a new setting."

And then the whole vision of people who had, for at least three generations, lived in a communal setting. What was that communal setting, and how was it set up? What were the women cooking? They were making their own tofu. They were in the garden experimenting with new breeds of watermelon. At the same time, there were stories about great love. There were stories about travel, and meeting the forest for the first time, and what it was like to come from Japan to this Brazil, and meeting Brazilians. There was murder. Everywhere I went there was a lot of activity—it was just fascinating to see, and I got carried away with the project. I became so wrapped up that I went from one place to another trying to figure out what went on and what happened.

MSM Then, this is as much a historical narrative as it is a fictional narrative?

KTY Yes.

MSM Do you see any separations between history and fiction, or are those two sides of the same coin?

Karen Tei Yamashita

KTY They're certainly woven. In this book, they are woven, and, in my mind, they've become more woven, but fiction was necessary not only to protect people but also to bring out ideas. You can hone the story and have it take a direction because reality won't necessarily take that direction. You can give little "whys," and you can ask questions within that framework, so fiction for me was a great freedom. My original intention when I went to Brazil was that I would do something anthropological and historical but that it would be journalistic. But, because of my inability to read the language and to get original printed material, which is so necessary for an academic piece, I took this direction. I could have simply done oral histories, and that would have been valid. But not to me.

MSM Why not?

KTY When I got to Brazil, I went to see an anthropologist who had also studied at Columbia, and he said, "You have a year for your research. What if you do oral histories? How about concentrating on Japanese women who immigrated from 1908 to 1924?" It all made very good sense. I started to do that, and every day or every other day I would meet one Japanese woman who would say, "Oh, I have a friend. She would be perfect." So I'd go visit this other woman. The stories they told were different, but they began to be very similar because the experiences of women from that period were similar. They would have been very young women who came with their families to work on plantations. If the woman was not a widow and her husband was still alive, invariably she would invite him to participate in the interview. I thought, "This won't be pure. How am I going to excise what he says?" But he was dying to talk. And sometimes we would sit there together, and, at an appropriate moment, she would serve dessert and bring her husband, and he would take over, and she would stop talking. Or she would not remember things and say, "Oh, I can't answer that." And so she would drag her husband in, and he would answer everything. The woman could tell me about raising her children or what she did in the home, but she could not tell me how much the family had paid for their parcel of land. Many of these people went from parcel to parcel. They leased land, and they left. All those decisions were made by men. They were not made by women unless it happened that the husband died or disappeared, and then the widow might have taken over.

So I couldn't get the full story. And I was thinking, "You know, I have a year to be here. I'm just going to hone in on this one very narrow subject and not get a larger picture. This is becoming ridiculous." So after about the first two months I thought, "It's not for me." I enjoyed being with these women, but after a while I just quit doing it. So I took some time off, and I said, "Ray, I want to see some rural life. What do you suggest?"[1] He said, "Why don't you go visit this commune? That's the easiest way for you to see rural life, the Japanese agriculture. You can also live at this place. There are many people there, and you'll find it interesting." He gave me some letters of recommendation, and I walked off with them. At the first commune I visited—there were two—this elderly man who came out to greet me said, "Well, what is it that you do?" I thought, "If I tell him that I'm doing oral histories of women, he's going to put me in the goddamn kitchen, and I'm going to be stuck there." So I said—I half lied and half didn't—"Well, I write." And he said, "You write? What have you written?" "Oh, short stories." Then he said, "Listen, I'm going to tell you my story because you write." I thought, "Oh no!"

So I sat down with him, and for the next week, day and night, he occupied my time telling me this story. I never got to the kitchen. I never got anywhere. I never got past the table. He sat me down and said, "Write this down. You don't understand? Look in your dictionary. Look here. Read it. You

335

Karen Tei Yamashita

know, your Japanese is getting better as the week goes on. This is good for you." It was hysterical. And he kept telling his story, and I kept taking notes, and I thought, "This might be good for something." After the week was over, I was able to get out and went on to the other commune. I said, "I met this very interesting man, and he was telling me his story." The people in the other commune said, "All lies! All lies! Oh, he told you that? No! It really happened like this." I was hooked.

Interspersed with all the storytelling were philosophical questions about use of the land, settlement, immigration, community, society, Japanese culture—all the big questions I wanted. I *knew*, then, that I couldn't do oral histories of women between 1908 and 1924. There was something to be had that was greater here.

MSM You talked earlier about not being able to access certain ideas through straight history that you can in fiction.

KTY Right. You can talk about the history, but I wanted to tell the stories. With straight history, you wouldn't have this line where someone would say, "At this point, my daughter died. I had to bury my daughter." You couldn't express the emotion. You couldn't express those extra things that illustrate history. You'd have to stick to facts. I also wanted to bring in a feeling for the sense of place, that scene, the smell—all those things that people have to deal with that tell more than just, "In 1925 there was an exclusion act here." How did it affect us here? What happened the year there was a frost that killed all the coffee trees? There is so much freedom in telling the story in a fictional manner, and I don't think I'd be very good at telling history.

MSM You mentioned a sense of "place." When I read the book, that was one thing that I felt was an issue throughout: What place do we call home? Clearly, Kantaro says, "We came to Brazil to settle." Not to escape conscription, or whatever the case may be, but to live here, set up something new, do something different. On the other hand, especially with Genji, there's almost no contact with Brazilians. They continue to think of themselves as just Japanese, not Japanese Brazilians. Where is the "place" in all that?

KTY I guess that's the question. What happens to this group of people is that there is this idea; but because of the situation in Brazil—the war, paranoia, their lack of practicing democracy, and an inability to face this reality even when it's presented to them—and also because of their arrogance and prejudice—their sense of themselves as being better—the idea is no longer clear.

When I started to write the book, I wanted less of the focus to be on Kantaro and particularization of what kind of life it was for that commune. I wanted it to be larger than that. That was part of the problem in earlier versions of the book where I diluted the story because I wanted to show this other thing that was happening. And, yet, he was right. He knew what the essence of his story was. He knew exactly how it could be best told. He knew exactly what to take out. He could write the screenplay for his life. And I laughed at myself because, when I was editing the book and pulling stuff out, it was like, "Yeah, he would take this out. Damn it!"

But I don't think he would have written about himself. It's sad because what happened was that this ideal became a very insular experiment, although that's not true of the children, of future generations, or even people in the other commune. Today, the communes exist, but they're smaller, and the children have left, and they've gone on to do other things. The story is really widening, and their relationship with the community is certainly larger and more complex. Many of them are in Japan.

MSM Emigrating back, now, in hard economic times?

Karen Tei Yamashita

KTY Right. They're in Japan working. And they do very well because they can speak Japanese pretty fluently. Probably more fluently than other Sansei or Nisei in the Japanese Brazilian community. So the adaptation to working in Japan is probably easier for them.

MSM You have four or five main narrators in the book, but only one of them is a woman. I was wondering, Why at that point? Why a woman narrator there?

KTY Haru was written in the last revision. She's always been in the book, but I'd never taken her voice. I had a friend of mine read one of the last versions of the book and got a lot of valid comment from her. We hashed through what I could do, and finally I came up with the idea of making Haru tell a portion of the story. It was very easy to drop into her voice. After writing this five times, her voice was the easiest to write. I knew who she was by the time I finished.

Some people have said that they wished there were more women's voices in the book, but in many ways this is a man's tale—this going forth with ideas, creating structures based on theories and ideas, building grand schemes. It's a male thing. Women come along, and, as Haru says, they clean up. They have to make it work, sweep out the houses, make everybody like each other.

I always said half facetiously that the Japanese men created the poultry industry because it was work that women and children could do. Women can gather the eggs, feed the chickens. Children can make sure that water feeders are out there. Men don't have to be there. They go market the stuff, drive the trucks, get the cash, make the money. But women have to stick around and do all the other things. Poultry was perfect because the women could stay near the house, take care of the house and their children at the same time. So I thought it was just the Japanese man's clever way to keep the women working and not the men. And women will tell you that. A lot of them will say, "We worked all day long. Even in the evening we would have to do the mending, and we would wake up early." I guess Haru shows this other side.

MSM Let's move from Brazil back to LA. I'd like to end by asking you a few questions about your newest book, *The Tropic of Orange*. How about the quirky characters in the novel?

KTY Someone wrote a review complaining that the characters weren't quite real. And it's true, they're not real. But they're not real in the same way that maybe Bart Simpson is not real, in the same way that all of us have ourselves become characters in the sense that we are increasingly defined by the entertainment we choose to surround ourselves with. Embedded in the characters are representations of entertainment because, after all, we're in LA. In a sense, this entertainment is driven by your understanding of it so that you as a reader are put in the driver's seat. The hypercontext at the beginning is sort of the map of the book. You have your map, you're in LA, and you have to drive. Now, what's the entertainment represented? There is literary entertainment—magical realism, noir; performance—dramatic and musical; the media—television, radio, and news; the newest toy of entertainment—the internet; and, finally, the movies—kung fu, Bruce Lee, and Jackie Chan.

MSM Yet characters such as Bobby, Manzanar, and Arcangel seem much more than embodiments of entertainment. They are such extraordinary inventions. . . .

KTY They also have their genesis in "real" people. In fact, as I wrote this book, I thought the truth of things that happen in LA is crazier than fiction. Bobby was inspired by someone I knew at work. I worked for many years at a public broadcasting station, KCET, Channel 28. There was a Chinese guy there who ran the mail run, who was raised in the Pico-Union

Karen Tei Yamashita

area, a Mexican-Central American area. He had a very strong accent: it was partly his Chinese accent, but it was mixed with Spanish because he was also speaking Spanish. I used to think of him as El Chino raised by Los Lobos.

Manzanar was inspired by someone my husband spotted on our way to work. I used to rideshare from Gardena over to Hollywood. I would ride with Ronaldo and sleep in the car. One day we were on the Harbor freeway, and he nudged me, "Wake up, wake up, wake up!" I looked up, and he said, "Oh, you missed it." What I had missed was apparently a man who was leaning over the overpass, conducting music. I never saw this man, but I had this image in my mind. At some point the image got put into a musical I did with Vicki Abe called *Godzilla Comes to Little Tokyo*. But we could never get the musical off the ground. I wanted to resurrect this character, Manzanar Murakami, so he's back in this book.

MSM You mentioned earlier that you can't write a book without a vision. What's the vision behind *Tropic of Orange*?

KTY I grew up in the fifties and sixties in Los Angeles, in what used to be the very center of Los Angeles, around Jefferson and Normandy, near USC. In those days, it was an African American place, and yet it had a Japanese American ghetto at the center of it. It was constituted of Japanese Americans returning from camps right after the war. These people were trying to get a jump start on their lives again. From LA I left for Minnesota and later traveled to Japan and then Brazil. When I finally came back to Los Angeles, I found a city that was very different, filled with people from all over the globe. I found living here very exciting. I reveled in being here again. I started to take a look at the literature of Los Angeles, but no one was talking yet about that change. I wrote the book to bring in those who have been invisible in the literature of Los Angeles. I also wanted to take a look at my experience because, returning from Brazil, I found myself adapting to my own country. I found my family part of this great movement of immigrants to the city, and I certainly identify with that movement. A friend of mine read the book and commented that there are no white characters in it. Well, someone else gets to tell the story for a change.

Note

1. Raymond Narusawa, a Free Methodist missionary to Brazil. Yamashita lived with him and his family for three months at the beginning of her stay in Brazil.

Selected Works by Karen Tei Yamashita

"The Bath." *Amerasia Journal* 3, no. 1 (Summer 1975): 131–152. Reprinted in *The Third Woman: Minority Women Writers of the United States,* ed. Dexter Fisher (Boston: Houghton Mifflin, 1980), in *Multitude: Cross-Cultural Readings for Writers,* ed. Chitra B. Divakaruni (New York: McGraw-Hill, 1993), and in *Uncommon Knowledge: Exploring Ideas through Reading and Writing,* ed. Rose Hawkins and Robert Isaacson (Boston: Houghton Mifflin, 1996).

"Tucano." *Rafu Shimpo* (Los Angeles), 20 December 1975, 11, 35.

Omen: An American Kabuki. 1978. This play was produced by the East West Players in Los Angeles in 1978. It is available through the New World Theater, University of Massachusetts at Amherst.

Hiroshima Tropical. 1984. This play was produced as a work in progress by the East West Players in Los Angeles in 1984. It is available through the New World Theater, University of Massachusetts at Amherst.

"The Dentist and the Dental Hygienist." *Asiam* (Los Angeles) (April 1987): 66–70. Reprinted in *Hermes* (Tokyo) 55 (1995): 125–135.

Hannah Kusoh: An American Butoh. 1989. This play was produced at the Japanese American Cultural Community Center, Los Angeles, and Highways, Santa Monica. It is available through the New World Theater, University of Massachusetts at Amherst. *Madama Butterfly: The Sense of Sound (Part 5),* a scene from *Hannah Kusoh,* appears in *Premonitions,* ed. Walter K. Lew (New York: Kaya Productions, 1995).

"The Japanese Brazilians." *Rafu Shimpo* (Los Angeles), 16 December 1989, A4–A8, B27–B31.

Through the Arc of the Rain Forest. Minneapolis: Coffee House, 1990.

Tokyo Carmen vs. L.A. Carmen. 1990. This play was produced at Taper, Too, Los Angeles, as part of "Thirteenth Hour: A Festival of Performance." Parts 1 and 2 have been published in *Multicultural Theatre: Scenes and Monologs from New Hispanic, Asian, and African-American Plays,* ed. Roger Ellis (Colorado Springs, Colo.: Meriwether, 1996). The entire play is available through the New World Theater, University of Massachusetts at Amherst.

Godzilla Comes to Little Tokyo. 1991. Musical produced at the Northwest Asian American Theatre, Seattle.

"The Orange." *Los Angeles Times Magazine,* 30 June 1991, 12–13, 36. Reprinted in *Chicago Review* 39, nos. 3–4 (1993): 12–16, and *Hermes* (Tokyo) 55 (1995): 121–125

Brazil-Maru. Minneapolis: Coffee House, 1992.

GiLAwrecks. 1992. Reading performance produced at the Japanese American Cultural Community Center, Los Angeles. *GiLAwrecks* is also known as *Godzilla Comes to Little Tokyo.*

Noh Bozos. 1993. Produced at the Japanese American Cultural Community Center, Los Angeles.

"Virtual Reality vs. Magic Reality." *Subaru* (Tokyo), no. 8 (August 1995): 180–184. Essay.

"The Last Secretary." In *2000 and What? Stories about the Turn of the Millenium,* ed. Karl Roeseler and David Gilbert. San Francisco: Trip Street, 1996.

"Siamese Twins and Mongoloids, Cultural Appropriation and the Deconstruction of Stereotype via the Absurdity of Humor." *DisOrient* (Los Angeles) 4 (1997): 60–68. Essay.

Tropic of Orange. Minneapolis: Coffee House, 1997.

19

Hisaye Yamamoto and Wakako Yamauchi

Interview by
KING-KOK CHEUNG

A lasting friendship between two acclaimed Nisei writers, Hisaye Yamamoto and Wakako Yamauchi, blossomed in the desert of Poston, Arizona, where the two women were interned during World War II. Yamamoto, author of *Seventeen Syllables and Other Stories* (1988), received the American Book Award for Lifetime Achievement from the Before Columbus Foundation in 1986. Yamauchi's *Songs My Mother Taught Me: Stories, Plays, and Memoir* (1994) received the Association for Asian American Studies' 1995 National Book Award in literature. But Yamauchi is best known as a playwright. Her plays include *The Music Lessons, 12-1-A, The Chairman's Wife,* and *And the Soul Shall Dance,* which won the 1977–1978 American Theatre Critics Association's first regional award for outstanding playwriting.

Some of the themes that recur in the work of these two writers—whose lives have been intertwined at various points—are remarkably similar. But their temperaments are markedly different, as becomes evident in the joint interview I conducted with them as part of the fiftieth anniversary commemoration of the Japanese American internment. I wanted to interview them together because they know each other intimately and I hoped that, being exceeding modest, they would speak more freely that way. Allowing them to talk about each other brought up information I would have had a difficult time eliciting in a one-on-one conversation. The interview took place at Yamauchi's home in Gardena after the hostess had plied us with a generous assortment of sushi. Throughout the interview, Yamamoto is referred to as Si (pronounced *Sai*), as she is called by her friends.

KKC When did you two meet, and how long have you known each other?

HY About 1940, when I went down to Oceanside. As soon as I got there, my brother, who was in the same class as Wakako at Oceanside Carlsbad High School, would tell me about this smart Japanese girl that was in his English class, and it turned out to be her.

WY When I was a girl, I lived in Brawley. I used to read Si's columns in the *Kashu Mainichi*,[1] and I thought, My goodness, who is this person? This was the first time I had read a Japanese American who spoke about our culture, the food we ate, and I thought, This is wonderful! You can be honest. So I read her column for quite a while, and then we moved to Oceanside because my father had suffered an enormous crop disaster, and it was like fate. Somebody said that Si Yamamoto lived here. I wanted to meet her, and I did, one day, at the meeting they were trying to develop for the young people's club. I'd already known Johnny, her brother, because we were in the same class, and I used to see her other brother, Jemo; and I met her.

HY She said at that time she got the impression I was cold, but I distinctly remember playing tick-tack-toe with her on the blackboard in the schoolhouse where we had the meeting.

KKC What was your impression of Wakako?

HY I thought Wakako and her sister really worked hard because they would come out with these sun hats and work out in the fields picking Kentucky beans while I just puttered around the house and went back and forth to the library.

WY Our family lived in town. My mother had a boarding-house, so, when the farmers came to pick up, we'd go out to the fields, too, and we'd get paid! We'd be so tired that at lunchtime we'd just lie in the dirt.

HY I didn't know that. I would have invited you in.

WY I didn't even know you lived there, and, yes, I did think you were cold. I was so effusive. I thought she should have been responsive to that, but she wasn't. She was very calm and very august.

KKC And you met again at Poston?

WY Yes. The first time we met in Oceanside I don't think I saw Si much then. But in camp we both were working for the *Poston Chronicle.* That's when we became friends.

HY Yes, and Jeanie Inokuchi. The three of us would try to scandalize the camp by walking around with red or blue kneesocks, all matching.

WY We were the beatniks of our day.

KKC How did each of you decide to become a writer?

WY Si was already a writer when we were in camp; I didn't even dream of being one. When I was a girl, I thought I would write an epic poem. I used to read Tennyson and say, "I'm going to write like that one day." But, as I grew older, I realized how difficult it was to write and how much you had to know; so I never aspired to be a writer. I thought maybe when I grew up I would get a job in an advertising agency and maybe wash brushes.

Hisaye Yamamoto and Wakako Yamauchi

HY She was an artist. That's how she came to the newspaper in camp—as a cartoonist.

KKC Why did you switch from painting to writing?

WY Si said the reason I gave was not valid, so I won't give that one.

KKC Do tell us.

WY Well, I was under the impression that Si stopped writing for a while. I thought maybe one of us should be writing, but she says that's not true. The reason why I did write was that there were stories I really wanted to tell. I didn't have to know a lot as long as I knew what I felt, and so I just wrote these stories. One of the first ones I completed was "And the Soul Shall Dance."

KKC How did you get started, Si?

HY Not long after I first learned to read, my father and mother brought in these bales of Japanese American newspapers so they could make hot caps to fit over young shoots in the fields. I had a field day looking through all the English sections, thinking, Oh, maybe I can write, too, one of these days and get my name in the paper. . . . All vanity.

KKC Which writers had the strongest influence on you when you started?

HY I don't know because I read one book after another in those days.

KKC But didn't you say somewhere that the Japanese American writers had had the strongest impact on you?

HY Because they were of the same background, and that didn't prevent them from writing, so that kind of encouraged me to do likewise eventually.

WY I started off just like she did. We would order these bales of newspapers—we called them brush covers—to cover the plants, to keep them from being attacked by the frost, and there was nothing to do in the country but read, so I would look through these papers, and I found Si, and I thought she was the best writer among them all. I just enjoyed her articles; they were humorous, intelligent, and grammatical—something that I discovered to be rare.

HY All that stuff I used to write couldn't have been very elevated.

WY Well, it was funny, and you were honest. You talked about things I knew about, like *gohan* [cooked rice] and *tsukemono* [pickles].

KKC But some of the stories in *Seventeen Syllables* are sad rather than funny.

HY I'm what you call a humorist manqué. Every time I started a story I would try to be funny, and it would always end up kind of tragic sometimes, so I don't know what happens between my intention and the outcome. Those characters take over and go down to destruction.

KKC Can you two say something about the influence of Japanese American tradition on you as women and as writers?

WY Well, I've always been a Japanese American, and, in those days, racism was so prevalent that, from early childhood, you naturally went toward your own, and from where I came from there were no Chinese, no Koreans, so all I had were Japanese playmates at school. When we came home, there was nobody but your sister and your brother. As a woman, I was very much influenced by the Japanese culture. My saving grace is that my mother was an extremely strong woman, a person in her own right; she took no guff from anybody, including white people, and I think that helps. Also, my position in the

Hisaye Yamamoto and Wakako Yamauchi

family—I was a third child after a sister and a brother; by that time my parents were just tired of disciplining the kids. They just let me go around. I was extremely strong willed, very headstrong, and I got away with it.

KKC Have your stories—about mothers—actually told the story of your own mother?

WY I was trying to tell it to myself. I was trying to figure out where she came from, what happened to her, and why. The way women were brought here in those times seemed so unfair, and I think I was trying to set it right.

HY They didn't fare much better in Japan.

WY I know, but this is all I knew: my mother was a woman who pined to go back to Japan, and she didn't seem to fit into this country, in this dry, hot, dusty area, and grubbing in the dirt like she had to to help my father. Maybe that's why I write about her, to see why, and to get it straight in my own mind.

KKC And you, Si?

HY I say I'm telling my mother's story in "Seventeen Syllables," but I'm probably telling my own, that women express their creativity under all kinds of circumstances, and the way that story has been reprinted so much I think she's behind it all, getting everybody to reprint it. So I call it her story. Yet it is not just about Japanese women here. All over the world I think women are kept from doing what they are capable of doing.

KKC Was your mother encouraging when you were writing?

HY Oh, yes. When she found me writing on either butcher paper or the back of paper bags or something, she said, "What are you doing?" And I said, "I'm writing a story." And she said, "Then you should live in a house on top of a hill where a cool breeze blows so you can write." I felt that was surely encouraging.

KKC What about the fathers? How did they react to your writing?

WY I never wrote until they were both dead. My father died when I was about twenty, and my mother died when I was thirty-one.

KKC You said earlier that it's unfair the way the women came to this country. What about the men?

WY I don't think they came because they had to. They wanted better for themselves. The women were kind of sold into it, as picture brides. But my mother was not a picture bride. She came here with dreams of returning rich; that's why she could never go back. She had promised her sister, "When I come back, I will be rich." So she could never go back because she was never rich.

KKC But did your fathers have any influence on your writing?

HY Mine never objected to it that I recall. Yes, once a neighbor in Oceanside was told by his children that I was writing unseemly things, so this neighbor asked my father to tell me to quit writing. I got very indignant and kept writing. I don't know what they were talking about.

WY She was very honest; she talked about her neighbors, her brothers, her friends.

HY I don't know if anybody complained to the English-section editor, who was Roy Takeno at the *Kashu Mainichi*, but I remember him writing to me, in a letter that enclosed five dollars—token payment for the whole year. He wrote, "Don't be so hard on the ubiquitous characteristics of the Nisei." So I must have been making fun of us.

Hisaye Yamamoto and Wakako Yamauchi

KKC Were either of you brought up according to any particular religion? Did your beliefs change later?

WY I was brought up as a Buddhist, and I haven't changed my belief. Religion was not that important to me, or else it was so ingrained that I didn't notice it.

HY I was brought up Buddhist, too. We didn't go to church exactly, but we went to Buddhist funerals and weddings. I was already in my thirties when I accepted the idea that Jesus Christ was the Son of God. That automatically makes me a Christian, right? But I don't reject any of that Buddhism. It's like taking Catholicism down to Mexico and coming up with Our Lady of Guadalupe. You can synthesize.

KKC What are some of your fondest memories of childhood or of adolescence?

WY I loved my mother very much, and I loved listening to her stories and listening to her songs. In adolescence, I loved being alive, and I loved falling in love, and those kind of things made life so exciting for a country girl.

HY For me, adolescence was painful. But during childhood we had all this outdoor space to roam around in, all kinds of food growing on the trees and bushes. In those days, there was no smog, except when they had to start up those fires for the orange groves when the temperature dipped too low. I had a wonderful time. But it was very hard for me to adjust to high school, and I remember more pain than pleasure from that period.

KKC How comfortable are you with the label *Asian American writer*?

WY I feel very comfortable. I'm an Asian American, and I write Asian American stories, so I am an Asian American writer. And Asian American people are interested in my writing. I don't think anybody else is.

HY Yes, it's all right. Whatever I'm called is not going to affect what I do.

KKC Do you think that, being women of your generation, you have had a harder time writing?

WY The women of my generation are brought up to hold down our emotions, to be more passive, and to censor before we even think. I have a very difficult time writing because of that. I have to try not to censor before I get it on paper. Nowadays, people have more freedom; they accept their passions, their emotions, their sorrows, and their joys. We were taught not to do that because you had to hold your head up; even if it hurts, you smile and say, "Oh fine, fine."

HY Yes, but she was one of the first Nisei I met that was so free about her feelings. I didn't think so much about my feelings then. In camp, when we got to be pretty good friends, she would confide things like sunset making her sad, and I never reacted to sunset that way. All these things were revelations, and I got an education in sensitivity from her that I never would have had otherwise. I never even thought about stuff like that. For me, the sun went down, and that was it. I just accepted the change of the seasons and rolled with the punches, so to speak.

WY But that's the nature of people like us that are very close to the earth, like the bear. They say that you get depressed in the winter. I used to feel like that every winter....

KKC Do either of you feel any political obligations as a writer? As an Asian American writer or a woman writer?

WY I try not to. I write as a person, as a woman, as an Asian American, and, if I fulfill my political obligations in being honest, then great. I try not to think like that because I'm a very simple person and I have to tell my story as simply as I

Hisaye Yamamoto and Wakako Yamauchi

can. If I feel politically inclined, or if something enrages me, maybe it will come out.

HY My politics are radical; I don't know if it comes out in the writing because I don't deliberately try to inject it. I don't even vote because I consider myself anarchist.

WY I believe that, whatever you write, your social consciousness comes out no matter how you try to camouflage it.

KKC Both of you started publishing in Japanese American newspapers. Now your work is read by people of different ethnic backgrounds. Does that shift in audience affect your writing in any way? Do you find yourself writing for a specific audience or trying to reach out to everyone?

WY I try not to think about audience. I don't know if everybody is reading my stuff. I don't think so.

HY I don't think a writer aims at any audience.

KKC But, when you wrote for Japanese American newspapers, you knew that people would understand all the Japanese American terms.

HY Sure, I'm writing for my fellow Japanese Americans. I don't know how I felt when I was sending stories to other places. Maybe I had to do a little more explaining about Japanese terms.

KKC How would you characterize the reception of your work? Are there any particularly upsetting or gratifying responses?

WY I never got any response. That's one of the reasons why I quit writing for *Rafu Shimpo*.[2] I thought, Nobody's reading my stuff; I'm going to quit, and then the paper will be deluged with people saying, Where's Wakako Yamauchi? But nobody said a thing.

KKC A lot of people are commenting on your plays now.

WY Oh, yes, a famous playwright. But it hurts me when they tear me up, and they do tear me up.

HY You mean the critics?

WY Yes. As far as the audience is concerned, I feel that what one likes the other hates. But, as far as the critics are concerned, if they don't give you a good review, nobody will come to see the play.

HY I never got published for many, many years; I just wrote for the Japanese newspapers.

KKC That's publication, too.

HY But nobody responded to my writing that I remember. I remember Henry Mori asking us every October to write something for the holiday issue, and I would always do it no matter what. And he got us pretty good payment.

KKC Good reinforcement.

WY/HY Uh-huh.

KKC How old were you when Executive Order 9066 came? Do you remember your reaction when you first learned that you were to be herded into camps?

HY I was twenty. I remember this neighbor girl who belonged to San Diego JACL [Japanese American Citizens' League] evidently coming around to ask us to sign these JACL petitions that said that, to prove our patriotism, we would willingly go to camp. I said, "No, I'm not going to sign any such thing." She was appalled because Nisei don't treat each other that way; they all try to get along with each other. I felt bad about making her feel bad. So I don't know if I signed it or not. I hope I didn't.

WY I was seventeen. My first recollection was reading the Japanese papers and seeing these pictures of people going to camp. I guess a lot of people went ahead to prepare the places—camps—for us, and these people were waiting in lines, holding tin plates for their dinner. I was not a very political person. I didn't know what was going on—I knew that Japan was at war with America, and I knew that, for many, many years, there were hostilities, and I knew that we suffered a great deal of racism—but I didn't like the idea of it. In civics classes, we were told that all men are created equal. But we went.

KKC Who started the camp newspaper *Poston Chronicle*? Were both of you recruited to work for it?

HY No, I was working as a waitress in the mess hall, and then my friend—my neighbor Jeanie—and I heard about them recruiting staff for the paper, so we went over there and started working, if you could call it that. It was called *Press Bulletin* to start with, and then it became *The Chronicle*. We got our sixteen-dollar-a-month allowance that everybody got. The doctors and other professionals got nineteen dollars a month, and apprentices got twelve dollars. Later on, everybody started gravitating toward the hospital for the three dollars extra.

KKC What did each of you do exactly for the *Poston Chronicle*?

WY There were three of us artists, and we were all teenagers, and I guess nobody who's a real artist would want to do that work. It's just mimeographing, cutting stencils, and getting textures: you put a little plate under there, and you just rub it, and you get little different textures. There was one fellow named George Okamoto who was very good. I was terrible, but I didn't want to work in the mess hall, and I'd heard they were looking for artists to do advertising, and I said, "Oh, I can do that." But how do you advertise in camp? What is there to advertise?

HY The editor would send me around from office to office asking for news, and I'd take anybody that wanted to come along. Wakako and Jeanie and I, we all walked around together to get my no-news from every office, making wry comments about this person and that person as we went.

KKC What was it like to be living with so many Japanese Americans all of a sudden?

HY You got used to it. I'd lived on this mesa where there were about twenty different Japanese families farming, so it wasn't that new to me. But you never saw that many Japanese all in one place at one time.

KKC With so many young men and women living together in camp, was there a surge in romance?

WY There were a lot, but guys didn't like me. I was sort of antisocial, anyway, so I didn't fit in very well. I pretended to; I wore this veneer of superiority.

HY In our block, we had this bachelor's dorm, where there were people like Howard Kakudo, a cartoonist at Walt Disney Studios, prewar.

WY Who was very, very handsome.

HY And Coburn Nakamura, the hairdresser. They would drop in once in a while and chat and see me picking at my athlete's foot. And some of them would make a suggestive remark. But I don't think I was interested in boys. I had this idea of being a writer first. So this was all extraneous stuff that you put up with.

WY But didn't you feel the natural juices? I mean, I didn't even want to think of guys; my nature would just feel that attraction.

HY Oh, these girls were always asking me questions like, "What Nisei would you rather be if you could be anybody?" I would say, "I don't want to be anybody but me." But one time they wore me down. And I said that, if I had to be some

Hisaye Yamamoto and Wakako Yamauchi

other Nisei, maybe Jim Yamada—who was at Topaz and wrote for *Trek* and wrote very nice short stories. So what do you know, he came to our camp.

WY And one of the things that happened to me—because I thought so highly of Si as a person and as a writer, when she told me that she would like to be this Jim Yamada, I immediately fell madly in love with the guy, and he didn't even know I was alive! But he used to come swimming at the swimming hole next to his block. We—Edith and I—would stand neck deep in this icky, muddy green water while we watched him swim. He did a wonderful swan dive, jackknife, and he sat on the barge and contemplated the sunset, and, finally, Edy—Edith, one of the reporters for the *Poston Chronicle*—called him over and asked him to teach us how to swim.

KKC What was best and worst about camp life when you look back?

WY The worst is the colonization of the mind. You think you are less than what other people are because you are there. Best, like Si said, are friendships that we made and the growing up we did, too. I learned a lot in camp. I was really, really green. I'm still not there, but I sure was green.

HY Just before the war, my father was finally able to resume farming in Oceanside, and he'd planted his first crop of strawberries. That was sold along with all the other stuff on the farm to this man named Pierson from El Monte who bought it all up, and then we all went to work just before we were evacuated, picking the strawberries and everything for him. I guess he paid the farmer's cooperative there for the produce, but I'm sure he made a lot of money.

WY After my father had this big fiasco in Brawley and we moved to Oceanside, my mother started to operate a boardinghouse for farm laborers, like the transient immigrants. They call them *buranke katsugi* [lit. blanket carriers]. They travel the length of California harvesting—in Oceanside, strawberries; in Bakersfield, Fresno, grapes and celery. My mother ran this boardinghouse, and it seemed like she was just paying the debts and, possibly finally, after all these years, making enough money to realize her dream of going back. And then the war came along, and we lost everything except the stuff that we carried in our hands to camp.

KKC How were the families affected in camp?

HY In some mess halls, they had the family system, but eventually most young people started eating with their friends.

WY Maybe some of these things would have happened anyway. Most of us were just at the median age of seventeen, just at that rebellious stage. We were asked to answer these very important questions at seventeen and eighteen without any knowledge of politics.[3] And we were asked to denounce Japan or agree to fight wherever they sent us. And that really tore up the families! In our family, my brother was the only one that went to Tule Lake. My sister went out to Arkansas, got married to a U.S. soldier, and I went to Chicago.

KKC Both of you lost a family member during the internment.

HY My brother Johnny was one of the first to leave with the young men that were going out to Colorado to top sugar beets. Evidently, they needed a lot of labor there because there was sugar rationing during the war. They made a lot of sugar beets then, and they would top them so that the beet would grow larger by itself without the leaf. When that season was over, Johnny went to Denver and worked washing dishes in a boys' seminary, and then he was candling eggs, and he was going to night school, taking accounting classes, and then all of a sudden we heard he'd volunteered for the 442d. Antiwar as I was or am, I didn't think he'd done a good thing. But it didn't take him long to get through basic and go over to Italy and get killed. He was only nineteen when he died; I don't know if that would have happened if we weren't in camp.

KKC Did your father try to stop him?

HY No, when young people want to go out, they go out, where there's promise of more money than the sixteen dollars a month.

WY There's the freedom, too.

HY Yes, freedom.

KKC What about your father, Wakako?

WY My father died during the last few weeks of camp, when they were pushing everybody out. He had a preexisting health problem—ulcers. He was a minor-league alcoholic. He was unable to express himself, so his pain just ate him up. When he got in camp, it got aggravated, and then it got better. Then Hiroshima was bombed. I believe the thought of going back out, starting from scratch, killed him. My mother said that, after Hiroshima was bombed, he got very sick and started to bleed, and he died in November, in camp. I was in Chicago, and, when my mother said, "He's going, come home," I came home, but it took about four days to get back on those milk wagons. (We called them *milk wagons,* those old trains.) By the time I got back, there was hardly anybody in camp. I could hear the voices of the people coming back from the wake, and I knew he died. Shortly after that he was cremated, and we left camp.

KKC Any other memories about camp?

HY Dust storms. One time, in the early months, there was such a bad dust storm, and nothing had been planted yet. This mud was rushing horizontally past the windows. I was horrified because I'd never seen weather like that before. Wide-open spaces. Major lightning storms, which were frightening but beautiful to watch. And the vegetation that was there, unique to that area, like mesquite and cotton-woods and tamarisks.

WY And ironwood and manzanita.

HY If you didn't have to go there, you would find it maybe a beautiful place to visit.

WY The big November strike.[4] As far as I remember, there were two guys who beat up on some of the JACL members suspected of being FBI informers. These two guys were put in the Poston prison, which was just another barrack with a lock on it. So the whole camp went on strike because the two guys were going to be taken to Tucson to be tried. There were other grievances, too, which were all put into one big package.

KKC What was your routine in camp? What did you do together?

WY Oh, walk around, and talk, and . . .

WY/HY [*Together.*] Argue!

WY One night, Si showed me a poem and said, "It's wonderful." I read it and said, "I don't think it's so good." And she said, "It's better than what you do." I was furious, and I rolled up this paper and started beating her up with it, and she was lying on a bench, letting it happen.

HY Well, I was laughing, too, because it was ridiculous.

WY I don't know how I stopped, probably grew tired or my arms flew off.

Hisaye Yamamoto and Wakako Yamauchi

HY But that taught me a lesson about criticizing other people's poetry.

WY You should have told me when you read my poem that it was no good, but you didn't.

HY And we don't even remember the poem now.

WY No, but I told this story to Garrett Hongo once, and he laughed about it because, in his mind's eye, he was seeing these two old ladies fighting.

WY/HY But we were young.

KKC Were there other writers in camp?

HY Quite a few. Fuku Yokoyama was in Camp 2; she still writes in Honolulu, under her married name, Tsukiyama.

WY Jim Yamada was there, but he didn't write when he came to Poston. He was deep in his sociological surveys.

HY There were these people who were writing their books, like Alexander Leighton, who'd be down at the Ad Building once in a while. Dorothy Swaine Thomas and Richard Nishimoto showed up, too.

WY Nikki Sawada Bridges, who wrote a poem about camp.

WY The real artists were in Topaz: Miné Okubo and all those writers. . . .

HY Toshio Mori and Jim Yamada and Toyo Suyemoto.

KKC Did the incarceration determine what you did after camp?

HY In between, my two brothers and I had gone to Massachusetts, and I worked as a cook. I didn't know anything about cooking, and here I was cooking. My brother Jemo was supposed to be the butler. The other brother, since he was so young, got to go to summer camp with other kids, so he had a fine time. I had asked for farm work because that's all I knew physically. They got us to Springfield to work for this millionaire lady whose mother had a farm out in a place called Longmeadow. But we never did get there because we got news of Johnny dying and our father asked us to come back to camp, so we went back. The following spring I went up to Manzanar to visit my aunt so that we could make relocation plans, and then on the bus down I met Emily, my good friend from Compton Junior College days. She had visited camp from Chicago, and she was coming down to Los Angeles. We both stayed at Evergreen Hostel, which was a place where a lot of the returnees stayed before they found places to go. And I found a job with the *LA Tribune* before I found a house, and then I found a house, and then about twenty people came to stay at the house at one time or another. Right?

WY I did. It was like a hostel at her house, and she did all the cooking.

HY I didn't do all the cooking. I remember Emily making stew and baking bread.

WY I had no idea, but every time I think about you and Jemo in Massachusetts as cook and butler it just makes me laugh.

HY The War Manpower Commission had sent the millionaire's chauffeur to work in the factory, and they had sent her cook somewhere else.

WY That's why the boys in our camp had to go out and top sugar beets, because all the white laborers were working in the defense industries.

KKC What happened to your home in Oceanside after the war?

HY Where we lived was called Stewart Mesa, and they had already been planning to turn that into Camp Pendleton (though we didn't know this). There were Engineer Corps

Hisaye Yamamoto and Wakako Yamauchi

marching down the dirt road to survey the place, and there were big pipes from a company from Irvine, everything lying around in big stacks. We were doomed, but we didn't know it. There was no home to go back to—it was all Camp Pendleton. I had this sense of déjà vu when they sent the Vietnamese and Cambodians that escaped Vietnam there, in the Marine tents. So there were these Asians where we used to live. It was a beautiful place. You can see and hear the ocean from there, and I thought I would like to live there the rest of my life. But not the way it is now. It's all barracks and Marine stuff.

WY Because of the Alien Land Law, Asian immigrants couldn't own their own land. We didn't even own the hotel. It was owned by a white landlord. When the farmers didn't come back, there was no point in having a boardinghouse, which was like an employment agency: farmers came in and picked up the guys and then took them home. After the war, there was nothing to go back to. So my mother just joined the last contingent out, and we went to San Diego. My older sister and I looked for a job. All the papers were advertising—like the telephone companies were advertising for women to come and interview, and the defense industries were still advertising. We went everywhere, but we couldn't get a job. We were housed in a trailer—where they put us after we came out of camp. It was a navy yard. My sister and I were coming home one day, and the bus stopped just short of the trailer park. We were walking from the bus stop, and we went by this warehouse-looking place that said: "Help Wanted." It was a photofinishing place, and we said, "Let's go in there, and, if they say they've already hired, let's go to the window and tear up that 'Help Wanted' sign."

So we went in there fully expecting to be rejected, but they said, "Come in; we'll hire you!" It turned out to be morons' work. All we had to do was to put all the numbers together.

362

The snapshots you take are printed with a number on them, a different number for each order. We just sat there and sorted these numbers: all the 158s go in one pile and the 159s in another and so on. But we started to get better jobs at this place, and my sister ended up being a printer for snapshots. She printed the negatives, and I sat doping [i.e., developing] them and threw them into the chemical solution. I sat all day, throwing. That's where I learned to smoke.

KKC How long were you at that job?

WY Off and on, I guess a couple of years, from one photofinishing plant to another. We struck, got thrown out, then found another job.

HY Didn't you do that in Chicago, too?

WY No, in Chicago I was running a candy-wrapper machine.

HY I thought in the end you worked in photofinishing.

WY Oh, yes, you're right. I wanted to get out of that candy factory, so I (when you're young, you have all kinds of guts) went to one of the bigger department stores called Carson Pirie Scott. I went to the photo department to ask if I could get a job doing retouching (which is not photofinishing). They said they sent their stuff out, but the lady was very nice, and she gave me the name of this guy they sent their stuff out to.

KKC Si, you said that you found your job before the house. Can you describe your job with the *Los Angeles Tribune*?

HY While I was staying at the hostel, I saw this ad in the *Pacific Citizen*—in those days a Negro newspaper—wanting a Japanese American man to work for them. I applied. Another applicant was Bean Takeda, a Nisei who had edited his own newspaper before the war. I thought, Shoot, I don't have a chance, because he was reeling off these names, like he went

Hisaye Yamamoto and Wakako Yamauchi

to school with Kenny Washington and Woody Strode, who were big football players. What do you know—they hired me instead of him.

KKC Why do you think that was the case?

HY I figure they recognized some kinship in me. They weren't very business minded. (Bean Takeda was very success oriented.) What they wanted the Japanese for was to maybe make contacts with the returning Japanese community so that they could have a sort of joint newspaper. During the war, Little Tokyo had become Bronzeville—the blacks had moved in. Once the Japanese came back, they took over again. But I didn't go out to get Japanese ads for them, so they just kind of tolerated me.

KKC Did you like that experience?

HY Oh, yes. After a while I learned an enormous amount— on top of grammar—which they taught me. But the oppression and discrimination [faced by blacks] finally got to me, and the weight was just too much to bear. So after two, three years I left. I said I was going back to school, but that's when I started writing the short stories.

KKC But then you joined the Catholic Workers. How did that happen?

HY This *Catholic Worker* newspaper used to come in as a *Tribune* exchange, and I used to go through all the exchanges and combine stories, like there would be a story in one paper about how to live to be a hundred, and somebody would say that they went to church and went to bed early and got up early; somebody else in another paper would say they lived to be a hundred by drinking and smoking and eating everything they felt like. I would combine stories like that, including combining all the lynchings that took place during the week. One of the newspapers that came in was the *Catholic Worker*.

I felt attracted to it and to the work of the Workers. After I quit the paper I subscribed; the more I read it, the more I wanted to go join, to live in a community like that and take part in the work.

KKC What were you attracted to, particularly?

HY Peter Maurin [one of the founders of the *Catholic Worker*] believed in a synthesis of what he called "cult, culture, and cultivation," which meant going back to the land. His ideal was that a person could work out in the fields maybe four days—four hours a day—and then go back to the farmhouse and paint or write or do printing or whatever, all centered around the Catholic Church. They were also pacifists who believed in living out the Sermon on the Mount as far as humanly possible, and these things just appealed to me.

KKC Still, it was a pretty radical decision to drop everything and join.

HY Well, it took a while, corresponding and meeting Dorothy Day here before I finally went.

KKC Tell us about your experience with the Workers.

HY Oh, golly, it was so variegated. We used to go to daily mass, and I went with Paul, my [adopted] little boy, who was born a Catholic. (I got him when he was five months old.) He would say, "I'm the Catholic, and my mother's the Worker." We would end the day with compline if things were going right, but sometimes things got pretty wild there, with people having emotional problems, and alcoholics, and religious fanatics, and people who went there for the same reason I did, who believed in the work. And I got to do things like going around killing tomato worms and feeding the chickens and rabbits. Eventually, they asked me to review books and do the farm column and . . . cook.

Hisaye Yamamoto and Wakako Yamauchi

KKC How many people were there?

HY It varied; maybe a core of about twenty to twenty-five, and then there were always people coming and going.

KKC Were you the only Asian?

HY I guess so, but there were visitors from Japan.

KKC And then?

HY Let's see. Oh, I got married and came back to California.

KKC I guess you don't want to talk about falling in love.

HY No, I don't want to talk about falling in love. . . . [*Sings.*] Falling in love. . . .

KKC Wakako, did the internment affect your career as a writer?

WY No, I didn't write until I was older. I started writing for *Rafu Shimpo.* . . .

HY You were doing the artwork.

WY Yes, and I was very happy with the work I was doing. I always wanted to write, but I didn't think I was good enough. One day, my ex-husband said, "Why don't you offer to do the artwork for free if they'll accept your stories?" That's the pressure I put on Henry Mori [postwar editor of *Rafu Shimpo*'s English section], who said "all right" as though he was doing me this big favor, and after a while I got really tired of his patronizing. And I wasn't getting any response from readers, so I said, I guess I'm not really a writer.

KKC Both of you have written about the internment, Si in "The Legend of Miss Sasagawara" and Wakako in *12-1-A*. Are any of the people and events described in these works based on your actual experience?

HY It's all so jumbled; nothing is really autobiographical because, for instance, in a story like "Yoneko's Earthquake," I've borrowed stuff that people said about Wakako and her relationship with her mother. In fact, I visualized Mrs. Hosoume as Wakako's mother. And then my own experience is in there and other people's, too.

KKC Then it is based on actual experience, even if it's not just your own.

HY Yes, that's right.

KKC What about *12-1-A?*

WY Everybody in there is somebody or parts of somebody I know, and everybody in there is me. Mr. Ichioka, who never came out of his barrack and who quietly died, is like my father. Yo I took from Si's character. Although Si certainly wasn't that active a feminist, she was nevertheless a feminist, and she taught me a lot.

HY I didn't recognize myself in her.

WY I hope you didn't. And Mitch, the young man that went to camp, I took from my brother. He did go to top sugar beets, and he did go to Tule Lake. I don't think that Mrs. Tanaka was my mother, but I took parts of her—the nagging parts.

KKC I read an essay by Dorothy Ritsuko McDonald and Katharine Newman about the two of you. They say that, whereas Wakako stresses personal involvement with her characters and writes totally within the Japanese American community, Si moves outward and sees the world in interaction. Do you agree with that assessment?

WY They are right about me because that's the only experience I have.

Hisaye Yamamoto and Wakako Yamauchi

HY Me, too. The statement about personal experience would be just as valid about me, right?

KKC Except your stories usually have characters besides Japanese Americans. I believe that's what they mean by your going outward. In your experiences both with the *Tribune* and the Catholic Workers, you were actually not surrounded by any Japanese Americans.

HY I guess not, but I don't look at things that way. As long as I write and I'm Japanese American, it's Japanese American experience, isn't it?

WY I didn't have too much involvement with other races. In fact, the first Chinese I met was Shawn Wong.

KKC Was that before or after you became a writer?

WY After I became a writer.

HY We had a meeting here with Shawn and Lawson [Inada]. They were making this film about Lawson.

KKC So, even though you both grew up in rural communities, your experiences have been very different.

HY The kids I went to school with were of all nationalities: Dutch, Armenian, French, Mexican, Italian, just about every nationality that was in southern California.

WY When I was going to grammar school, the schools were segregated, but, because of the Japanese government's intervention, we were considered white. The Mexicans, the Indians, the East Indians, and other races were in a separate school— the bus would drop them off and then take us to the other school. But we Japanese Americans just congregated together because children do recognize their own and feel more comfortable with them. And then the kids in the segregated school were permitted to join us at the main school at sixth grade. During sixth grade, I remember falling in love with a Mexican guy.

KKC You both grew up experiencing so much racism. Do you feel that the situation has improved?

HY No. Well, yes, in the sense that there's such a thing as multiethnic literature now and groups that promote it.

WY And also in the sense that most people are now aware of racism.

HY But discrimination is worse than ever, and hate crimes are proliferating. Does literature have any impact on what goes on day to day?

WY I remember going to the store and not getting waited on. But people are more aware of racism now. Although you have a lot of police brutality and so-called suicides in jail, if you have a lynching now, it's publicized, and those of us that care say something about it.

HY I remember in Oceanside when we were going to be evacuated, the Japanese community had to put up with a lot. Some businesses wouldn't take their checks. One girl asked the clerk for a certain style of clothing, and the clerk told her, "Where you're going it's not going to matter anyway." But there was this Mr. Zahniser that rescued everybody: he had this Red and White grocery store, and he cashed everybody's checks and sold them groceries, and he stored everybody's stuff in one of his warehouses, and then he brought it all to camp for us later.

KKC I've always been struck by the parallels (as noted by Stan Yogi) in "Yoneko's Earthquake" and "Songs My Mother Taught Me": both these stories describe rural families, both use a naive narrator, and both contain an illicit love affair and an unwanted pregnancy. And now Si discloses that Mrs.

Hisaye Yamamoto and Wakako Yamauchi

Hosoume (in "Yoneko's Earthquake") is based on Wakako's mother.

HY I didn't realize that somebody could see the stories as similar because they seemed totally different to me.

WY Si wrote hers first. I didn't think of mine as being similar. That was a very traumatic year for me—the year that my little brother died—and I just had to tell it. I tried to be as honest as I could.

HY And mine is fiction. My idea was to reproduce the trauma of the earthquake, and I started out writing a funny story, right? And it turned tragic in between and went to that kind of conclusion.

WY We had an earthquake in Brawley, too, a very big one. "Yoneko's Earthquake" was very evocative for me.

KKC Despite the similarity, I thought there was a very interesting difference in the two stories, namely, that the lovers were attractive in very different ways. Marpo in "Yoneko's Earthquake" seems very Westernized: he's Christian, very chivalrous, and so forth. Yamada in "Songs My Mother Taught Me" is almost the opposite: he's more attractive than the husband precisely because he's more Japanese, being a Kibei (a Nisei educated in Japan). When you were growing up, did you fluctuate between Japanese masculine ideals and the Western masculine ideals?

HY I really based the physical aspects of Marpo on a Kibei fellow who was actually a friend of the family. I just made him Filipino.

WY I always liked Japanese men because we were brought up on Japanese movies. We looked at those samurai movies when we were kids. The samurai are masculine. They wear the kimonos tied with the low belt—open up to the navel; they split their legs, and you can see their thighs.

HY Their hairdo with the one ponytail. . . .

WY Their wild, wild eyes, and their grunts and their groans.

KKC What about the American movies? Weren't you brain-washed by those as well?

HY Oh, yes. Gary Cooper and Fred Astaire. We were impressed by those.

WY Sure. And Erroll Flynn, my God. But they were foreigners to me. Japanese were my people. You could feel an intimacy exuding from the screen.

KKC In "And the Soul Shall Dance," the narrator says, "It's all right to talk about it now. Most of the principals are dead." Since both of you write about real people and real events all the time, do you feel uneasy about publishing your stories right away?

HY No, my people aren't real, like Marpo is a composite of several different people. So who recognizes who?

WY When I started the story saying "all the principals are dead," it was because I was going to tell this very personal story—more or less autobiographical. The kind of thing I had in mind was just like the problem Si had with people resenting her talking about them. Now I realize—like Si was saying before—people don't recognize themselves.

KKC Both of you have written stories that have been turned into films. What is lost and gained in the process of cinematic adaptation?

WY I wrote "And the Soul Shall Dance" into a play first.[5] Mako, the artistic director at East West Players at that time, asked me to do it. It got such great reviews that the producer of Hollywood Television Theater came to see the play and really loved it. So he approached me and Mako. I said, "I've heard about what Hollywood does to your stories; you have

Hisaye Yamamoto and Wakako Yamauchi

to promise not to change one bit of it." He said he wouldn't change a word. There are a few things changed because it's a movie instead of a play. You could go all over the place in a movie, but in a play you have to stay on stage, on one or two sets, right? But he was true to his promise, and he made some good suggestions. He said, "Why do they have to move every two years?" Like most white people, he didn't know anything about the Alien Land Law. So the question and answer are inserted into the movie. More could have been changed. I could have dropped a lot of the dialogue and shown it just with eyes, shrug of the shoulders, but what did I know then?

KKC What about you, Si? What do you think of the changes made by Emiko Omori in *Hot Summer Winds*,[6] the film based on "Seventeen Syllables" and "Yoneko's Earthquake"?

HY Emiko Omori is a woman I used to baby-sit when she was about a year old down in Oceanside, and she eventually grew up to become a cinematographer. She mentioned that she wanted to do a full-length film and wanted to know if she could do something with my stories, and I said, "Sure, go ahead." It took her several years. She wrote her own script and incorporated all these notes about Japanese Americans that she'd been saving, and she used the two stories as a loose frame on which to hang all her anecdotes. I like it; it's a beautiful film, but there are people who think it should have remained more faithful to one story or the other. And, since she liked happy endings, she tacked a happy ending onto it. So it is not really supposed to be my stories.

KKC What's your impression of *Hot Summer Winds*, Wakako?

WY I loved it very much. The happy ending didn't bother me. People have to live with what they have got. You might as well be happy with it; you might as well accept the situation. I loved the way Emiko did the love affair, and I loved the kids. They were not too precocious and not too cute, and

Natsuko Ohama and Sab Shimono were great. They went out there, and they got those tomatoes bobbing in the water—it was wonderful.

HY The set was already there because a Japanese production company had made this film called *Strawberry Road.* They leased the land for a year and grew strawberries on it. They were through with the movie, so they said Emiko could use the land. They had put a shack there, and she built it up even more and built a palm bathhouse and the packing shed.

WY It's very effective. I've seen movies made by Japanese producers doing our lives, and, Lord, they have some silly inconsistencies.

KKC What are the different demands for writing plays and writing short stories?

WY In the short story, you could take the reader anywhere—to the desert, to the sea. In the play, you have to consider the limitations of the stage, and everything has to be done by dialogue, and you can't do too much exposition because people fall asleep. But Momoko Iko said to me once, "I see why your plays work. It's because you write short stories and the short story is the most abbreviated form; to adapt it into a play would be easier than adapting a novel." A short story could be five minutes in a person's life. And so could a play.

KKC Did you ever try writing plays, Si?

HY No. Poetry is what I would like to write, but nobody likes my poetry. So I keep it hidden now. I don't even have time to write these days, the older I get, the . . .

WY The more fun it is to live!

HY No, the more time it takes me to do everything else.

WY I haven't written for years! Well, the good thing about plays: they get recycled without your putting one extra line in

Hisaye Yamamoto and Wakako Yamauchi

there. I have to feel pretty bad before I write. And, lately, I've been feeling very good! I have to be depressed to write. That's why my stories probably are depressing.

HY People have to ask me for something, and then out of guilt I go to the typewriter when I can and put it together. With "Florentine Gardens," for instance, I sent it to David Wong Louie for his anthology. Once I sent it off, I became aware of all the mistakes in it, so I asked for it back, and about then my nephew asked me for something for the English section of *Hokubei Mainichi* [a Japanese American newspaper published from San Francisco since 1947], so I sent it to him. Meanwhile, I had gone up to the University of California, Santa Barbara, and they were starting a magazine and asked me for something. My nephew hadn't been able to use this story because he had a whole bunch of material for that holiday edition, so I asked for the story back, and I gave it to the people at UC Santa Barbara.

KKC Wakako, you said writing can be a pain, but isn't it also a pleasure?

WY It is. Once I get started, I find I am on a roll; I feel so good. It's one of the few pleasures I have left, besides going shopping! If I have a story I want to tell, it's generally already made in my mind, and it's just, How am I going to approach it? How am I going to present it? Once I've decided, it's very easy, and it's very much a pleasure. If I don't have a story to tell, it's very painful to write. Or, when I have a story to tell like "Songs My Mother Taught Me," it was still very painful for me to write. I found myself crying when I was typing.

KKC So you're not like Si, who can write as long as she is guilty.

WY I'm a little bit more emotional. There's got to be something that makes me want to talk and talk, and I think to myself, Who wants to hear these old stories over and over again?

HY I would get about five stories started simultaneously in a notebook, but I haven't finished any of them yet.

KKC But you enjoy writing?

HY Ah, yes. If I had the time, I would have spent a lot of time doing it, but the yardwork takes me all day basically, and cooking, ironing—everything else takes a lot of time. The older I get, the slower I get.

KKC Don't you feel that your writing should have priority?

HY No, no, that's what I get to when I finish everything else.

WY It's a dessert. It's true. I sat at the typewriter, looked, and said, Oh, cobwebs! I got to clean that up. Then I got to go over there and mop the floor. And then I think it's just putting it off one more day.

KKC In the public eye, both of you are successful writers, but what is success for you personally? What do you consider as your most successful work?

HY I don't think I'm that successful, just that these old stories that I wrote a long time ago have been printed and reprinted, and I'm amazed. I didn't do anything to do that. If I had it printed once, that was enough. The rest is flabbergasting.

KKC But what's your personal idea of success?

HY If I get through the day! At my age . . .

WY Success? I don't know. You write a play, and some people like it, and some people don't. If you can get it in the theater, get it put on at all, that's a step. I have plays that have never been put on. I don't see myself as being well known,

Hisaye Yamamoto and Wakako Yamauchi

and I don't consider being well known as [being] a success for me. I would just like to be happy. I am trying, and I find that, if my personal life is good, that's enough or that, if my professional life—my writing—is good, then that's enough. I don't have to have everything. I'm not used to getting everything; it's just a little here and there, and it's enough. If I can straighten out my personal life or the things that haunt me, I would consider that a minor success. Life is a series of pitfalls and successes.

KKC Of all the works you've written, which one is your favorite?

WY Let me think about that.

KKC Which one of Wakako's works do you like best, Si?

HY Oh, I love "The Handkerchief." I tried to write this short story called "The Yellow Serpentine." But she wrote it instead, and her story is so great. It's about this young fellow growing up while his mother leaves the house for a while.

WY What happened was my ex-husband told us this story of himself as a little boy, how his mother had left to go to Japan.

HY He used to go in the closet and look at the serpentine streamers and weep for his mother.

WY And Si wrote this beautiful story!

HY But nobody would print it. I tore it up.

WY So I said, "Well, if you are not going to use that story, I'll write it." And I wrote "The Handkerchief."

HY That's one of her best stories; I love it.

WY That's the only story that I knowingly took.

HY No, it wasn't my story; it was yours.

WY My ex-husband's. But there were some wonderful things in your story about going to the burlesque show, going to the bar, ordering fruit cocktail, thinking "he" was getting an alcoholic drink, and it turned out to be fruit salad.

KKC Si, I am disturbed to learn that you actually destroyed your own work just because no one wanted to print it.

HY I threw away lots of stories if they didn't get accepted the first time or, once in a while, the second time. Well, it's no good, so . . .

WY I sent that short story "And the Soul Shall Dance" out many times, and I finally said, "Nobody wants it." So I gave it to *Rafu Shimpo*. And then Si told me that these fellows—Chin, Chan, Inada, and Wong [the editors of *Aiiieeeee!*]—were putting this anthology together. She advised me to send them five stories, and I did. They chose "Soul." That's how it worked out.

KKC Speaking of "And the Soul Shall Dance" and "The Handkerchief," I notice that many of your stories are about the plight of women stuck in unhappy marriages; some stay, some leave. Do you feel that the situation for women is better now?

WY For the younger people there's a lot of options. Many Nisei have put up with unhappy marriages and will continue to do so.

HY Not just Nisei. That's in all cultures.

WY That's true. But then the Nisei, because of the culture, are much more prone to put up with bad marriages, endure, and *gaman* [persevere].

HY I read somewhere—it was either Ann Landers or Dear Abby—that, after answering tens of thousands of letters every weekday for years, the columnist has decided that any successful marriage means the woman is a martyr.

Hisaye Yamamoto and Wakako Yamauchi

WY I don't believe in that; I don't think that's true at this day and age. There are more options. I mean, if you want to be a martyr, you're a martyr, but, if you don't want to be, you don't have to be.

KKC You feel that you would be more free if you were to start all over now?

WY I don't know if I want to be young again. There's so much pain, and there are so many perspectives.

HY Also, I would recall this one young starlet being interviewed on one of these talk shows, and somebody asked her about the men in her life, and she looked around, and she said, "There must be something else." And I said, "Right."

KKC Wakako, what is your favorite work?

WY Of Si's?

KKC Of yours, and also of Si's.

WY Of Si's, I like "Epithalamium." I like my play *12-1-A*. Of the short stories, "A Veteran of Foreign Wars" is one of my favorites.

KKC And, Si, what's your own favorite?

HY The one I wrote last, or I wouldn't have written it.

KKC What are you working on now?

WY I started a one-act comedy, and it has been sitting there for a little while. Now what I'm going to do is probably let it sit for a little while longer and then rewrite the play that I was working on about a Nisei woman because I know what I need to do for it and I don't mind rewriting. I don't even have a computer, but I don't mind retyping over and over again; it makes me feel close to the play.

HY I'm working on at least five or six short stories. One is going to be called either "Sunflowers" or "Monet's Garden." And another about peacocks, and another one I've started about transportation—trains, planes, taxicabs. And what is another one? I can't even remember all of them. I've got the beginnings or ends or the middles of about five stories, but I haven't gone to the typewriter with them yet.

KKC Do you feel it's easier to be an Asian American writer now because of all the interest surrounding Asian American literature?

WY I suppose. It never occurred to me to ever be published, except in the *Rafu Shimpo,* and Henry Mori only did it because I drew pictures for him. This may sound like a lot of false modesty, but I think my reputation is undeserved because I have no training. I am just persistent, and I just try to tell it as truthfully as I can.

HY One of these days I'll figure out why I write. I'm comfortable being an Asian American writer because that's what I am, a Japanese American writer. You can write only out of your own experience because I've tried to write fantasy or use other background and it just doesn't ring true to me.

KKC Do you have any advice for young Asian American writers who are starting to write?

WY You just have to practice, practice, practice. You have to keep doing it, and you can't give up. Because the time will be ready, right for you, when you get the feel of yourself, your material, the language—and it takes a long time. Some people are more mature at an early age, have more command of the language and more idea of what life is all about. I was totally ignorant. Whatever story you have to tell, as long as it's honest, it's valid, and it's a matter of how to present it, how to give it its best shot.

HY I don't feel qualified to advise anybody else. If people

Hisaye Yamamoto and Wakako Yamauchi

have this urge to write, they will, no matter what; wild horses can't stop them.

WY Wild horses can stop you.

HY Not permanently.

Notes

1. A Japanese American newspaper published in San Francisco.

2. A Japanese American newspaper based in Los Angeles.

3. Yamauchi is referring to two questions designed to test the loyalty of interned Japanese Americans: "Are you willing to serve in the armed forces of the United States on combat duty wherever ordered?" and "Will you swear unqualified allegiance to the United States of America and faithfully defend the United States from any attack by foreign or domestic forces, and forswear any form of allegiance or obedience to the Japanese emperor, or to any other foreign government, power, or organization?" Positive answers to the two questions made male Nisei of draft age eligible for service in the army and made citizens and aliens of Japanese ancestry eligible for resettlement outside the West Coast exclusion areas. Dissidents were deemed disloyal and segregated in Tule Lake, one of the ten internment camps.

4. The Poston strike was a manifestation of long-standing tensions. The Community Council in the camp consisted entirely of young Nisei (only Nisei were allowed to hold elective office) and those who were seen as stooges for the administration were sometimes physically attacked. On 14 November 1942, a Kibei (a Japanese educated in Japan) council member was beaten almost to death. About fifty evacuees were investigated, two of whom were detained. A general strike occurred on 18 November out of sympathy for the two detainees.

5. *And the Soul Shall Dance*, directed by Paul Stanley, produced by KCET (Los Angeles) for PBS, and aired nationally in 1977–1978.

6. *Hot Summer Winds*, directed by Emiko Omori, produced by KCET (Los Angeles) for the PBS American Playhouse Series, and aired nationally in 1991.

Selected Works by Hisaye Yamamoto (DeSoto)

"After Johnny Died." *Los Angeles Tribune,* 26 November 1945, 20–21. Reprinted as "Life and Death of a Nisei GI: After Johnny Died," *Pacific Citizen,* 1 December 1945, 5.

"Seventeen Syllables." *Partisan Review* oo (November 1949): 1122–1134. Reprinted in *Seventeen Syllables and Other Stories* (1988) and *Seventeen Syllables* (1994).

"The Legend of Miss Sasagawara." *Kenyon Review* 12, no. 1 (1950): 99–114. Reprinted in *Seventeen Syllables and Other Stories* (1988).

"The Brown House." *Harper's Bazaar,* October 1951, 166, 283–284. Reprinted in *Seventeen Syllables and Other Stories* (1988).

"Yoneko's Earthquake." *Furioso* 6, no. 1 (1951): 5–16. Reprinted in *Seventeen Syllables and Other Stories* (1988) and *Seventeen Syllables* (1994).

"Morning Rain." *Pacific Citizen,* 19 December 1952, 46, 50. Reprinted in *Seventeen Syllables and Other Stories* (1988).

"Epithalamium." *Carleton Miscellany* 1, no. 4 (1960): 56–67. Reprinted in *Seventeen Syllables and Other Stories* (1988).

"Las Vegas Charley." *Arizona Quarterly* 17 (1961): 303–322. Reprinted in *Seventeen Syllables and Other Stories* (1988).

"Writing." *Rafu Shimpo,* 21 December 1968, 14–15, 26, 30, 39. Reprinted in *Seventeen Syllables* (1994).

"Life among the Oil Fields: A Memoir." *Rafu Shimpo,* 20 December 1979, 13, 24–25. Reprinted in *Seventeen Syllables and Other Stories* (1988).

"A Fire in Fontana." *Rafu Shimpo,* 21 December 1985, 8–9, 16–17, 19. Reprinted in *Rereading America: Cultural Contexts for Critical Thinking and Writing,* 2d ed., ed. Gary Columbo, Robert Cullen, and Bonnie Lisle (Boston: Bedford, 1992).

Seventeen Syllables and Other Stories. Latham, N.Y.: Kitchen Table/ Women of Color, 1988.

"Eucalyptus." *Gidra,* 20th anniversary issue, 34–36. Reprinted in *Charlie Chan Is Dead: An Anthology of Comtemporary Asian American Fiction,* ed. Jessica Hagedorn (New York: Penguin, 1993).

"Florentine Gardens." *Asian America: Journal of Culture and the Arts* 1 (Winter 1992): 10–25.

Seventeen Syllables. Edited by King-Kok Cheung. New Brunswick, N.J.: Rutgers University Press, 1994.

Selected Works by Wakako Yamauchi

"Something Better for Miwa." *Rafu Shimpo,* 20 December 1958, 23–24.

"The Handkerchief." *Rafu Shimpo,* 20 December 1961, 13–14. Reprinted in *Songs* (1994).

"And the Soul Shall Dance." *Rafu Shimpo,* 19 December 1966, 9, 11, 18, 22, 28. Reprinted in *Songs* (1994).

"In Heaven and Earth." *Rafu Shimpo,* 21 December 1968, 24–25, 29, 34. Reprinted in *Songs* (1994).

"The Boatmen on Toneh River." *Amerasia Journal* 2, no. 2 (1974): 203–207. Reprinted in *Songs* (1994).

"Songs My Mother Taught Me." *Amerasia Journal* 3, no. 2 (1976): 63–73. Reprinted in *Songs* (1994).

"Makapuu Bay." *Bamboo Ridge* 3 (1979): 2–11. Reprinted in *Songs* (1994).

"That Was All." *Amerasia Journal* 7, no. 1 (1980): 115–120. Reprinted in *Songs* (1994).

"A Veteran of Foreign Wars." *Rafu Shimpo,* 19 December 1981, 7, 10. Reprinted in *Songs* (1994).

And the Soul Shall Dance. In *West Coast Plays* 11–12 (1982): 117–164.

"Maybe." *Rafu Shimpo,* 22 December 1984, 28–29, 35, 39. Reprinted in *Songs* (1994).

The Chairman's Wife and *12-1-A.* In *The Politics of Life: Four Plays by Asian American Women,* ed. Velina Hasu Houston. Philadelphia: Temple University Press, 1993.

The Music Lessons. In *Unbroken Thread: An Anthology of Plays by Asian American Women,* ed. Roberta Uno. Amherst: University of Massachusetts Press, 1993. Reprinted in *Songs* (1994).

Songs My Mother Taught Me: Stories, Plays, and Memoir. Edited by Garrett Hongo. New York: Feminist, 1994.

Contributors

Zainab Ali was born in Hyderabad, India, and was raised in both India and America. Her work has appeared in *Iowa Woman: A Retrospective; Our Feet Walk the Sky; Speaking in Tongues;* and *Literacy Matters: Reading and Writing in the Second Wave of Multiculturalism.* She has been awarded the Barbara Deming Memorial Fund Award for fiction. A recent graduate from the University of Oregon's M.F.A. program, she is currently working on a novel entitled *Madras on Rainy Days.*

King-Kok Cheung is an associate professor of English and Asian American studies at the University of California, Los Angeles. She is the author of *Articulate Silences: Hisaye Yamamoto, Maxine Hong Kingston, Joy Kogawa* (1993) and the editor of *An Interethnic Companion to Asian American Literature* (1997), *Seventeen Syllables* (1994), and *Asian American Literature: An Annotated Bibliography* (1988).

Stacey Yukari Hirose is a graduate student at the University of California, Los Angeles. She received her M.A. in Asian American studies and is currently working toward her Ph.D. in U.S. history.

Khanh Ho is a graduate student in the English Department at the University of California, Los Angeles, writing his dissertation on the idea of paradox in Asian American literature. He has published several stories and essays in *Amerasia Journal*. His short story "Bittermelons" is reprinted in *Perspectives: Authentic Asian American Voices,* ed. Maureen Devine Sotoohi (1996).

Tamara Ho was born in Rangoon, Burma (now Yangon, Myanmar). She received her M.A. from the Program in Comparative Literature at the University of California, Los Angeles. Her dissertation investigates the intersection of Asian American and postcolonial studies and explores immigration, diaspora, and gender. She has written a book review of Wendy Law-Yone's *Irrawaddy Tango* and a piece on *The Coffin Tree,* forthcoming in *A Resource Guide to Asian American Literature,* ed. Sau-ling Wong and Stephen H. Sumida.

Grace Kyungwon Hong is assistant professor of English and American studies at Princeton University. She received her M.A. in Asian American studies from the University of California, Los Angeles, and her Ph.D. in literature at the University of California, San Diego.

Robert B. Ito is book editor at *Los Angeles Magazine.* He writes on Asian American topics for *Mother Jones, International Documentary, Asian Week,* and *Bright Lights Film Journal.*

Scott Kurashige received his M.A. in Asian American studies from the University of California, Los Angeles, where he is now a Ph.D. candidate in history. His interview with Amy Uyematsu is part of a broader study of activists from the Asian American movement of the sixties and seventies.

Brenda Kwon was born and raised in Honolulu, Hawai'i. She received her B.A. in creative writing at the University of Southern California and her Ph.D. in English at the University of California, Los Angeles. Her poetry has appeared in *Amerasia Journal, disOrient,* and *Making More Waves.* Her book *Beyond Ke'eaumoku: Koreans, Nationalism, and Local Culture in Hawai'i* has been published by Garland (1999). She currently lives in Honolulu, where she is writing and teaching.

Emily Porcincula Lawsin is on the Board of Trustees of the Filipino American National Historical Society and was an M.A. student in Asian American studies at the University of California, Los

Angeles. She has taught composition and Filipino American history in the Asian American Studies Department at California State University, Northridge, and at the University of California, Los Angeles. An oral historian and performance poet, her poetry and essays on war brides and students have appeared in *Flippin': Filipinos on America,* the *Filipino American National History Society Journal, Seattle Arts,* the *International Examiner, Forward Motion Magazine's Asians in Struggle, Homegrown 3,* and the *Seattle Times.*

James Kyung-Jin Lee is a doctoral candidate in the English Department at the University of California, Los Angeles. His dissertation examines U.S. racial and cultural politics during the eighties. His essays on Alejandro Morales and Hisaye Yamamoto are forthcoming respectively in *Re-placing America: Intercultural Conversations and Contestations,* ed. Ruth Hsu et al., and in *Blackness and the Mind/Body Split,* ed. Lindon Barrett.

Rachel Lee received her Ph.D. in English from the University of California, Los Angeles, where she is currently an assistant professor of English and women's studies. Her works have appeared in *Cultural Critique, African American Review,* and several volumes of collected essays. Her book *The Americas of Asian American Literature: Gendered Fictions of Nation and Transnation* has been published by the Princeton University Press (1999); it includes a chapter on Gish Jen.

Michael S. Murashige is an assistant professor of literature at the University of California, San Diego. His book *Race, Resistance, and Contestations of Urban Space in Los Angeles* is forthcoming from the Duke University Press.

Dharini Rasiah is currently doing her graduate work in Asian American studies at the University of California, Los Angeles, and is teaching video production in ethnic studies at the University of California, Berkeley. She is coeditor of *Our Feet Walk the Sky: Women of the South Asian Diaspora* (Aunt Lute Books, 1993) and has produced a number of videos on women and labor issues.

Darlene Rodrigues received her M.A. in Asian American studies from the University of California, Los Angeles. Her M.A. thesis focuses on Al Robles; a portion of that thesis will appear in *Amerasia Journal*. A poet and a performer with Kalo Projects, she currently lives in Honolulu, Hawai'i.

Rahpee Thongthiraj is a doctoral candidate in American culture at the University of Michigan. She received her B.A. in English and M.A. in Asian American studies at the University of California, Los Angeles. S. P. Somtow is the main author explored in her dissertation, "Re-conceptualizing Asian American Literature through the Works of S. P. Somtow, Wanwadee Larsen, and James T. Hamada."

Nancy Yoo obtained her B.A. from Bryn Mawr College and is currently pursuing a Ph.D. in English at the University of California, Los Angeles.

Index

East Coast and California, 30–31, 221; Filipino American, 30–31, 154–161; Hawai'i, 303–304; Japanese American, 13, 177, 183, 256–257, 266, 349–350, 367; Japanese Brazilian, 324, 326, 332–333; Jewish, 228–229; South Asian American, 74, 144–145, 147–151; Korean American, 96; Thai American, 58, 66; Vietnamese American, 111; writer, 192, 216, 221–222, 228–229. *See also* African Americans; Burmese Americans; Chinese Americans; Filipino Americans; Japanese Americans; Korean Americans; South Asian Americans; Thai Americans; Vietnamese Americans

Conrad, Joseph, 289
Coover, Robert, 210
Cornell Symposium on Asian American: Issues of Identity (1990), 38n. 1, 306
cultural anthropology, 63
cultural workers, 5, 234
cultures, 63, 95–96, 107, 109, 112, 114–115, 118–119, 141, 147, 310; between, 59–60, 62, 94; Jewish, 229; and language, 114; mixing of, 11–12, 37, 59, 62–63, 94–95, 112–113, 156–157, 165–166, 229, 303, 310–311. *See also* ethnicity, multiculturalism; traveling
Cuyugan, Tina, 25

Day, Dorothy, 365
Desai, Anita, 149
diaspora, 7, 69, 103. *See also* "Overseas Chinese"
diasporic literature, 278
Ding, Loni, 244
displacement, 33–34, 72, 141, 293–294
Divakaruni, Chitra Banerjee, 12, 140–153; *Arranged Marriage,* 141, 148, 150–151; Bengali, 152; *Black Candle,* 141–142, 147; *Dark like the River,* 151; *Mistress of Spices,* 141, 148, 150–151; *Reason for Nasturtiums,* 141; teaching, 152
diversity, 11
Doctorow, E. L., 307
domestic violence. *See* violence
Dong, Jim, 236
Dostoyevsky, Fyodor, *Crime and Punishment,* 292
Douglass, Frederick, 209
drama. *See* performance; performance; poetry; theater
DuBois, W. E. B., 89

East Meets West Foundation, 105, 109, 113
East West Players, 179, 324, 371
emasculation, 5–6, 134, 207, 243–244
Emerson, Ralph Waldo, 86
empowerment, 141, 149, 166–167, 201, 207, 279
Erdich, Louise, 150–151
ethnicity, 12, 13, 67, 77, 83, 86, 90, 141, 209–211, 215–216, 229–230, 240, 303, 315. *See also* cultures; multiculturalism

madness. *See* insanity

Maitri, 140, 142–144

Mako, 371–372

Mamet, David, *Oleana*, 46

Manangs, 167, 169. *See also* community, Filipino American; Filipino Americans; Manongs

Manilatown, 164. *See also* community, Filipino American

Manongs, 13, 30, 154–158, 162–165, 167–168. *See also* community, Filipino American; Filipino Americans; Manangs

Manzanar (California), 254, 267. *See also* Japanese Americans, internment

Mao Tse-tung, 203, 239, 262

Márquez, Gabriel García, 307

Maurin, Peter, 365

McCarthy, Nobu, 180–181

McDonald, Dorothy, 367

media, 2, 13, 43, 52, 77, 135, 178–179, 241, 244

Mehta, Ved, 149

memoir. *See* genre

memory, 86, 117, 142, 155, 158, 270, 284, 301–302

Miller, Arthur, 53

Mirikitani, Janice, 1, 10, 12, 123–139, 236; "Generations of Women," 131; "Healthy Choices," 131; "Jade," 131; "Jade Junkies," 131; "Ms.," 136; self-image, 125–126; *Shedding Silence*, 130, 138n. 1; war imagery, 132

Mishima, Yukio, 245–246

missionaries, Christian, 238, 240; in Hawai'i, 312

Miss Saigon, 183–184

Mistry, Rohinton, 149

model minority, 125, 228. *See also* stereotypes

Moraga, Cherríe, 209

Mori, Henry, 353, 366, 379

Mori, Toshio, 360; *Yokohama, California*, 246

Morrison, Toni, 202, 209

Moss, Thylias, 264

movement, anti-war, 259; Asian American, 10, 123–125, 179, 236, 252, 259–260, 262; black power, 4, 129, 252, 259–260; Chicano, 260; civil rights, 4, 129; Third World, 259; women's, 260. *See also* empowerment; Third World Strike

movies, American, 371. *See also* media

Moyers, Bill, 272, 280n. 1

Mukherjee, Bharati, 149, 194

multiculturalism, 10, 30, 34, 77, 109, 157, 165, 228–229, 247. *See also* cultures; ethnicity

multiracial/"mestizo," 27

Mura, David, 81

Murase, Mike, 261

Murayama, Milton, 306

Murguia, Alejandro, 165

Myanmar. *See* Burma

narrative, 51, 93–94, 103, 210, 271, 273–275

Narusawa, Rev. Raymond, 341

national allegiance, 4, 7, 9, 11–12, 34, 40, 42, 44, 59–60, 79, 102–103, 112. *See also* "home;" homeland

trade unions, 318
tradition, 113, 220, 299
translations, 152, 194
Transpacific, 243, 245
traveling, 28–29, 62. *See also*
    cultures, between, mixing of
truth, 49, 111–112, 114, 178
Tsukiyama, Fuku Yokoyama,
    360
Tule Lake (California), 380n. 3.
    See also Japanese Americans,
    internment

universal, 146, 234, 309
Uyematsu, Amy, 8, 10, 14,
    252–269; "Emergence of
    Yellow Power in America,"
    252, 259–261; "Harvest,"
    266; "Sansei Line Dance,"
    266; *30 Miles from J-Town*,
    14, 253, 262–263, 265;
    "Three Pulls of the Loom,"
    265–266; "War Stories," 257,
    266

Valéry, Paul, 195
Vietnam, 109–112, 117–118
Vietnamese Americans, 105,
    107–108, 110–112, 114–115,
    117–118. *See also* community,
    Vietnamese American
Vietnam War, 10, 12, 46, 107,
    110–111, 118, 258–259; and
    women, 118
violence, 52, 87, 100–101, 124,
    132; anti-Asian, 180, 311; cycle
    of, 90, 144; domestic, 140,
    143–144; ethnic, 77, 90; and
    South Asian women,
    142–144; against women,
    76–77

Walker, Alice, "womanist," 136
war, 2, 132, 191, 252, 303
War Manpower Commission,
    361
Weathermen, 161
Williams, Cecil, 129, 132–136,
    168
Williams, Tennessee, 52–53
Wollstonecraft, Mary, 76
Wong, Sau-ling Cynthia, 7
Wong, Shawn, 5–6, 159,
    235–236, 247, 368
Woo, Merle, 236
Wordsworth, William, 76
World War II, 40, 46–48, 130,
    259, 380; Nisei participation
    in, 380n. 1. *See also* Japanese
    Americans, internment,
    resettlement
writer. *See* Asian American
    writer
writing, 24, 33, 49, 64–66,
    70–71, 78, 80–81, 87–88,
    94–97, 102–103, 108, 114–115,
    141–142, 148–149, 152, 155,
    192–194, 217, 236–243, 258,
    271, 276, 279, 295, 299, 305,
    307–309, 312, 315–316, 350,
    374–379; advice on, 15, 56,
    65–66, 74–75, 152, 175,
    178–179, 184, 192–199,
    203–204, 207, 224–226,
    379–380; process, 50, 56, 64,
    72, 80–81, 85, 93–94, 96, 104,
    107–111, 115–116, 133–134,
    141–143, 155, 165, 284–285,
    294–295, 271–272; reasons
    for, 155, 158, 190–192, 218,
    296; revision, 271, 331–332;
    style, 177, 326–327, 329;
    voice, 130, 217, 272. *See also*

402